For John
With Best Wishes,
Thelma Jennings

*The Nashville Convention*

# *The Nashville Convention*
## *Southern Movement for Unity, 1848-1851*

*Thelma Jennings*



Memphis State University Press

Library of Congress Cataloging in Publication Data

Jennings, Thelma, 1920-
The Nashville Convention.

Bibliography: p.
Includes index.
1. Southern Convention, Nashville, 1850.
2. Southern States—Politics and governments—1775-1865. 3. United States—Politics and government—1849-1853. 4. Secession. I. Title.
E423.J5 975'.03 80-12917
ISBN 0-87870-097-8

# Preface

"Inconsequential," "insignificant," "of little moment" are adjectives that historians have traditionally applied to the Nashville Convention of 1850. But the 175 delegates from nine southern states who met "to devise and adopt some mode of resistance to northern aggression" had a greater impact upon the course of our nation's history than has been acknowledged heretofore. True, the convention adopted no mode of resistance and the Compromise of 1850 temporarily stalemated the slavery conflict; but the convention did bring national attention to the section's grievances and undoubtedly influenced passage of the Compromise. In addition, and equally important, the meeting brought together representative minds of the South—fire-eater to conservative—and forced them to subject their attitudes to debate, to reason, and to the democratic process. Finally, the convention showed the loyalty of the South to the Union and the willingness of southerners to compromise to preserve national unity.

Southerners had meandered toward unity since 1820, when they had first begun to develop a sectional consciousness. They had often conferred at commercial and planters' conventions, initiated to determine ways to attain independence from the North. In times of political crisis certain leaders had suggested an all-southern convention to promote unity. When the triumph of Manifest Destiny in the Mexican War brought about a new sectional crisis, southerners realized the importance of unity more than ever before. In the struggle for an equitable division of the West the minority South faced an increasingly aggressive North. On 22 December 1848 sixty-nine southern congressmen, representing every slave state except Delaware, launched the southern movement for unity. A few months later the Mississippi Convention met at Jackson and issued the call for the Nashville gathering. At first southerners in general responded favorably, but events in Washington pointing toward compromise lessened support for the convention around the first of March.

The first session of the convention, far more temperate than early observers had predicted, adopted no mode of resistance. The delegates, whose views ranged from fire-eating radicalism to Unionism and conservatism, set forth a platform based on the extension of the 36°30' line while adopting a series of moderate resolutions and a more radical "Address to the People" of the southern states. Although the members expressed willingness to wait and see, their adjournment was conditional. Should Congress fail to meet their demands, the delegates were to reassemble at Nashville. The fact that the convention met and agreed to meet again undoubtedly influenced the passage of the Compromise; the second session might have been entirely different without its passage. But events combined to bring about the collapse of the southern movement for unity. Moderates defeated radicals in the Georgia elections to a state convention a week after the November session, and the "Georgia platform" soon served as the South's model for acceptance. The South conditionally acquiesced, and the Union was saved.

This study, based on primary sources hitherto unexplored and on a wide selection of secondary material, represents a reappraisal of the convention. It rests upon a variety of manuscripts, the edited works of leading contemporaries, the official journals of both sessions, the census records of 1850, contemporary newspapers, and other sources. This first book-length study of the Nashville meetings as seen by contemporaries concludes that the Nashville Convention was more significant than most historians have formerly thought. On the surface it might appear that the convention accomplished little in the way of action, but the above reasons indicate that in other, less tangible, ways the convention was indeed successful.

I wish to express my appreciation to the many people who have been helpful in the preparation of this study. My special thanks are extended to the library staff at the University of Tennessee, Middle Tennessee State University, Tennessee

State Library and Archives, and Joint University Libraries, Nashville. Mrs. Frances Hunter, interlibrary loan director at Middle Tennessee State, deserves an extra "thank you." The courtesy and assistance of the staffs at the Library of Congress, National Archives, Duke University, University of North Carolina at Chapel Hill, Universities of Virginia, South Carolina, Georgia, and Alabama, the state archives of Georgia, South Carolina, North Carolina, Alabama, and Mississippi, and the Virginia Historical Society are also deeply appreciated. I am also grateful to staff members of the libraries at the University of Texas, the University of Florida, the Historical Society of Pennsylvania, the South Carolina Historical Society, Harvard University, and the New York Public Library for supplying me with research materials.

I especially want to thank Dr. Holman Hamilton and Dr. Charles P. Roland of the University of Kentucky, who read the manuscript and offered many helpful suggestions; Miss Mary Lee Tipton, who assisted with editing the manuscript and improving its style; Mrs. Wilma Barrett, Mrs. Shirley Reed, and Miss Joye Elrod, who cheerfully typed many versions; Dr. Ralph W. Haskins, who first suggested the topic and directed my Ph.D. dissertation; Dr. Robert E. Corlew, my dean, and Dr. William T. Windham, my chairman at Middle Tennessee State who have encouraged me, and many friends too numerous to mention.

My cousin, Miss Lois Grippin, has constantly aided and encouraged me, and to her I am most grateful.

Thelma Jennings
Middle Tennessee State University

*To The Memory of My Mother and Father*

# *Contents*

*The Nashville Convention*

# 1

# *1850: The South and the Nation*

After the adjournment of the Nashville Convention in June 1850, James H. Hammond, South Carolina delegate to the meeting, concluded the results "do not amount to much." William L. Sharkey, who had served as president of the convention, revealed that he had decided even before it met that "the convention movement would result in a total failure." Various southerners had denounced the convention as "iniquitous in its purposes, and treasonable in its designs—having in view nothing less than a dismemberment of the Union, and an overthrow of the Federal Constitution."[1] Such negative verdicts have overshadowed positive analyses of participants and other contemporaries, as historians for the most part have repeated such terms as "unrepresentative," "insignificant," and "failure" to describe the Nashville Convention. The "ill-assorted" delegates had contented themselves with "mild" resolutions and slipped quietly home, scarcely making a ripple on the course of human events.[2]

In the view of many contemporaries and some historians, however, the convention, far from being a failure, had positive results. Southerners met and consulted at Nashville, declared their rights in the territorial controversy, and set forth a platform based on the extension of 36°30′. Most important was the fact of their meeting and that they agreed to meet again after Congress adjourned. Moreover, their adjournment was conditional, and the second session in November might have been entirely different if the Compromise of 1850 had not passed. Contrary to dire forecasts of disunionist domination, southerners weighed the merits of secession and in the final analysis agreed to give the Union another trial.

A new sectional crisis had occurred as an outgrowth of the expansionist desires of President James K. Polk, agent of Manifest Destiny and an American Nationalist in the Jacksonian tradition. This crisis fostered feelings of inequality with the North among southerners that eventually resulted in a movement for southern unity for which the President had no sympathy.[3] Nevertheless, this movement gave birth to the Nashville Convention.

In an atmosphere of increased northern resistance to proslavery measures, an angry South demanded respect and an equitable division of the West. Not only did northern threats present sufficient cause for fear, but the situation in the South itself was alarming. The section continued to lag behind the North in population, wealth, and political strength.[4] Undoubtedly John C. Calhoun was more deeply concerned than any southern leader, for he understood, as many of his contemporaries did not, that the imposition of moral odium in the slavery quarantine of the Wilmot Proviso would make the position of the South in the Union intolerable. Admission of enough free states could eventually lead to a constitutional amendment to abolish slavery. When Calhoun became convinced that acquistion of territory in the Mexican War, which he had opposed, was inevitable, he felt constrained to deny congressional power to restrict the institution of slavery in the territories. On 19 February 1847 he presented in the Senate a set of resolutions, prefaced by a speech opposing the Wilmot Proviso as inconsistent with the Constitution. Calhoun contended that the South must rest its defense on the Constitution of the Founding Fathers, as the section demanded equality in the territories and protection of minority rights in the face of northern aggression. The situation required a united front on a vital issue, and his doctrine that neither Congress nor a territorial legislature could exclude slavery from a territory prior to its admission as a state became one of the fundamental tenets of southern orthodoxy and operated as one of the key factors of southern unity.[5]

When the Senate ratified the Treaty of Guadalupe Hidalgo in March 1848, Calhoun made a dire forecast: "The slave question will now come up and be the subject of deep agitation. . . . If it [the South] yields now all will be lost." Calhoun was correct, for the question of organization of the newly acquired territory became hopelessly entangled with slavery extension. Convinced that the South was on the verge of "the crisis of its fate," Calhoun became extremely alarmed. For him the southern problem was essentially that of retaining equal rights for the South in the Union and preventing the destruction of the South's socioeconomic system and whole way of life. What could possibly save both the South and the Union? Calhoun's answer was a southern convention.[6]

As early as 1845 Calhoun had attempted to organize a third party based on southern rights. On his return home from Washington in March 1847, Calhoun had spoken in Charleston for a united South. All party distinction must cease and members of both parties in the South should unite in resistance to northern aggression. When Calhoun had gone to Washington in December 1848, he was doubtlessly determined to achieve a coalition among southern congressmen as a step toward union of the whole South. He may have been the prime mover of the southern movement in Congress that began with a meeting of sixty-nine southern congressmen, representing every slave state except Delaware on the evening of 22 December.[7] South Carolina Senator Andrew P. Butler claimed that the idea of a southern movement did not originate with his state, and that three preliminary meetings occurred before Calhoun was consulted. According to Butler, Senators Henry Foote of Mississippi and R. M. T. Hunter of Virginia initiated the movement in Congress. As chairman of a subcommittee of five, Calhoun wrote an address to the southern people that was a powerful plea for unity. Although the address did not directly call for a southern convention, it hinted at the idea as a future device to combat northern aggression on southern rights.[8]

Calhoun played a major role in the call for the Nashville Convention, but he did not originate the idea of such an assemblage. Other leaders had also suggested such a course during the South Carolina nullification controversy. Southerners had often conferred at commercial and planters' conventions—devised to find ways to bring about commercial, industrial, and financial independence from the North—to rid the South of the everlasting colonial status of its economy. During the heated discussion over the admission of Texas, certain leaders had even suggested a conclave at Nashville.[9] Considering the outcome of the nullification crisis, Calhoun's desire to place some other state in the forefront is understandable. South Carolina was still the most radical of the southern states in 1849. To avoid charges of radicalism, therefore, the movement for a cooperative endeavor in the form of a southern convention should come from another state.

Mississippi made the move. A bipartisan convention at Jackson in October 1849 issued a call for an all-southern convention in Nashville in June of the following year. Early response toward the convention was generally favorable. Sectional feeling was intensifying, and unless the crisis was settled in a manner the South could accept, the Union was in danger. Around the first of March, however, a change of sentiment occurred. Support for the convention began to wane. The introduction of Clay's resolutions, Webster's speech on 7 March in favor of the Compromise, and the apparent willingness of some northerners to settle ths differences all figured in the change. Since the people were tired of sectional strife, their interest—never as great as that of the politicians—lagged as hope of compromise progressed. Only in South Carolina and Mississippi did public sentiment continue favorable to the convention, and even in Mississippi the Whigs were unenthusiastic.

Contemporaries disagreed on the purpose of the convention; its opponents maintained that the originators and delegates were plotting to dissolve the Union. But to label the convention "disunionist" or "treasonable" in purpose is an obvious oversimplification. If Calhoun is considered the "father" of this gathering, an analysis of his motives in 1849-50 is imperative. He did not urge the meeting at Nashville in order to dissolve or weaken the Union; Calhoun loved the Union and hoped to preserve it. He hoped that a united South would strengthen the national fabric, as well as protect its own rights. But though Calhoun loved the Union and desired its preservation, he loved the South even more—to save the South was his foremost objective. Early in the winter of 1850 he wrote that the object of the pending convention was to make "a solemn statement" of southern wrongs and appeal to the North to desist. In case the North refused to change its course, the meeting should "devise some means of action."[10] By the time of his death, two months before the assemblage, Calhoun appears to have been almost convinced that secession was necessary. According to Senator James M. Mason of Virginia, Calhoun said shortly before his death on 31 March, "The Union is doomed to dissolution there is no mistaking the signs."[11] Was Calhoun ready to cross the Rubicon at Nashville? Perhaps.

The Mississippi delegates, who issued the call for the Nashville Convention, believed the time had arrived for the southern states to counsel together for their "common safety." The proposal stated that the purpose of the convention was "to devise and adopt some mode of resistance to northern aggression."[12] "Some mode of resistance" did indeed mean secession to certain delegates; to others, it did not. The politicians, the press, and the public all put various interpretations on such a vague definition of purpose; events and circumstances influenced and sometimes changed their attitudes as they influenced those of the delegates. In the minds of those who conceived it, the purpose of the convention may have been radical; the meeting itself, however, was quite moderate.

From beginning to end, ambivalence marked the Nashville Convention. The first session proved far more temperate than anticipated, and the failure of the delegates to adopt a mode of resistance has doubtless led to an overemphasis on the moderation, and hence insignificance, of the proceedings. But the "wait-and-see" attitude of the delegates cannot be interpreted as submission. Although they preferred to adopt resolutions rebuking congressional acts and northern aggression rather than to promote disunion, the declarations produced by the convention were not mere threats, and the proceedings were not so insignificant that the nation's lawmakers could ignore them. Webster called the address, written by South Carolina's Robert Barnwell Rhett and adopted by the delegates, "a studied disunion argument."[13] Many contemporaries, even delegates who disliked parts of the address, insisted that the convention should be judged by the resolutions alone. The address was, however, a part of the proceedings, receiving the negative vote of only eight delegates. Public reaction to the meeting manifested itself in various ways; few Americans completely ignored it.

By the time the second session met, however, the southern movement had virtually collapsed; indeed the November session attracted little attention, probably less than the Georgia elections held a week after its adjournment. Perhaps in reaction to the apparent doom of "fire-eating" motives, this session was more radical than the first. Many moderates boycotted Nashville, yet some of the most prominent disunionists also failed to attend. Hammond, Beverley Tucker, R. F. W. Allston, and Walter Colquitt, among others, were conspicuous for their absence. Many of them probably believed, as Hammond did, that no state except South Carolina was ready to act. Even in this more radical environment, however, Avery Craven speaks of "a conciliatory temper" in November.[14] The resolutions and preamble were similar in principle to those in June, with the additional rejection of the Compromise. The delegates bypassed South Carolina's resolution advocating united secession but agreed on the most important recommendation for a southern congress.

Although the Nashville Convention failed to unite the South in 1850, the experience increased the feeling of southern nationalism and undoubtedly paved the way for a Southern Confederacy in 1861. Yet, ironically, the convention also promoted consolidation in favor of the Compromise and against secession. But southerners all the while regarded their acceptance of the Compromise as conditional, and most of them undoubtedly felt they had received the little end of the bargain. In return for this magnanimity, the South expected the North to honor its part of the deal.

Considerable uniformity of sentiment existed on northern enforcement of the new fugitive slave law, and the Georgia Platform—a qualified acceptance devised in response to the Compromise—united the South more successfully than the Nashville Platform. Allan Nevins suggests, however, that the fourth resolution of the Georgia Platform, which listed a series of encroachments on southern rights that would justify secession, "seemed to many Southerners writ in letters of burning light."[15] If the North broke the new compact, resistance would follow. The possibility of renewed sectional strife remained in the background; compromise did not dispel the grievance. Neither the territorial problem nor the great problems of slavery and the Union had really been solved. The Compromise was only a truce, an armistice, in the sectional conflict.[16]

The future action of the South in case of renewed northern aggression remained a moot question. Southern nationalists had realized the difficulty of securing the cooperation of all the southern states in defense of southern rights, and southern fire-eaters had found the convention too slow and unlikely. As far as they were concerned there would be no more southern conventions; when the time came one state must lead in secession and the others of necessity would follow.

Both the question of purpose and the failure to achieve southern unity relate to the theme of the divided mind in the South—the peculiar and tragic burden of ambiguity and ambivalence to which David Potter refers in his analysis of the whole southern experience.[17] The majority of southerners did not advocate disunion but sought unity in the face of what they considered northern aggression, while a minority desired disunion and concluded that cooperation among the states was an unlikely method to achieve their goal. Many southern Unionists looked askance at the proceedings in Nashville and optimistically to the thirty-first Congress, as South Carolina

Unionists had looked to Congress in 1832. But Unionist delegates were also present at Nashville, as they had been at the nullification convention at Columbia almost two decades before. In fact, with the exception of a preponderance of Democrats, the delegates at Nashville represented a good cross-section of southern political opinion, as divided in sentiment as the South itself. Analysis of the personnel clearly reveals that they were not an "ill-assorted group"; on the contrary some of the South's outstanding leaders participated in the convention. Their views ranged all the way from the radical fire-eating sentiments of Robert Barnwell Rhett and Nathaniel Beverley Tucker to the Unionist conservatism of William L. Sharkey and Thomas Gholson. The victory of the moderates in June reflects the change of sentiment in the South; the delegates were not "unrepresentative" of the people. But each state group had its fire-eaters and southern nationalists. A few, like Tucker, longed for a Southern Confederacy; others, like Hammond, realized "the fruit is not ripe."[18]

Calhoun's dream of an all-southern party dedicated to sectional rights was an impossibility. Southern Whigs did not wish to injure the administration of Zachary Taylor, a Whig, and some southern Democrats like House Speaker Howell Cobb hesitated to form any combination that would separate them from their northern Democratic allies. Members of both parties participated at Jackson in issuing the call for the Nashville Convention, but Democrats generally assumed leadership, both before and at the convention. Moreover, as soon as Clay introduced his resolutions, southern Whig sentiment for the convention began to diminish. Partisanship was a serious obstacle, therefore, not only among Whigs and Democrats, but to a somewhat lesser extent among Democrats themselves, throughout Calhoun's attempt to unify the South. Herein lies the important key to understanding the southern movement for unity since, at its peak, the convention cannot be interpreted as a popular nonpartisan movement. In many cases the people were apathetic; in some instances they had little or no opportunity to participate in the selection of delegates. Herman V. Ames has correctly noted, however, that while the convention project was largely a movement of the politicians rather than the people, so was the Compromise.[19]

The Nashville Convention promoted political realignment. President Taylor's policies that seemed to favor the North placed southern Whigs in a dilemma, and those Whigs who united with the Democrats in 1850 for the protection of southern rights found it easier to do so later. The formation of a Constitutional Union party composed of southern Whigs and southern Democrats also occurred, as southern Whigs experienced increasing difficulty with northern Whigs. Thus the Nashville Convention indirectly contributed to the downfall of the Whig party.[20] It promoted the growth of the Democratic party in the South, but the convention contributed to the disruption of the Democracy in the nation. For the fifteen years before 1850 the South had experienced the most active two-party system in its entire history. But the events of that year marked the beginning of an important change in the opposite direction and doomed the era of bisectional parties in the nation.[21]

The Nashville Convention also foreshadowed state and personal alignments a decade later. Many opponents of the convention in 1850 sided with the Union in 1861; likewise states that wavered in 1850 hesitated in 1861. Several delegates would become leaders in secession and participants in the Civil War. Predictably those most favorable to the 1850 gathering were the secession leaders of 1861, which suggests that the 1850 movement had a lasting effect. The November session of the convention was not at all the "dying gesture" of the southern movement for unity; it did mark a decade-long period of dormancy. Like a prophet of the future, Hammond confided to his diary on 30 November 1850, "The true crisis is not yet and he who husbands his strength now can expend it to much more effect in a few years hence." Though no state would follow South Carolina in 1850, disunion sentiment was not dead, and given time and further aggression his state "would be sustained in open secession."[22]

The fact that the convention met and agreed to meet again was actually more important than its accomplishments. Undoubtedly the convention influenced the passage of the Compromise, not through intention but through portent. Various state resolutions that were not "mere gasconade," the convention call, and the early favorable response influenced Henry Clay and other moderates to try to settle the crisis. Although the majority of the delegates at Nashville opposed Clay's measures, that same majority consented to make concessions to save the Union. The fire-eaters could not sway the convention to radical measures. After passage of the Compromise they even failed to carry Mississippi and South Carolina—the states in which their strength was greatest. Pragmatism prevailed over idealism and common sense over passion. The predominantly moderate tone at Nashville may have surprised many Americans, but it symbolized the national consensus—both northern and southern—and strengthened those who worked for compromise.

Instead of disrupting the Union, the convention may have saved it for another decade. But at the same time, most southerners retained the belief that secession was a legal right that the states could use in the face of intolerable aggression. Neither a southern convention nor an American compromise would mark the secession crisis of 1861. It was too late. But the Nashville Convention was a landmark in regional cooperation; it represents a climax or watershed in the perennial conflict between nationalism and sectionalism. Ambiguous to the end, it paved the way for a Southern Confederacy at the same time it was strengthening the forces that saved the Union.

# 2

# *Meandering Toward Southern Unity*

When Calhoun set forth the southern platform in February 1847, he began a chain of events that eventually led the southern states to greater unity and to the Nashville Convention. On 8 March the Virginia General Assembly passed a series of resolutions asserting that passage of the Wilmot Proviso would cause "submission to aggression and outrage on the one hand, or determined resistance on the other, at all hazards and to the last extremity." Virginia pledged to support the second alternative and called upon the people of the South "to take firm, united and concerted action in this emergency." As the first legislative protest from the South, the Virginia Resolutions became the model for the remonstrances of the other slave states.[1]

The day after Virginia's proclamations, a group of Charlestonians who had met to welcome Calhoun on his way home adopted resolutions reiterating verbatim the Virginia Resolutions; they also declared that submission to the proposed extinction of slavery, beyond what had already been yielded by the Missouri Compromise, "would be unwise, dangerous, dishonorable and debasing." Public meetings were held throughout the state and unanimously demanded resistance; few outlined any action. Governor David Johnson recommended, in

November 1847, that the South Carolina legislature adopt the Virginia Resolutions. The two houses could not agree on what stand the state should take, however, and the group took no official action at this time.[2]

The Democrat State Convention in Alabama formally approved the Virginia Resolutions in May 1847, and the Georgia Democratic Convention followed suit a few weeks later. Although the Mississippi legislature did not convene in 1847, Governor Albert G. Brown wrote to Virginia Governor William Smith that both political parties in his state would heartily approve the resolutions. In February 1848 the Alabama legislature not only adopted resolutions but also declared that Congress was obliged to protect slave property in the territories. In addition, the legislature promised that Alabama would act in concert and make common cause with the other slaveholding states to defend the institution of slavery in any necessary manner. On 2 February 1848 the Texas legislature declared unconstitutional any proposition prohibiting slavery in the territories and a few weeks later asserted that it would not honor any such restriction on future territory acquired from Mexico.[3]

Meanwhile, newspapers in South Carolina began to urge a convention of southern states to announce a southern platform to which each state should solmenly pledge its adherence. By late summer 1848, South Carolina leaders began to debate on the value of such a meeting. In Abbeville on 4 September, Representative Armistead Burt said that a convention was the only means whereby the South could save itself. Calhoun was also carefully considering the propriety of a southern convention, but he believed the initiative should come from another state. Thus he exercised a certain restraining influence. Robert Barnwell Rhett urged separate state action, as he had in 1844. He told the Democratic Party of Charleston on 23 September that the South must "meet the question at once, and forever." A southern convention was highly unlikely and might even "breed confusion and weakness in the South." If abolition should dominate congressional legislation, the southern states should request their congressmen to vacate their seats immediately. If other southern states should fail to maintain their rights under the Constitution and thereby submit to aggression, South Carolina "unaided and alone should meet the contest."[4]

When the legislature convened in November 1848, controversy over the state's position again divided South Carolinians. Governor Johnson attempted to show that action was impractical at this time; however, he made his own position clear by declaring that "unity of time and concert of action are indispensable to success, and a southern convention is the most direct and practical means of obtaining it." On 15 December, after Calhoun had visited Columbia, the legislature unanimously adopted resolutions declaring that the General Assembly of South Carolina was prepared to cooperate with the other southern states in resisting the application of the Wilmot Proviso at any and every hazard.[5]

In the presidential nominations and election of 1848, the struggle between sectionalism and nationalism, in which slavery became the dominant issue, began to emerge. Torn by dissension, the Democrats finally nominated Lewis Cass, whose position on popular sovereignty made him acceptable as a compromise candidate to most party members in both North and South. For the Whig nomination, most southern Whigs supported Zachary Taylor, southern planter and slaveholder, in preference to Henry Clay, who to a certain extent was the candidate of the northern antislavery Whigs. Clay, however, was not without loyal supporters in the South, and Taylor attracted many southern Democrats. After Taylor's nomination, the antislavery groups of the two major parties, with no place to go, formed the Free Soil party and nominated former President Martin Van Buren as their candidate. Throughout the entire South, with the exception of South Carolina where there were very few Whigs, the most strenuous partisans of Taylor were the rich planters and owners of slaves. Calhoun, who said he trusted neither candidate on the subject of slavery, called upon his fellow Carolinians to take no part in the election, but to work instead for nonpartisan unity in the South. The election results gave Taylor and Cass each fifteen states.

Taylor carried eight slave and seven free states while Cass carried seven slave and eight free states. Voters were still more loyal to their party than to their section.[6]

On 22 December, after the election, some sixty-nine southern congressmen, representing every slave state except Delaware, met to determine a course of action. The Whigs gave this southern movement in Congress very little suppport. Why? Because the southern Whigs did not want to jeopardize the results of their presidential victory before Taylor took office. Robert Toombs, Georgia Whig Congressman, reported to Kentucky Governor John J. Crittenden that the Whigs had "completely foiled" Calhoun, whose project was "a bold strike to disorganize the southern Whigs." Toombs had told Calhoun that the "union of the South was neither possible nor desirable" until southerners were ready to dissolve the Union. For the present they should look to the national government for the "*prevention* of apprehended evils."[7] Of a total representation of 121 from the slaveholding states, 48 signed the Southern Addresss; only two of them were Whigs (Alabama and Mississippi). The South Carolina, Mississippi, and Arkansas delegates gave the Address their united support. Calhoun was evidently satisfied, however, for he wrote to his daughter that his address was "a decided triumph under the circumstances." In spite of opposition from the Polk administration, as well as the "most rabid of the Whigs," Calhoun believed the South was "more roused" than he ever saw it on the subject.[8]

Was the South "more roused" than ever? One prominent South Carolinian, H. W. Conner, toured the South and West and reported to Calhoun, "The people of Georgia of both parties are up to the mark and ready to act." They considered a confrontation with the national government inevitable, and the sooner it happened the better. In Alabama the people as a whole were "sound," but the politicians were blocking action. Conner feared for Louisiana, as New Orleans was almost freesoil in opinion, and the "theory" existed there that restricting slavery to its present limits would cause the lands and Negroes of Louisiana to increase in value. Louisiana would be "the last if at all to strike for the defense of the South." Conner had not traveled far in Florida, but he felt that the state was "right." Yet a feeling of despondency among the people in general—a willingness "to cower before the storm"—greatly disturbed Conner. This was "the *only danger* of the South," and he was convinced that "*prompt decided and efficient action on the part of the South*" was imperative.[9]

Other correspondents told Calhoun that the people of the South were more militant than their representatives in Congress. They deplored the lack of unanimity of southern congressmen, the "demoralizing influence of party organization," and the "treachery of both Whigs and Democrats." James Henry Hammond, former governor of South Carolina, declared that the value of the Union was "calculated hourly in every corner of the South," and the conviction was growing rapidly that the Union was a disadvantage to the South. He continued, "I met one five years ago who agreed with me, I now meet fifty." To Hammond the fate of the Union seemed sealed as a decree of Providence.[10]

Although the Southern Address, on 22 January 1849, did not create "any popular excitement," the South, as a whole, reacted favorably to it. Virginia was again in the vanguard, having taken a position not yet assumed by any southern state; both Virginia senators and half its representatives signed the Address.[11] In his annual message to the General Assembly in December 1848, Governor Smith had declared that if the Proviso or a similar measure passed Congress "then indeed the day of compromise will have past [*sic*], and the dissolution of our great and glorious Union will become necessary and inevitable." He hoped unity in the South would diminish the danger.

Two days before Calhoun's address, the Virginia legislature passed a new set of resolutions reaffirming those of March 1847 and providing that passage of the Wilmot Proviso or abolition of slavery or the slave trade in the District of Columbia would allow the governor to convene the legislature "to consider the mode and measure of redress." Virginians, responding through county meetings, approved both the Address and these resolutions. Richard K. Crallé, however, wrote to Calhoun from Lynchburg that he doubted whether Virginia would live up to these resolves. Should Congress pass the anticipated legislation, he feared that the state would submit "after a few patriotic groans." Crallé believed that South Carolina would have to look to states farther South for support of decisive action.[12]

On the same day that leading newspapers published Calhoun's Southern Address, North Carolina passed more moderate slavery resolutions. States' rights Whigs introduced in both the House and Senate measures declaring unjust and unconstitutional the abolition of slavery or the slave trade in the District of Columbia and the prohibition of slavery in the territories. To preserve peace and promote the perpetuity of the Union, the legislators expressed willingness for an extension of the Missouri Compromise line to the Pacific. Representative Edward Stanly proposed an amendment expressing the attachment of the people of North Carolina to the Union. The Whig-controlled legislature adopted the resolutions with the Stanly amendment. Whig Senator George E. Badger, however, described the southern meeting as "a most unwise and dangerous proceeding—out of which no good can come, but much evil may," and he intended "to have nothing to do with it."[13] A. W. Venable was the only North Carolina congressman who had attended the southern caucus, and only Venable and J. R. J. Daniel (both Democrats) of the North Carolina delegation signed the Southern Address.

The Address received little notice among the citizens of North Carolina. Democratic meetings in Greene and Washington counties approved it, but it was ignored at a large number of meetings in the spring of 1849. The editor of the Wilmington *Journal* wrote "that the action of the southern members was proper and judicious, still it would have been perhaps wiser, in view of the necessity of unanimity, to have given the address as little of a sectional character as could well be done." Moreover, North Carolinians were apparently indifferent to the possible exclusion of slavery from California and New Mexico. W. H. Haywood Jr., a prominent Democrat of Raleigh, thought that the people cared very little whether slavery went to California, and they would never be willing to dissolve the Union over such an issue. In May 1849 he wrote, "Of one thing I feel sure and that is that our people (NC) will rise up against Disunion and Disunionists the moment they see that there is any peril of action." The editor of the Whig *Weekly Raleigh Register and North Carolina Gazette* found "unsound" the opposition of the Democrat Raleigh *Standard* to the Wilmot Proviso upon constitutional grounds. The *Register* advocated protecting southern rights by leaving the question to the people, while the *Standard* was "for taking care of *itself* and *its party*" by entrusting the question to radical politicans or "constitutional hair-splitters."[14]

Farther to the South, the General Assembly of Florida, also Whig-controlled, passed resolutions in January 1849. Similar in tone to those of North Carolina, the Florida resolves opposed the abolition of slavery in the District of Columbia and declared that the South showed no party division about southern rights and the preservation of slavery. Florida would cooperate with the other southern states in the defense of these rights by any feasible plan, whether a southern convention or some other means. These resolutions also proclaimed firm opposition to any congressional act that would exclude slavery from the territory south of the Missouri Compromise line. They were much milder in tone, however, than the sentiments expressed by retiring Governor William D. Moseley, a Democrat, the preceding November, when he had told the State Senate that the South would submit to much to preserve the Union but this forbearance was limited; there were rights and liberties dearer than the Union. On the other hand, the inaugural address of Whig Governor-elect Thomas Brown on 13 January emphasized the preservation of the Union, although he pledged adherence to the sovereignty of the states, the rights of the South, and the compromises of the Constitution. He believed northern fanatics had done much to weaken the attachment of the people to the Union, yet southern demogogues had also done great harm.[15]

To a great extent response to the Address in Florida followed party lines. In Madison County a public meeting adopted resolutions critical of the congressmen who had not signed the

Address. A similar meeting in Gadsden County heartily endorsed the Calhoun document.[16] Governor Moseley regretted that he could not "*warrant* the cooperation of Florida in such measures as are . . . calculated to give security to the South," but he cherished hope that the state could cooperate. A Whig correspondent assured Governor Crittenden of Kentucky that Florida would always show an anxiety for the preservation of the Union.[17] Florida's reaction to the Southern Address along party lines was indicative of the response of other states with the exception of South Carolina and Mississippi to a little less extent. Generally, the Whigs opposed the southern movement as a dangerous way of increasing sectionalism in the South. They had opposed the Mexican War—a war of conquest waged by a Democratic administration. With a broad nationalistic outlook, the Whigs had no desire to agitate the slavery question. Moreover, they did not wish to embarrass President Taylor by endorsing Calhoun's Address.

Of the Florida delegation in Congress, only Senator David Levy Yulee (Democrat) had signed the Southern Address. Yulee wrote Calhoun that he thought "some movement of a more systematic character" than "the occasional meetings" was needed, but he solicited Calhoun's advice. Should there be a "convention of the United States?" If a southern convention were called, how should delegates be chosen? Yulee suggested preliminary consultation among the states before a southern convention.[18]

The Southern Address met with more universal approval in the cotton states of the deep South, where necessity for action seemed more urgent. Most of the southern counties of Alabama acquiesced almost unanimously, without party distinction, while North Alabama demonstrated more reticence.[19] A meeting in Huntsville, led by the previously anti-Calhounite Clement Clay family, however, promptly endorsed the Address and urged the Alabama legislature to prepare the state to sustain Virginia. A similar meeting of both Whigs and Democrats, described by the editor of the Greensboro [Alabama] *Beacon* as "one of the largest ever assembled in Mobile," gave hearty approval to the Southern Address and fully concurred with its sentiments. At other meetings throughout the state, Democrats and Whigs generally united in denouncing antislavery measures before Congress and recommending resistance if they passed, but these local gatherings also adopted resolutions pledging allegiance to the Union.[20]

Six of Alabama's nine-member congressional delegation signed the Southern Address. One Democrat who did not sign was George Smith Houston of the Florence District. Returning to his district, he began a contest to secure the leadership of the Democratic party by making the Southern Address an issue in the state election of 1849. He discovered, however, that sentiment in favor of Calhoun's position was strong, even among the North Alabama Democrats. Henry W. Hilliard, Whig congressman from the Montgomery District, had also attempted to defeat the southern movement in Congress. But some of the Whig leaders refused to support him for reelection as they did not want to create the appearance in the North that the South approved Hilliard's course. James L. Pugh even became an independent Whig candidate, with Democratic support, against Hilliard. His campaign was one of the first efforts to follow Calhoun's advice and unite, irrespective of party, on a candidate pledged to demand southern rights. Senator William R. King (Democrat) deplored the fact that Calhoun's pleas for unity had not been followed in Congress. Near the end of the session he asserted that if the whole South had "presented an undivided front" the slavery question would have been settled by compromise. Divisions among southerners encouraged the antislavery advocates "to persevere in their mad career, and where it is to terminate God only knows."[21]

While Howell Cobb, the great leader of the Union Democrats of Georgia, who did not sign, was corresponding with Houston about saving the Union, the states' rights Democrats were corresponding with Calhoun. Hilliard W. Judge wrote, "Your suggestion, as to the necessity of a Convention of the southern states is perfectly obvious. We cannot get along in any other way." Judge believed that Alabama, next to South Carolina, was better prepared for resistance than any southern state.[22]

Like Alabama, Georgia presented a picture of divided sentiment—sectional, partisan, and personal. Cobb and his intimate friend, Georgia Representative John Henry Lumpkin, and two Kentucky Congressmen, Linn Boyd and Beverly Clarke, attempted, in a statement to their constituents, to explain their failure to sign the Southern Address. The main point of the letter was a remonstrance against the formation of a southern sectional party. They condemned the Address for its failure to give justice to those Northern Democrats who had stood by the South. Cobb himself wrote to James Buchanan that his Democratic constituents approved his course. He continued, "It is in other portions of the State that the effort is made to make the Calhoun Address the test of democratic fellowship."[23]

Many Democrats in upper Georgia approved Cobb's position and supported his opposition to Calhoun; others, however, disapproved. Even Hopkins Holsey, editor of the Athens *Banner*, the Cobb organ, feared that many friends of the Georgia leader seriously regretted his position. Holsey believed that southerners were more aroused than ever in defense of their rights and wrote Cobb, "We will not *follow* Calhoun, but must cooperate with him in resisting the encroachment." The *Banner* editor thought that the southern Whigs would eventually join the resistance movement. Simpson Fouche, Democratic editor of the *Southerner* at Rome, however, opposed any public approval of Calhoun's Address.[24]

Democratic editors in the remainder of Georgia, especially the central portion, apparently favored the southern movement. Both the Calhoun Address and the Virginia Resolutions received immediate support from Democratic newspapers in the Black Belt.[25] In the spring of 1849 a few extreme leaders in central Georgia accepted the inevitability of secession or "secession *per se*." Such a person was Henry L. Benning of Columbus, who declared, "The only safety of the South from abolition universal is to be found in an *early* dissolution of the Union." Two of Calhoun's most ardent followers in Georgia were Senator Herschel V. Johnson and Wilson Lumpkin. Before the Southern Address appeared, Lumpkin had written to

Calhoun, "Nothing can resist this fire of Hell but the united resistance of the South." But he strongly doubted whether the South would unite, as he had confidence in no state except South Carolina. Johnson also expressed the fear "that the people of the South are not properly awake to the danger—not thoroughly nerved to united resistance." He took great pride in the fact that he signed the Southern Address, as the signers were "true friends" of both the South and the Union.[26]

When the Democratic state convention met on 11 July 1849, the Calhoun faction attempted to adopt the Southern Address, but Cobb threatened them with a bolt of his Cherokee delegates and the "uncompromising hostility" of the former Polk administration. The delegates, therefore, compromised for the sake of harmony by adopting the Virginia Resolutions instead of the Southern Address. This intraparty feuding among southern Democrats in most states was a major reason for Calhoun's failure to form a united front of southerners. Why? For many southern Democrats the preservation of the Union was more important than the preservation of slavery and the southern way of life as Calhoun thought. Personal enmities and rivalry for state control, as well as sectionalism within some states, were also significant.[27]

The majority of the Georgia Whigs tended to oppose the southern movement. Whig editors echoed the Democrats of upper Georgia by declaring that the movement appealed only to politicians and editors and the masses were indifferent. After all, the Whigs were the largest slaveholders, and if they were not alarmed, why should others be? Referring to Calhoun's Address, the editor of the *Georgia Journal and Messenger* declared, "The South needs no inflammatory appeals . . . no paper bulletins—no vaporing manifestos." The movement had lost its moral force and failed to unite the South.[28] Although Whigs demonstrated less division than Democrats, especially on sectional lines, the Whigs also had to recognize divergent action among their congressmen in the southern caucus. The contrast between Robert Toombs' and Alexander Stephens' efforts to break up the southern congressional caucus and Senator John M. Berrien's desire for a more conciliatory address was quite obvious. Berrien was the leader of the Clay faction of the Whigs; he expected no favors from Taylor and did not trust him to protect southern rights. Thus it was natural that this faction should tend to accept the southern rights views in opposition to the majority Whig faction, who did not wish to embarrass Taylor by endorsing Calhoun's Address. But the Berrien Whigs, unlike the Union Democrats, were very few in number and were not concentrated in any one particular section. None of the Whig congressmen and only Senator Johnson and Representatives Alfred Iverson and Hugh A. Haralson of the Democratic delegation has signed the Address.[29]

Meanwhile, district meetings occurred in many parts of South Carolina during February and March, with citizens of Columbia and Charleston responding more slowly than their rural counterparts. The delegates adopted resolutions endorsing the Southern Address and the Virginia, Florida, and North Carolina resolutions, and reiterating South Carolina's willingness to cooperate with the other southern states. The chief progress, though, was the beginning of organization for resistance. Most of these meetings provided for the appointment of Committees of Safety and Correspondence reminiscent of the struggle between England and the colonies. Charged with the duty of reconvening the meetings when necessary, these committees corresponded with one another and with other states for the purpose of devising proper measures for common safety.[30]

The next step after local organization was to form a central committee. In accordance with such an idea, the Richland County Committee of Safety and Correspondence invited the district committees to send delegates to a meeting at Columbia on the second Monday in May. Naturally, the leaders solicited Calhoun's advice on proper action. His opinion was that the meeting should aim toward adoption of measures to prepare the way for a southern convention, but the delegates could best decide what these measures should be. If anything could arrest the aggression of the North, "it would be the South to present . . . to the North the alternative of dissolving the partnership" or of ceasing to disregard the Constitution and violate southern rights. In order to present an "unbroken front," a convention of southern states was essential. The object of the southern convention would thus be to give the North a solemn warning and, in Calhoun's words, should the "warning voice fail to save the Union, it would in that case prove the most efficient means for saving ourselves."

On 14-15 May 1849 some 109 delegates assembled in Columbia. They adopted resolutions moderate in tone as compared with those of many of the district meetings and that of the press. They approved the Southern Address, provided for a five-member Central Committee of Vigilance and Safety, expressed confidence in the state authorities, and recommended a special session of the legislature, should Congress pass any of the proposed objectionable legislation. Furthermore, South Carolina should stand prepared to enter into council with the other southern states for united and concerted action. Yet the delegates extended no invitation for a conference to consider joint action. The meeting was conservative as a whole, and for some months South Carolina was outwardly very quiet.[31]

South Carolina's apparent calm was a ploy. Because the state was known to be more radical, the leaders thought it should remain quiet and promote southern unity elsewhere. Governor Whitemarsh B. Seabrook was already corresponding with other southern governors about their common problems. Franklin H. Elmore, Chairman of the Central Committee, advised Seabrook to send C. G. Memminger to Kentucky; in the same letter Elmore promised to go to Richmond. At the same time, the Executive Committee was making arrangements to purchase arms for South Carolina. Elmore told the governor to do nothing until he could see a plan for the defense of Charleston which the Central Committee desired to present to him.[32]

Mississippi probably ran close behind South Carolina in its resentment of northern aggression and fear of congressional interference. Shortly after the Southern Address, the *Mississippi Free Trader* called for a general southern states convention immediately after Congress adjourned. Pleading for unity, the editor declared, "The issue has to be met, the sooner the better, and it would be worse than folly for us to divide, in regard to the mode, the manner, or time in which it should be met." Because the important questions must be settled unanimously, he urged "upon the people a Southern Convention." Members of the Democratic party from one end of the state to the other endorsed the southern movement. In public meetings they warmly approved the Southern Address and expressed gratitude to the congressmen who had signed it. One prominent leader wrote to Calhoun, expressing the desire for an immediate settlement of the slavery question, for he believed the South was much stronger than it would be two or five years hence. As the Whigs saw opposition to southern demands growing stronger in the North, they also became convinced that the South must unite in opposing such measures.[33]

After several months of agitation in Mississippi, a movement calling for definite action began to materialize. Forty-five leading men of both parties invited the citizens of central Mississippi, without political distinction, to meet at the capital on 7 May 1849. The assemblage would consider recommendations to Congress and the state legislatures and ascertain whether Mississippi would cooperate with certain other states to arrest what appeared to be "the fixed determination on the part of the North to assail, if not destroy, the equality, independence and existence of the southern states."

In spite of inclement weather, a respectable delegation from central Mississippi united with Jackson citizens on 7 May. The delegates chose Governor Joseph Matthews (Democrat) as president of the convention. A committee of prominent men of both parties, headed by Chief Justice William L. Sharkey, described by a contemporary as Mississippi's "most talented and eminent Whig," proceeded to draft resolutions and prepare an address. Moderation and dignity prevailed at the gathering. The purpose of the meeting, stated by Sharkey in the address, was "not to agitate—not to act, but to prepare for action when the occasion may be forced upon us," in hopes that in defending southern rights the Union might also be saved unimpaired. The speech supported both the doctrine of state sovereignty and the institution of slavery and positively denied congressional authority over slavery. Upon recommendation of the committee, the delegates unanimously adopted resolutions requesting Mississippians to choose county delegates to attend a convention at Jackson on the first Monday in October for the purpose of expressing the voice of the people on the slavery question. In order to reach a united sentiment, the committee further recommended that the delegates should number twice the membership of the state House of Representatives, with an equal number of Democrats and Whigs.[34]

Division of sentiment was apparent in some of the remaining southern states, while others made little or no response to the movement. In Tennessee, perhaps more than any other state, the two political parties were the most nearly balanced. Whigs and Democrats vied with each other in efforts to discredit the opposition party; accusations of abolitionism and support of the Wilmot Proviso did serious political damage. The Whig Nashville *Republican Banner* placed the responsibility for the whole deplorable position of the South upon Democratic "follies," protesting that the Democrats were ready to dissolve the Union because they could not *compel* the southern Whigs, who were in no way responsible, to follow Democratic leadership. The editors continued, "We are ready to stand up to the rights of the South, to the 'last shot in the locker,' but we claim the right of choosing our leaders in doing it." On the other hand, the editor of the Democrat Nashville *Union* noted that as soon as Taylor won the election, the antislavery feeling in the free states gained momentum.[35] Yet intraparty divisions plagued both parties and increased the complexity of Tennessee politics. Whig Senator John Bell had ardently supported Taylor for President and had great influence with the new administration. Some Tennessee Whigs, who were friends of Clay, however, disliked the idea of a President under Bell's influence. Democratic Senator Hopkins L. Turney, who had signed the Address, was a controversial person within the state's Democratic party. He had been elected to the Senate in 1845 with Whig votes over A. O. P. Nicholson, the candidate of the Democratic caucus and a friend of Polk who was then President.

Jackson and Polk had left to Tennessee a Democratic tradition of strong devotion to the Union. Nullification had found little favor in the state. Only two Tennessee congressmen had signed Calhoun's address, but such men as former Governor Aaron V. Brown, A. O. P. Nicholson, and others were meeting "northern aggression" with a distinctly southern point of view. At their state convention in April, the Democrats passed resolutions and disclaimed all threats of dissolution of the Union but declared that it was "the duty of all Southern men, without regard to party distinction to deliberate and determine upon the true and safe line of policy to be adopted."[36] Tennessee Democrats also declared they would join the other southern states in such measures as a southern convention might advise. At the same time, a few Whigs in West Tennessee advocated nonsubmission.[37]

The three southern states west of the Mississippi River showed little interest in the proposed congressional measures and the southern movement. The presidential election of 1848, as well as the struggles in Congress, failed to arouse much emotion in Arkansas. Late in December 1848, however, the legislature considered resolutions recommending support for Taylor as long as his administration conformed to the principles of the Baltimore Democratic Convention and recommended that Arkansas congressmen oppose any efforts to interfere with slavery in the states, territories, or the District of Columbia. Before the session adjourned, the senate passed another set of resolutions expressing concern over the interference of many northerners with slavery in the District of Columbia and the territories, and reaffirming the principle that slavery was a local institution subject to local laws.[38]

On 23 February 1849, the *Arkansas State Democrat* published the Southern Address, accompanied by a favorable editorial. William E. Woodruff, *Democrat* editor, commented that the entire congressional delegation, all of whom had signed the Southern Address, could be assured that not one of their public acts would meet with "a warmer or more unanimous approval" than their endorsement of this "important document." In the same issue, a letter from Senator Solon Borland strongly denied that the southern movement was designed to dissolve the Union and urged everyone who desired "equality of the states and people" to "rally and speak out, as one man, to stay the black tide of aggression" which threatened to "overwhelm" the South. The *Arkansas State Gazette*, an intensely partisan Whig paper also located in Little Rock, ignored Calhoun's address and the southern movement.[39] Thus it appears that much of the reaction in Arkansas, like that of most southern states, was along party lines.

Louisiana had never advocated southern and states' rights, as strong economic and social ties bound it to the nation. The Mississippi Valley provided its commerce; a tariff protected the sugar industry; and the North furnished many of the state's leading citizens. Although the New Orleans *Picayune* (Whig), one of the most prominent southern newspapers, had covered the Mexican War in great detail and published articles on the great future of California, it paid little attention to the issue of slavery and the growing sectional crisis. The editor considered the Wilmot Proviso as primarily an attempt to prevent the acquisition of territory and dubbed "preposterous" the idea that such a measure could endanger the Union. In his legislative message of January 1848, Governor Isaac Johnson declared the Wilmot Proviso "utterly repugnant to the letter and spirit" of the Constitution, as it deprived the inhabitants of the right to organize their institutions as they desired. The issue should be met "respectfully and temperately" but with "a firm and uncompromising resistance." Somewhat later, J. D. B. DeBow, a much more forceful champion of southern rights and editor of the influential *DeBow's Review of the Southern and Western States*, set forth the southern position in an essay on slavery in the territories.[40]

Democratic reaction in Louisiana to the Southern Address reflected intraparty division as in the other states. Bitter enmity and rivalry for state control had developed between John Slidell and Pierre Soulé when the legislature elected Soulé rather than Slidell as United States Senator in January 1848. Soulé was an ardent follower of Calhoun; Slidell opposed the southern movement. His former association with the Polk administration as an unsuccessful emissary to Mexico probably also influenced Slidell's opposition. Louisiana Whigs opposed the southern movement because of their desire not to embarrass Taylor (a Louisiana resident), their intense rivalry with the Democrats, and their pronounced national conservative as opposed to states' rights attitude.

The editor of the *Picayune* did not endorse the southern movement in Congress, but he did recommend southern "unity, firmness and dignity of action." The *Picayune's* special correspondent in Washington wrote more strongly, predicting that a successful coalition would provoke rather than intimidate the North, divide the Democrats, and give the Whigs power for twenty years. Calhoun had evidently "outlived his time," and probably few would follow the old leader. In fact, the correspondent believed most southern congressmen regretted the whole movement. The editor of the New Orleans *Bee,* a conservative Anglo-French newspaper, called the southern proceedings in Congress a struggle between the friends of the Union and factionists who would dissolve it. With cordial approval of the opposition to Calhoun and the southern movement, he declared, "We consider his address . . . ill-advised, ill-timed, intemperate and grossly unjust." Although the idea of slavery restriction was as repugnant to Louisianans as to any other southerners, they found even this evil preferable to dissolution of the Union. According to James K. Greer, the Wilmot Proviso could not be made a party issue in the 1849 election. Nevertheless, four of Louisiana's eight congressmen added their signatures to the Southern Address.[41]

Generally speaking, Texans found the debt, the railroads, and the boundary question, on which they were expected "to act boldly," more vital than the slavery issue. Although slaves composed 27 percent of the population of Texas in 1850, the plantation system had not yet developed to such an extent that the great owners could control state policy and make slavery the paramount issue. But a few militant Texans such as Louis T. Wigfall, formerly of South Carolina, supported Calhoun's movement. Wigfall headed a committee that formulated resolutions reiterating the southern platform; the Galveston

County Democratic Convention passed these in February 1848. Soon after the presidential election, Wigfall sent Calhoun a copy of similar resolutions adopted at a public meeting in Marshall, Harrison County, the most populous county in the state. He told Calhoun that the state probably would not spearhead the opposition to the Proviso, but that it would unanimously follow the lead of any other state.[42]

The two Texas representatives in Congress signed the Southern Address, but neither of the senators endorsed it. Senator Thomas J. Rusk (Democrat), a member of the committee of fifteen created by the southern caucus, vehemently opposed Calhoun's Address, calling it "an attempt to create a new political party organization." Calhoun regretted most the lack of support from Rusk, who had been his protégé and was one of the strong men of the South.[43] Senator Sam Houston, a devoted Unionist, declared that Texas was "among the last to come into it [the Union], and being in, we will be the last to get out of it." In an address to his constituents on the anniversary of Texas independence, 2 March 1849, Houston stated his opposition to the Southern Address and questioned Calhoun's authority to act as "guardian of the whole South," whose interests he sacrificed for his own selfish ends. A public meeting at Marshall on 27 October, however, adopted resolutions pronouncing both Houston and Rusk guilty of "dereliction of duty to Texas" in not supporting the Southern Address. A short time later Houston again opposed the southern movement in a speech before Congress, declaring that the Southern Address was not intended to achieve "any valuable end." Rather it was designed "to create sectional parties, a step toward dissolution of the Union."[44]

In Missouri, the remaining slave state west of the Mississippi River, slavery was a domestic rather than a commercial institution. Yet losses in runaway slaves were disproportionately high in this border state. As the slavery issue came to overshadow all others in national politics, Missouri tended to agree more with the South. The Southern Address, therefore, met with wide acceptance. On 10 March 1849, the Missouri legislature had passed resolutions denying that Congress had the power to legislate on the subject of slavery in the states, the District of Columbia, or the territories, and instructing her senators to oppose any such legislation. Approving a settlement based on an extension of the Missouri Compromise line, these resolutions also pledged the state to cooperate with the other slaveholding states in any necessary measures.

In a speech at Jefferson City a short time later, Senator Thomas Hart Benton, vehemently opposed to the southern movement, claimed these resolutions were a mere copy of those offered by Calhoun in the Senate in February 1847; their purpose was disunion and thus he could not obey them. Benton accused the proslavery group of using these legislative resolutions to cause his defeat for reelection the following year as his avowed sympathies with the free-soil wing of the northern Democracy had put him out of step with his constituents.[45] One resident wrote Speaker Cobb that the "extreme resolutions" had been "smuggled through the legislature" in an effort to defeat Benton. Samuel Treat, Missouri's representative on the Democratic National Committee, wrote Calhoun, however, that "the tone and temper of the Southern Address suit Missouri at this time."[46] Senator David R. Atchison, the sole Missouri congressman to sign the Southern Address, became the leader of the proslavery group of the Missouri Democracy, which sought to wrest party control from Benton's hands. Antagonism between Atchison and Benton in Missouri politics duplicated the Calhoun-Benton rivalry on the national level.

No congressman from the remaining border states of Kentucky, Delaware, and Maryland had signed the Southern Address, although emancipation of slaves was one of the most controversial questions to be considered in a Kentucky constitutional convention in October 1849. Position on slavery influenced delegate selection in every county; Democrats were generally for slavery, Whigs, antislavery. Governor Crittenden expressed devotion to the Union in his first message to the legislature and shortly thereafter stated his opposition to the southern movement, especially "sectional conventions," in a letter to his friend John M. Clayton, prominent Delaware Whig. According to the governor, "no alarm or agitation" existed in Kentucky.[47] Since Crittenden was a close friend of President Taylor, he would naturally not have anything to do with Calhoun's plans. In Delaware, emancipation of slaves had been defeated by only one vote in the legislature two years before.[48] Former Congressman J. C. Weems of Maryland suspected that the nearly equal balance of the parties in his state precluded support for the southern movement. The Baltimore *Sun* expressed no sympathy for the movement itself but conceded that the Address contained certain acceptable principles.[49]

Meanwhile, a new administration had assumed office in Washington. Zachary Taylor failed to specify his position respecting slavery extension in his inaugural address, and he made no allusion whatsoever to the Wilmot Proviso. His cabinet comprised a rather "commonplace body of men," all of whom except George W. Crawford of Georgia opposed slavery extension. Neither the President nor numerous congressmen had been able to persuade Crittenden to accept a cabinet post. Alexander H. Stephens was convinced the administration would be "most desperately assailed" but pleaded vainly for Crittenden "to take the head of General Taylor's Cabinet." Administration policy quickly materialized. Taylor and the cabinet resolved to secure the early organization of both California and New Mexico as states, thus omitting the territorial stage, and to urge Congress to admit them to the Union. The plan probably originated with Secretary of State Clayton. Crittenden had earlier told him that Congress could not settle the question and had written, "The mode you suggested in a late letter is the only one of certain success—and that is to let it settle itself by admitting those territories as states, at the earliest practicable period."[50]

Before he had been in office a month, Taylor sent his friend, Whig Congressman T. Butler King of Georgia, to California as a special agent with instructions to encourage the people to form a constitution and petition Congress for statehood. By mid-October a group of delegates had framed a constitution forever forbidding slavery. Taylor could, therefore, announce in his first annual message to Congress in December

1849 that California's request for statehood would shortly arrive. In late autumn, the administration had encouraged the residents of New Mexico to follow a similar procedure. During the summer of 1849, Taylor had also thwarted the hopes of southern expansionists by his firm stand to halt the Cuban filibustering expedition. The freesoil Whig influence over the President became even more apparent in August, when he told citizens of Mercer, Pennsylvania, that the "people of the North need have no apprehension of the further extension of slavery." This statement confirmed the worst fears of southerners, both Whigs and Democrats.

President Taylor thus unwittingly aided the southern unification movement by supplying the driving force that it had lacked. Every new evidence that the President shared the views of the antislavery-extension forces and could not be trusted on the crucial question by many southerners gave momentum to the movement. The Whigs increasingly involved themselves in the activity, and the South became increasingly tense as summer progressed. Fears and criticisms of the administration rose from all parts of the region.[51] Senator Herschel Johnson of Georgia no doubt expressed the fears of many southerners when he wrote, "I confess I look to the future with sad foreboding for the South." Calhoun himself wrote, "The appearance is that Taylor's administration will prove a failure. I fear he is in the hands of the Northern Whigs exclusively." Thomas Claiborne, Nashville Democrat, declared that Taylor's administration was "the most wrecklessly [*sic*] persecuting of any other this nation has ever seen . . . The American people have never been more thoroughly humbugged." Even supporters of the administration found themselves on the defensive. Toombs attempted to explain the President's errors by the fact that he was in a new position with vast duties and responsibilities, and "surrounded by strangers whose aims and objects are not known to him."[52]

The admission of California as a free state would be an unacceptable victory for the provisionists. Senator Johnson urged a policy of compensation and firmness, requiring as a "condition precedent" to the admission of California the assurance of an honorable adjustment in New Mexico and total abandonment of all further interference with slavery in the District of Columbia and the states. "If we yield now we are gone," declared the Georgia senator. Although a southern convention was "the best and perhaps the only mode of securing harmony and concert of action among the southern states," Johnson doubted very much the feasibility of obtaining such a convention, for cries of "disunion" would probably kill the idea.[53]

After a summer during which the South saw little national recognition of its needs and desires, the second Mississippi convention met on 1 October 1849. Most of the counties of the state, as well as the two great political parties, were represented. The convention was not a unanimous expression of support for the southern movement, however; some Mississippians advocated waiting until Congress had acted. Upon recommendation of a committee of ten, President William L. Sharkey, Vice President Joseph W. Matthews, and Secretaries J. A. Orr and W. A. Purdom were named permanent officers.[54]

On motion of General T. N. Waul, the delegates seated Congressman Daniel H. Wallace of South Carolina upon the floor of the House. Wallace's purpose was to obtain from Governor Matthews an explicit declaration of the course of action he intended to follow, in the event Congress passed "obnoxious" legislation, and to get Matthews' permission to allow South Carolina's Governor Seabrook to quote him in his next legislative message. Wallace's effectiveness was hampered, however, by the suspicions of the Whigs, who were very much prejudiced against South Carolina, that Wallace was a secret agent whose presence would influence the proceedings of the convention or the approaching legislation. Although Wallace was never able to get a commitment from either Governor Matthews or John A. Quitman, Matthews' possible successor, he trusted the convention's action would undoubtedly create a coalition between Mississippi and the Palmetto state.[55]

Chief Justice Sharkey's address to the convention upon assuming the chairmanship stated unequivocally his position on the southern platform. He told the delegates that they could not and dared not submit to further encroachment. Resistance by every means in their power was necessary to self-preservation. Wallace informed Seabrook that no public man in South Carolina had ever delivered a more "ultra" speech on the subject at issue.

The next day, Edward C. Wilkinson introduced a resolution for appointment of a committee to prepare and report specific matters for convention action. The committee, of which Wilkinson served as chairman, comprised twenty members—four from each of the four congressional districts and four from the state at large. At first the committee submitted two reports—majority and minority—but the convention soon withdrew the minority report. After various amendments the majority report and resolutions received unanimous approval.

Although the resolutions contained a statement of devotion to the Union, they clearly indicated that Congress had no authority to abolish slavery in the District of Columbia, to prohibit the internal slave trade, or to forbid the introduction of slavery into the territories. Passage of the Wilmot Proviso or a law abolishing slavery in the District of Columbia would make it the duty of the slaveholding states to take care of their own safety. In view of the increasing determination of the North to disregard constitutional guarantees, and to agitate the subject of slavery for the purpose of effecting its abolition, the delegates believed that the time had arrived when the southern states should counsel together for their common safety: "A convention of the slaveholding states should be held at Nashville, Tennessee, on the first Monday in June, next, to devise and adopt some mode of resistance to these aggressions." The meeting appointed delegates and alternates equal to twice the number of senators and representatives in Congress, and invited other slaveholding states to use the same ratio. The convention further recommended that the legislature pass a law requiring the governor by proclamation to call a general convention of the state, upon passage of the objectionable legislation. He should then issue writs of election, based upon representation in the legislature, for delegates to consider the mode and measure of redress. The delegates omitted the most radical statement, declaring southern resistance should California be admitted to the Union as a free state.

Wallace reported that the author of the resolutions was Colonel W. R. Hill, formerly of York District, South Carolina. Because of Hill's origin, the committee first received and accepted the resolutions informally; the convention adopted them without knowing their authorship.[56]

Sharkey, George Winchester, Anderson Hutchinson, C. R. Clifton, John I. Guion, Hill, and Wilkinson, serving as a committee, prepared an "Address to the Southern States." No doubt Judge Sharkey wrote the long and able address. He rested his defense upon the rights of the South under the Constitution, referring to Hamilton, Madison, and Jefferson at length. Resistance to usurpations by the free states, through the federal government as their agency, was the "moral, social and political duty" of the slave states. If the slave states should submit to an attempt by the free states to destroy slavery in the South, they would cease to exist as sovereign parties to the Union. The Mississippi convention suggested, therefore, as a "possible ultimate resort" the call of state meetings which might lead to a convention of all the slave states to provide for separation and the formation of a new Union for protection of their rights. The convention thus ended on a note of southern militancy that surely gratified Calhoun and promised realization of his dream. Mississippi, not South Carolina, had issued the call for an all-South meeting; both Whigs and Democrats espoused the principles of southern unity; a southern conference *would* take place. That Calhoun originated the plan to have Mississippi issue the call for the convention has never been proven; his influence, direction, and advice, however, are indisputable.

After the meeting of Central Mississippians in May, Colin S. Tarpley, an eminent lawyer and an ardent Democrat of Hinds County, had forwarded the proceedings to Calhoun and requested his opinion as to what course the second convention should follow. Calhoun replied that the fixed determination of the North to push the abolition questions to the extreme left only one alternative for saving both the South and the Union—

"a Southern Convention, and that if much longer delayed, cannot." The convention should be held the following autumn if possible; certainly it must not be delayed beyond the next year. The great object would be to inform the other states of the causes of the South's grievances and to warn them of the consequences of failure to redress those injuries. Moreover, the convention should plan a course in case the injustices were not corrected. Calhoun further instructed Tarpley to address the call "to all those who are desirous to save the Union and our institutions, and who in the alternative, should it be forced upon us, of submission or dissolving the partnership would prefer the latter." He indicated that no state was in a better position to assume leadership than Mississippi, and that the proper time for a general call would probably coincide with the October Convention.[57]

When several newspapers the following year attributed the proposition for the southern convention to Calhoun, Tarpley attempted to show, in an open letter to the editors of the *Mississippian,* that Calhoun's letter to him had no influence whatever on the action of the Mississippi Convention. Tarpley said that he had shown the letter to only three individuals, none of whom were prominent in the convention. The convention acted, therefore, without any knowledge of the letter.[58] This may be true, but Calhoun's influence on the Mississippi convention came from an additional source.

In August 1849 Calhoun had urged Mississippi Senator Henry S. Foote to see that the October meeting issued the call for a southern convention—to save the Union if possible, but at all events to save the South.[59] Foote assured him that leaders of both political parties in the state had promised to follow Calhoun's recommendations at the October Convention. Yet the following winter Foote told Congress that Mississippi had acted "upon her unbiased judgment, without instigation from any quarter." Sam Houston's intimation to the Senate on 8 February 1850 that South Carolina had influenced Mississippi to issue the call for the convention met with stout denials from both Foote and Jefferson Davis. Davis claimed that the Mississippi Convention developed from the "spontaneous sentiments" of the people and that Mississippi looked to the leaders of no other state to direct her action.[60]

By December 1851, however, Foote was frankly admitting the Calhoun influence. He reported that during 1850 he had ascertained that several gentlemen in his state had corresponded with Calhoun; he had heard only recently of Calhoun's letter to Tarpley. Although he failed to mention his own correspondence with Calhoun, Foote reported that all of the letters he had seen satisfied him "that the *modus operandi* of the convention was more or less marked out by his [Calhoun's] great intellect."[61] This was by far the most truthful statement that the wily senator had made throughout the proceedings, and it explains very well the origin of the Nashville Convention.

But why were the Mississippi leaders so vehement in denying Calhoun's influence? The answer lies in southern politics—and in the southern mind. To admit South Carolina's influence would have made that state the instigator of the Convention, a course already deemed unwise. In addition, the Mississippi convention was not a movement of the people but an action of politicians, particularly certain Democratic party leaders, who felt that the Calhoun influence should be kept secret from most of the Whigs and undoubtedly some of the Democrats. Southern pride, sensitivity, and honor underlie the defensive replies of Foote and Davis. The implication that, in a section that insisted upon a Union of coequals and state sovereignty, one state would subject itself to the leadership of another, was unacceptable to the South's notion of itself.

According to Wallace, the Mississippi gathering selected Nashville for the site of the proposed convention as a "stroke of policy," in order to make a favorable impression on the public mind of Tennessee and Kentucky. Privately, friends informed Wallace that if South Carolina had *"attempted to lead"* in the struggle for southern rights, the result would have been disastrous to the cause. In order to maintain the support of the Whigs, the Democrats needed "to keep South Carolina *as much out of sight* as possible." Judge Anderson Hutchinson informed Wallace that he had a letter from Calhoun, but he dared not show it except to a few confidential friends.[62] Wallace confided to Seabrook, "I saw clearly *that our old statesman* was perhaps at the bottom of the movement."

If the South was approaching such a crucial point in its history as Calhoun feared, the political leaders, primarily the Democrats, had prepared the way for a cooperative endeavor. But in order to meet the challenge, the southern states *must be united.* Calhoun repeated this again and again; the hour demanded it. How would the southern states respond to Mississippi's invitation? Meanwhile, what attempt would Congress make to resolve the most serious sectional crisis the nation had experienced? The two questions were intertwined, and the response of either the South or the Thirty-first Congress could affect the other.

# 3

# *Congress Faces the Crisis*

During the two months between the Mississippi Convention and the assembling of the Thirty-first Congress in December 1849, sectional feelings were growing in intensity. The early response in favor of the Nashville Convention, Democratic victories in the South during the fall elections, and the bold messages of several slave state administrators all indicated tendencies toward resistance. Meanwhile, the northern determination to check the spread of slavery and remove it from the District of Columbia had also increased throughout the summer and fall. Writing to a fellow Tennessean, Representative Andrew Ewing of the Nashville District declared, "The spirit of anarchy is abroad and the Union is threatened on all sides." Ewing considered all the northern Whigs and many northern Democrats as "pledged" to an "unholy crusade against our Southern institutions."[1]

On the day before the opening of Congress, Alexander H. Stephens reported that the North was "insolent and unyielding"; he had never seen greater sectional feeling. A few days later he reported the opinion that the feeling among southern congressmen for a dissolution of the Union—if the antislavery measures were pressed to extremity—was becoming much more general. Some members, who a year before would hardly have allowed themselves to think of secession, were beginning to talk seriously of it. After visiting the nation's capital, James Johnston Pettigrew of North Carolina was amazed at the rapid progress that the spirit of disunion had made during the past year and became convinced that the Union could not possibly last longer than five or six years. Another North Carolinian, Calvin H. Wiley, expressed dismay at the number of "demagogues" in Congress who felt free to agitate the sectional questions for their own personal interests.[2] The success or failure of the Nashville Convention would thus depend, not only upon the response to Mississippi's invitation, but also upon the response of the incoming Congress to the crisis. Before any action could take place, however, the House of Representatives had to organize and choose a Speaker.

In the House, composed of 112 Democrats and 105 Whigs, the 13 Free Soilers held the balance of power. A caucus of each of the two major parties revealed serious sectional divisions. After a vain fight against Georgia's Howell Cobb in the Democratic caucus, the southern rights faction generally accepted him, only to have many northern Democrats deny his bid for the Speakership. On the other hand, Toombs, Stephens, and other southern Whigs became convinced that William H. Seward's influence would turn the Whig party into an antislavery movement committed to passing the Proviso. The Whigs could, therefore, recoup their strength in the North at the expense of the Northern Democrats. Assuming that President Taylor would not veto the Proviso, Toombs called upon him, and they discussed the subject fully. Although Taylor denied pledging himself to either side, he specifically indicated that he would sign the Proviso if Congress passed it. Toombs found that his own course "became instantly fixed and settled," as he would not hesitate to oppose the Proviso even though it required dissolution of the Union. On the night of 1 December Toombs presented to the Whig caucus a resolution, apparently drawn up by several southern dissenters, committing the party against the passage of the Wilmot Proviso and against the abolition of slavery in the District of Columbia. Intense excitement followed, during which the moderate southerners indicated agreement with the sentiments of the resolutions but said that the time was wrong for such action. The caucus postponed consideration at their suggestion, whereupon Toombs, Stephens, Allen F. Owen of Georgia, Edward C. Cabell of Florida, Henry W. Hilliard of Alabama, and Jeremiah Morton of Virginia withdrew. The remainder of the caucus nominated Robert C. Winthrop of Massachusetts as the Whig choice for Speaker.[3]

Election for the Speakership required 63 ballots over a three-weeks span. Although there was occasional shifting of the votes, Cobb and Winthrop remained the principal contenders, with the Free Soilers and dissident Whigs refusing to support either man. On 13 December, in the midst of "indescribable confusion," Toombs made a powerful impromptu speech. Toombs, more than any other person, had kept the southern Whigs from signing Calhoun's Address. Only a year later the man who had blocked southern unity declared that he "was unwilling to surrender the great power of the Speaker's chair without obtaining security for the future." If Congress abolished slavery in the District of Columbia and deprived southerners of the right to migrate with their slaves to California and New Mexico, Toombs advocated disunion. In another speech Stephens vowed, "We do not intend to submit to aggressions on our rights." Throughout the contest Stephens expressed deep pessimism over the outcome of the dispute. Even though a temporary settlement might come about he expected no final adjustment. Never again would harmony exist between the two sections of the Union; dissolution was "inevitable." On 22 December Cobb won the Speakership by a plurality of 102 votes to Winthrop's 99.[4]

The election of a Speaker did not allay sectional and party strife; in fact Calhoun described the strife between the two sections as "daily becoming more menacing." He continued, "The South is more roused and united than I ever knew it to be; and I trust that we shall persist in our resistance, until the restoration of all our rights, or disunion, one or the other, is the consequence." Northerners were just beginning to believe the South was in earnest. Moreover, the President's message added fuel to the furor. Taylor's insistence upon the admission of California, while trying to ignore or avoid other important sectional questions, such as the continuance of slavery in the District of Columbia, was bound to irritate resolute congressmen, especially many southerners.[5] Former Senator Herschel V. Johnson of Georgia expressed the fear that the admission of California alone would allow future division of California and Oregon into additional free states. Many southerners agreed with Calhoun that the admission of California was "worse than the Wilmot Proviso. What the latter proposes to do openly the former is intended to do covertly and fraudulently. It adds insult to injury." Southerners were keenly aware that California as a free state would destroy the balance in the Senate.[6]

Why was the entire territorial issue so critical for the South? The answer lies in southern fear for the future. If the South was not allowed an equal share in the new territory, the North stood to gain politically and economically at the South's expense. The central government would be further strengthened; it would lose much of its federal character. The minority South could ill afford to let this happen. Given a few years the slave states would be hemmed in by free territories—then free states—if the Wilmot Proviso became law. With additional representation from the free states, a northern dominated Congress could not only abolish slavery in the District of Columbia, but it could abolish slavery everywhere. Meanwhile it could outlaw the internal slave trade and further prevent the return of fugitive slaves. Instead of being hemmed in with the expectation of strangulation, the South needed to expand. The fruits of victory in "a southerner's war" were about to be snatched away. And even if slavery could not thrive in the new territory, there was the constitutional principle of equality in the Union. Southern pride and honor demanded no less than the "right" to carry slaves to the desert sands of New Mexico. A Union of coequals or no Union at all became a bugle call for high-spirited southerners in the political power struggle that continued intermittently for over a decade. Whether the fear was real or imaginary, it seemed indisputable to many southerners in mid-nineteenth century America. It mattered little to some that no act of aggression had been committed. Neither did it matter in 1861 for basically the same reason—fear for the future.

On 22 January Representative Thomas Clingman of North Carolina warned northerners that they must give the South a fair settlement at once. Congress should impose no restrictions on the newly acquired territory, although the South "might acquiesce in the Missouri Compromise Line." Senator William R. King of Alabama feared continued northern violation of southern rights would drive the South to desperate acts. The course of aggression must be stopped at once, only divine interposition could prevent dissolution of the Union. As if in answer to this fear, Representative Albert G. Brown of Mississippi declared in one of the most threatening speeches of the session, "I tell you candidly, we have calculated the value of the Union. Your injustice has driven us to it. Your oppression justifies me today in discussing the value of the Union, and I do so freely and fearlessly. Your press, your people, and your pulpit may denounce this treason; be it so." Brown delivered a final warning: "We ask you to give us our rights by *nonintervention*; if you refuse, I am for taking them by armed occupation." Stephens wrote to his brother that the Union offered no hope to the South. He did not believe much in resolutions. The argument was exhausted; the South, if it would capitulate to antislavery doctrines, must stand by its arms in the very near future. He would support the fight if the country would sustain him. Although not quite as outspoken, Senator John M. Berrien of Georgia agreed that the South must meet the situation, "Not by bravado—not by resolutions expressive merely of our indignation," but in a manner to convince the northern people that its determination was sincere. Berrien doubted whether anything short of actual resistance could produce this conviction.[7]

Ewing wrote home to Nashville seeking advice, as he plainly saw the dilemma southerners would face regarding the admission of California. He asked, "Can we and our friends on our grounds of non-intervention refuse her application for statehood?"[8] But unlike the President's nonintervention plan, southerners advocated the usual territorial stage. Calhoun's solution was to allow slavery to exist in all territories until the territory became a state, then decide the question by constitutional convention. Adherents of the doctrine of "popular sovereignty," as presented by former Senator Lewis Cass of Michigan, advocated letting the people of the territory decide the question of slavery or freedom. Both Calhoun and Cass, for opposite reasons, of course, denounced as unconstitutional the Missouri Compromise or any interference with slavery in the territories. Within a few months' time, however, the Nashville Convention would recommend the extension of the Missouri Compromise line.

Suppose the convention had been held in January or February, when southern sentiment was so high, and the South had united in favor of the extension of the Missouri Compromise line instead of demanding nonintervention. Might Congress have agreed to such a compromise? James Buchanan said the Democrats, at least in Pennsylvania, would have sustained it. Many southerners realized that California and New Mexico could never be slave territory. But to admit California as a free state under the Taylor plan, without any compensation in regard to other outstanding issues, was a greater concession than most southerners, Whig or Democrat, were willing to grant. Besides establishing a dangerous precedent, the President's plan left unsolved the other important questions. Herein lay the possibility for compromise through a broad settlement. California should not be admitted without a price; the North must be made to realize that the South was serious and mutual concessions were necessary. Such was the thinking of many southerners who cared about the safety of both the Union and the South. Southerners themselves were debating whether the admission of California as a free state, with or without concessions, would be sufficient cause for resistance.[9]

Henry Clay had returned to the Senate after an absence of seven years. According to the old compromiser's own account, patriotic duty had motivated him to serve. A year before, he had written, "God knows that I have no personal desire to return to that body, nor any private or ambitious purposes to promote by resuming a seat in it." Even then, he was thinking "of some comprehensive scheme of settling amicably the whole question." On the evening of 21 January Clay called on Webster to present his compromise plan and ask Webster's aid. After an hour-long interview Webster agreed in substance, though not in all details, with Clay's proposal and said that the plan should be acceptable to the North and to reasonable men of the South.[10]

Eight days later, with Senate galleries crowded and the Capitol lobbies full, Clay presented a series of eight resolutions covering the great controversial questions. California should be admitted with its free constitution, and territorial governments would be established in the remainder of the area acquired from Mexico without any slavery condition or restriction. The third and fourth resolutions would reduce the area of Texas and pay its debt, though the amount of payment was not specified. The fifth and sixth resolutions proclaimed the inexpediency of abolishing slavery in the District of Columbia but provided for termination of the slave trade there. The remaining points advocated a more effective fugitive slave law and prohibited congressional interference in the slave trade between slaveholding states. Even though Clay did not desire debate at this time, eight Senators, all southerners, interrupted at several points. Thomas J. Rusk of Texas insisted on the Rio Grande boundary, while Henry S. Foote declared the treaty with Mexico carried the Constitution with all its guarantees. "Is a measure in which we of the minority are to receive nothing, a measure of compromise?" derided Jefferson Davis; "I here assert that never will I take less than the Missouri Compromise Line extended to the Pacific Ocean, with the specific recognition to hold slaves in the territory below the line." Solomon W. Downs of Louisiana protested against the Compromise, because not one single point benefited the South. Clay defended his resolutions in a lengthy speech on 5 and 6 February. He appealed to both sections to compromise for the sake of the Union and pleaded especially with the North to cease demanding the Wilmot Proviso. "You have got what is worth more than a thousand Wilmost Provisos, you have nature on your side."[11]

Southern Whig sentiment in Congress began to change,

and the majority's willingness to accept the admission of California, if the Wilmot Proviso were not applied to the Mexican Cession, soon became apparent.[12] Why? Because the Compromise represented a national rather than a sectional solution to the crisis. The southern Democrats reacted differently, however. Speaker Cobb wrote of Clay's speech, "I fear no good is to result from it." His address would have a "bad effect" on northerners, as they would believe that Clay expressed southern sentiment, which was certainly untrue. On the second day of Clay's speech, Calhoun indicated that the so-called Compromise would get little support.[13] President Taylor soon made clear his own hostility to the combined plan, as he felt Congress should consider each question on its own merits. Furthermore, he hotly resented what he considered Clay's usurpation of leadership.[14]

Soon after Senate debate on Clay's resolutions began, Calhoun wrote James H. Hammond that the discussion would cover the whole issue between the North and South, and he trusted that it would be "of a character to satisfy the South, that it cannot with safety remain in the Union, as things now stand and there is little or no prospect of any change for the better." With the exception of Clay, Thomas Hart Benton, Sam Houston, and a few others, the tone of southern Senators was "high," revealing an increasing disposition to resist all compromises and to make no agreement that would not settle the entire issue in accordance with the southern position. Calhoun believed that sentiment for disunion as the only alternative was very general and increasing. The South had never before been placed in so trying a situation. "Her all is at stake," he concluded.[15] Berrien spoke first for the South in "the great debate." He declared to the North, "We do not ask your legislative aid. What we deprecate is your legislative interference." Those who sustained the power exercised by Congress in the Missouri Compromise did not understand it to be constitutional. They thought the pressure of the occasion warranted the assumption of power. In an extremely defensive speech on 13 and 14 February, Davis placed the sole responsibility for sectional difficulties upon northern desire to gain political power.[16]

Meanwhile, the battle in the House centered initially around an attempt by the supporters of the Taylor plan to admit California as a free state without compensation to the South. After a filibuster by southern Whigs had prevented a vote, Senator Stephen A. Douglas of Illinois contacted his lieutenants in the House, Illinois Democrats John A. McClernand and William A. Richardson, and suggested that they confer with Toombs and Stephens to try to formulate an acceptable program. At a meeting at Cobb's house on the following evening, 19 February, Toombs, Stephens, Cobb, and Linn Boyd (Kentucky Democrat) from the South and McClernand, Richardson, and Ohio Democrat John K. Miller, representing the North, agreed to attempt to resolve the sectional crisis in three ways: to support the admission of California, to support the southern stand on the organization of the territories, and to block any attempt to abolish slavery in the District of Columbia.[17]

In an effort to win Taylor over to their compromise plan, Toombs, Stephens, and Clingman called on him a few days later and argued strongly against his "California-without-compensation-plan." When the President remained inflexible, the southern congressmen intimated that the South would not "submit" unless he complied with their demands. One account reports that Taylor replied angrily that he would personally head the army to enforce the laws if necessary and would not hesitate to hang as traitors anyone involved in a rebellion against the United States. Shortly after the southerners left, New York Whig politician Thurlow Weed found Taylor in a rage. The chief executive declared that during previous years southerners had convinced him that the North was the aggressor. Since he had assumed office, however, he had become convinced that southern purposes were "intolerant and revolutionary" and that Jefferson Davis was "chief conspirator" of the southern group. Whig Congressman Edward Stanly of North Carolina did not believe that many persons approved the "violent course of Toombs Clingman and Co." He thought the whole agitation proceeded from a malignant wish to embarrass the Taylor administration.[18]

The real spokesman of southern opposition had been too ill

to attend the Senate sessions during this period. Returning to his seat on 18 February, Calhoun was eager to join the debate. As he doubted his ability to speak, he wrote an address that someone else could read. Webster called on Calhoun two days before its presentation, and for two hours they privately confided to each other. Webster apparently already had a very good idea of the contents of Calhoun's speech, and on this visit he outlined the main points of his own forthcoming message.[19]

On 4 March Calhoun tottered into the crowded Senate Chamber on the arm of James Hamilton of South Carolina. Wrapped in blankets, he sank into his chair and listened while James Mason of Virginia read his speech. No longer gratifying any ambition or fulfilling any hope, the dying man was making a final effort to save both his beloved South and the Union. The introduction caught and held the audience: "I have, Senators, believed from the first that the agitation of the subject of slavery would, if not prevented by some timely and effective measure, end in disunion." Such agitation had been permitted to proceed until it had brought into question the preservation of the Union. An almost universal discontent afflicted the southern people, who believed that they could no longer remain, as things now were, with honor and safety in the Union. Besides the continued agitation of the slavery question by the North, the primary cause of southern unhappiness was the disappearance of the equilibrium in the government—the decided ascendancy of the North. The South had no compromise to offer except the Constitution and no concession or surrender to make. Only a final and full settlement based on the principles of justice could save the Union. What was "a final and full settlement"? Equality in the territories, fulfillment of the fugitive slave law, an end to all agitation on the slave question, and amendments to the Constitution restoring the South's former powers of protection. In conclusion, Calhoun charged the North, who could save the Union without any sacrifice whatever, to accept the responsibility. If the question were not settled now, it might never be. California would become the test question.[20]

Calhoun was pleased with reaction to his speech, writing

to his son-in-law a week later that his address had "made a decided impression." Representative David Outlaw of North Carolina declared, "It has an 'awful squinting' at a Southern Republic, let the question of slavery be settled as it may." Senator William R. King expressed the opinion that in general the speech was "able, but in some particulars met with no approval from a large majority of southern men." Former President John Tyler of Virginia considered it "too ultra and his ultimata impracticable." Mayo Cabell of Virginia expressed the ordinary citizen's viewpoint that Calhoun's speech could "effect nothing." Cabell declared that Calhoun "always overshoots the mark and ever has on the slavery question." A northerner, William L. Marcy of New York, Polk's former Secretary of War, reported that "Calhoun had failed to take the South with him in his extreme positions." Ironically, Foote was the first to disagree with part of Calhoun's speech. He wanted it understood that he had not been consulted and despite his general agreement with Calhoun, he felt that an amendment to the Constitution was unnecessary; surely the entire North was not hostile to the South.[21]

Sometime late in February, Webster recognized that perils endangering the Union were rapidly developing. On 7 March he argued for the preservation of the Union on the basis that the law of nature excluded slavery from the West. Why insist upon the Wilmot Proviso? None of the conflicting issues justified secession, and peaceable secession was impossible. The object of the Nashville Convention, according to Webster, was to adopt conciliatory measures, to advise both the North and South "to forbearance and moderation," and "to inculcate principles of brotherly love . . . and attachment to the Constitution." If the convention met with a purpose hostile to the Union, the meeting place was "singularly inappropriate." Andrew Jackson would no doubt turn in his coffin if disunion was the motive of the convention.[22]

While New England antislavery leaders denounced Webster as a traitor, Outlaw reported that southern men generally received the speech favorably and it had produced "a very salutary effect." Calhoun remarked that Webster's speech showed "a yielding on the part of the North," and it would do much to discredit Clay and southern senators who had offered less favorable terms of settlement. If Webster's constituents and New England in general should support him, the question might be adjusted or "patched up for the present to brake [*sic*] out again in a few years."[23] The actual impact of Webster's oration on subsequent events is difficult to determine. There is no proof that his words changed a single vote in the Senate, but his personality and boldness, combined with what he said, tended to encourage the idea of compromise. As Stephens expressed it, "The friends of the Union under the Constitution were strengthened in their hopes, and inspired by its high and lofty statements."[24]

On 11 March King wrote Buchanan that southern men were showing a diversity of opinion and a drift toward compromise. Southern members, he thought, would generally prefer an extension of the Missouri Compromise line. Feeling this unattainable, however, they were "turning their attention to some other mode of adjustment." Toombs assured a friend that a proper settlement of the slavery issue would be a strong prospect, except that Calhoun's followers apparently desired no settlement and would probably oppose any adjustment that would pass. Representative Henry A. Edmundson of Virginia informed one of his constituents that the chances for settlement were "brightening," but he regretted that the South had lowered its tone. "If all had been true we could have dictated our terms," Edmundson declared. The South's moral force was now gone, and settlement would only invite further northern aggression. Another southern reporter from Washington indicated the likelihood of settlement, but he cited a small group in Congress, both northern and southern, whom nothing could satisfy except a dissolution of the Union. Although former President John Tyler preferred an extension of the Missouri Compromise line, he generally approved the Compromise as the best possible settlement. He, as well as many other southerners, was willing to compromise for the sake of the Union.[25] The crisis had been reached and tensions eased.

As if to counterbalance the conciliatory effect of a fellow

northerner's speech, William H. Seward set forth his higher-law doctrine in the Senate on 11 March. He refused to yield an inch, exclaiming, "I am opposed to any such compromise in any and all forms in which it has been proposed. . . . I think all legislative compromise radically wrong and essentially vicious." Seward's speech aroused hostility in both North and South, and even the President condemned his advisor's address. David Potter has correctly noted that Seward threw away an opportunity to defend the President's program in the Senate.[26]

Meanwhile, Tennessee Senator John Bell introduced a set of alternative compromise proposals on 28 February. According to William G. Brownlow, prominent East Tennessee Whig, President Taylor found Bell "the right arm of the Administration in the Senate." Bell's known conservatism on slavery extension also added some importance to his position. Bell believed the extension of the Missouri Compromise line, even if possible, would be a "barren victory" of no value. He proposed the creation of a new state from Texas, with its consent. This new slave state would balance the admission of California as a free state. In regard to the organization of the remainder of the Mexican Cession, Bell's proposal resembled Clay's, but he purposely omitted from his resolutions any proposals relating to slavery in the District of Columbia and fugitive slaves.[27] Opinions varied as to what prompted Bell, a southern senator, to introduce a second plan. Some persons considered it the result of consultation among southerners who preferred an extension of the Missouri Compromise line but realized they could not get it. Others saw a "modified form of the Executive policy" in Bell's plan. This was partially because the chief organ of the administration, the Washington *Republic*, enthusiastically supported Bell's proposals.[28]

John C. Calhoun slipped quietly away in death on the last day of March. Even in South Carolina many shared the feelings of Benjamin F. Perry, who confided in his journal, "I regard his death as fortunate for the country and his fame. The slavery question will now be settled. He would have been an obstacle in the way." Colonel William Preston called it "the interposition of God to save the country," while Joel Poinsett felt that Calhoun "was bent on the destruction of the Union." Others in the nation agreed, but the more common feeling was one of irreparable loss.[29]

A week after Calhoun's death, on the night of 7 April, a large number of southern senators and representatives met at the Capitol and issued a fiery new address to the southern people on their perilous situation. A party bent upon the overthrow of the South's domestic institutions had aroused sectional emotions; a successful attack would destroy the South. The group took steps to establish in Washington *The Southern Press*, a newspaper representing the radical southern position. The group fully recognized the necessity and propriety of the Nashville Convention; all of those present unanimously approved the gathering at the time and place proposed.[30]

Senator Foote insisted upon the creation of a Committee of Thirteen to act as counsel on all resolutions relating to the sectional crisis. The chief opposition to such a committee came from those senators who wished to consider the California question separately. Ironically, Thomas Hart Benton, Democratic Senator from Missouri, led the opposition forces. "I am opposed to this mixing of subjects which have no affinities," he declared, "and am in favor of giving to the application of California . . . a separate consideration, and independent decision, upon its own merits." During the ensuing debate, Benton described Calhoun's 1849 Southern Address as "agitation." Foote, who had earlier denounced Calhoun, now came to his defense: the "lamented" Calhoun was "illustrious" and his address "holy work."[31] The Senate finally approved Foote's proposal on 18 April by a vote of 30 to 22. Clay was chairman; other members included six men from the free states and six from the slave states.[32]

On 6 May Outlaw reported "little prospect of any satisfactory adjustment." The great difficulty, he explained, was in the House of Representatives, for the House would probably table any bill passed by the Senate. He further commented, "The Nashville Convention is dead for the present." If Congress adjourned, however, without any satisfactory settlement of the "distracting question," the Nashville Convention would "have new life and energy fused into it." He predicted "more excitement than at any previous time.[33]

Two days later, Clay read the report of the Committee of Thirteen. The main recommendation consisted of the omnibus bill, which not only provided for California statehood and for two territorial governments, but also offered solutions for the Texas boundary and debt questions. Separate measures included the fugitive slave bill and limitation of slave trade in the District of Columbia. Formal debate on the bill began 13 May. Outlaw predicted "strange bedfellows" in the ensuing conflict, if the southern senators continued to adhere to their opposition, and rubbed "cheek by jowl with Hale, Chase, Seward and Co." A few days later he reported, "Ultraism meets ultraism, and I am forced to the conviction, and so will the country be, they do not want a settlement." After visiting in Washington, Edmond W. Hubard, a leading Virginian, wrote his brother that a majority of the Virginia delegation opposed the Compromise because they believed the North would use southern approval to justify other improper legislation. On the other hand, Florida Representative Edward C. Cabell believed the South should unanimously support the Compromise because the North would then defeat it. Hubard thought this would simply weaken the southern cause. John J. Crittenden's faithful reporter, Orlando Brown, described the Capitol as "a perfect hum of wonder, speculation and conjecture," where the wisest knew the least and opinions on the result of the Compromise were as various as the men who entertained them. Congress was "a muddle": there was no Whig organization, and Democratic harmony was equally hard to find. Chaos abounded both inside and outside the legislative halls. Brown concluded, "Old Zach is the only one who stands unmoved like 'the red moon in a summer's night unshaken in the sky amidst the hurrying clouds.' "[34] The crisis was indeed critical; the Union was in danger and the South was in earnest. Mississippi's invitation had provided a means for southern consultation, and it behooved Congress to resolve the crisis in a manner that was acceptable to the South.

Meanwhile, as Congress proved its inability to resolve the sectional crisis, southern feelings had also grown in intensity. Southerners were debating the purpose and merits of an all-southern convention. Should they continue to look to Washington in hopes of a just settlement? Or should they counsel together to resist the continued aggressions of the North? Reactions within the individual states reveal the divided mind of the South. In the face of the greatest crisis that had ever threatened their way of life, some southerners were bold; others were cautious; while still others were outright hostile to the convention that was now only a few days in the future.

# 4

# *Southern Response to the Call for a Convention*

Mississippi's call for a southern convention met a generally favorable initial response. Democrats, as a rule, took the lead as the movement gained momentum; the Whigs, in keeping with their characteristic conservatism and a desire not to embarrass the Taylor administration, were less inclined to approve the convention. Yet in some instances the Whigs supported the meeting proposal to avoid being branded as enemies of the South. Moreover, some states' rights Whigs had already begun to calculate the value of the Union. When southern legislatures met for the winter session, the question of representation at the Nashville Convention became a controversial topic in many states.[1]

Southern states responded on economic and social as well as party lines. Reaction was generally most favorable in the lower South—those states that, with the exception of Louisiana and Texas, had a greater ratio of large cotton planters and Negro slaves. A definite correlation exists between reaction to the Nashville Convention and reaction to secession a decade later. On the whole, the first five states to secede, South Carolina, Mississippi, Alabama, Georgia, and Florida to a lesser extent, appeared most interested in a southern convention. Upper southern states—Virginia, North Carolina,

Arkansas, and Tennessee—with a lower ratio of slaves to total population showed less interest in the proposal. Nashville's selection as the site for the convention, however, affected Tennessee's response. In 1850, the border states of Maryland, Missouri, and Kentucky indicated their future action a decade later. The southern movement was also sectional in some states; backcountry yeomen showed little interest compared to that of low country planters.[2]

Although it may have been politic for South Carolina to be among the last to respond to Mississippi's call, Calhoun did not think that his state "should hold back and wait for the movement of the other states." Failure of the convention to meet for lack of endorsement would be unfortunate and would give the North "conclusive evidence" of southern indifference. If South Carolina did not respond, other states would hold back, for they still looked to the Palmetto State "to give the signal." Without South Carolina's support, the convention would "almost certainly fail"; therefore Calhoun urged James H. Hammond to urge the legislators to appoint delegates.[3]

In his annual message to the legislature, Governor Whitemarsh Seabrook reviewed the slavery agitation and predicted the probability of disunion upon the passage of any one of the opposed measures. Since the South finally realized the dangers of its position, southerners should forego party distinction and cooperate for the sake of safety or participation in a common fate. He applauded Mississippi's proposition for a southern convention and predicted a warm and unanimous response. According to Seabrook, the preservation of the Union was the paramount object of the convention. If that was impossible, the meeting should resolve "to protect and defend at all hazards, the freedom, sovereignty, and independence" of the states. Furthermore, he suggested that the legislature authorize the governor to call a special session, or to issue writs of election for a convention of the people, should the Wilmot Proviso or any similar measure be enacted by Congress.[4]

On the evening of 7 December 1849 the members of the legislature met in caucus and endorsed the Mississippi call, expressing their confidence that the people of South Carolina would support any measure that the convention might propose. The legislative caucus recommended that the people meet in their respective parishes and districts the following April to elect representatives, who would then meet at some convenient location in each congressional district and choose two delegates from each district to represent South Carolina at Nashville. Three days later the caucus chose Langdon Cheves, Franklin H. Elmore, Robert W. Barnwell, and James H. Hammond as delegates at large to the Nashville Convention. The legislature in regular session did not recommend any action for the convention; it did, however, accept the governor's proposal that he convene the legislature in case of the passage of the Wilmot Proviso or similar measures.[5]

Although the proposed convention met no open opposition within the state, thought in South Carolina was not completely unified. From the capital, Calhoun's nephew reported strong feeling on the southern question but a decided lack of concert, much of which he blamed on factionalism. The press and the public expressed various views on the convention's purpose and the action it should take. The conservative Charleston *Courier* believed the assemblage was a measure "of present security to the South, and ultimate harmony and prosperity to the Union." For once, the Charleston *Mercury* assumed a moderate position when it counseled the state to accept the leadership of others, for she could not advance further without endangering the success of the movement. When the Columbia *South Carolinian* proposed that the convention nominate Calhoun for the presidency, other state papers immediately protested, and Calhoun himself declared that he would not accept such an offer. William Gilmore Simms, author and editor of the *Southern Quarterly Review,* regarded the southern convention as, in fact, a southern confederacy. He believed that to secure one was certainly to secure the other; southerners wanted "few words and stern acts only."[6]

Georgia Governor George W. Towns, another southern rights Democrat, declared in his first message to the legislature that "further aggression was not to be endured." As a southern rights leader, he was anxious to promote the southern movement. He urged that the state take a firm stand and requested the legislature to pass an act authorizing the governor to call a convention of the people that would consider the proper measures for "safety and preservation" if Congress passed the Wilmot Proviso or similar measures.

Most of the Democratic papers in Georgia enthusiastically welcomed the call to Nashville and urged the legislature to respond favorably to it. The *Federal Union*, sole Democratic press at the capital, expressed the hope that before the legislature adjourned Georgia would be "standing among her sisters of the South on the same platform now occupied by Mississippi."[7] More outspoken was the Savannah *Georgian*, which declared that the union of the South and Southwest would save the Union by its moral influence or it would lay the foundation of a new Republic. One of the most militant of the southern rights organs, the Augusta *Republic*, formerly a Whig paper, expressed the opinion that a southern convention, which would simultaneously declare its attachment to the Union and demand justice for the South, would do more to check northern aggression and adjust the sectional crisis than "any and all other agencies combined." Howell Cobb's organ, the Athens *Banner*, did not support the convention; the Whig papers either attempted to discourage the movement or maintained a discreet silence.[8]

Senator John M. Berrien agreed that the legislature should provide for the election of delegates to Nashville and, to increase prestige for the measure, should authorize the governor to pay the delegates' expenses, either from the contingent fund or a special fund. He further suggested that the legislature might by joint resolution appoint a day for popular election of delegates, but he advocated recommending a list of names. Since Berrien opposed separate state action and favored united southern action, he desired to make Georgia's course dependent upon the proceedings of a southern convention.

Former Senator Herschel V. Johnson hoped to see every slave state represented at the Nashville Convention, but he feared that the preference of Toombs, Stephens, and Cobb for the admission of California would emasculate the moral power of the state, either in or out of a southern convention. Moreover, to admit California with the help of southern votes would render the convention "utterly impotent." Since Johnson had little hope that the Georgia Legislature would appoint delegates, he wanted the governor authorized to call a state convention to ascertain the proper course. The South must unite "as one man" and define its ultimatum, for the more southerners yielded, the "more unscrupulous" their "tormentors" would become. Johnson believed that unity would save both the South and the Union.[9]

During January, the Democratic-controlled Georgia legislature reaffirmed the southern position in a series of ten resolutions and approved a bill authorizing the governor to order an election to a state convention within sixty days, should Congress pass certain objectionable legislation, including the admission of California. The Whigs opposed using the admission of California as a basis for such action, but Charles J. Jenkins, leading Georgia Whig, introduced other resolutions to make clear the party's loyalty to the South. The measures concurred with those of Mississippi in the necessity of a southern convention and the hope that the meeting would devise measures calculated to preserve southern rights and honor, and if possible the Union. Jenkins' resolutions also provided that the Georgia delegates should be chosen by an electoral convention for that purpose—a move which House Democrats opposed. As finally amended and passed by both Houses, the resolutions provided that the legislature would choose four delegates at large for the state, while the people would select two delegates from each congressional district on the first Tuesday in April. The governor should fill any vacancy that might occur by an appointment from the party in which the vacancy occurred. On 7 February the legislature chose by acclamation William Law and Charles Daugherty, Whigs, and M. H. McAllister and C. J. McDonald, Democrats, as delegates for the state at large. McAllister declined from press of business, whereupon Judge Walter T. Colquitt succeeded him. In accordance with the resolutions, Governor Towns issued on 4

March a proclamation advising the people to meet in the several counties of each congressional district on 2 April to elect two delegates, one from each political party, to the Nashville Convention.[10]

Georgia's initial response to the Nashville Convention was characteristic of other southern states, with the exception of South Carolina. The same partisanship that had been exhibited in the response to Calhoun's Address was evident and for practically the same reasons. Many southern Whigs, however, were in somewhat of a dilemma, as President Taylor had come under the influence of antislavery Whigs. The southern Whigs had looked to him for the protection of southern rights. But they still desired a national solution. After all, the Union was more important than California and New Mexico and as yet Congress had passed no antislavery legislation. Furthermore, disunion would probably result in civil war. Many southern Whigs and some southern Democrats opposed the convention because they feared it would weaken the strength of their respective parties nationally. Among a majority of southern politicians, party interests still took precedence over sectional interests, as they had for the past two decades.

Meanwhile, Alabamians were also wrestling with the issue. On 15 January 1850 Bolling Hall, a member of the Alabama House Committee on federal relations, sought Calhoun's advice on the action Alabama should take. Hall was personally disposed to take the strongest possible southern position, and he believed his state was prepared for a dissolution of the Union in the last resort. Governor Reuben Chapman had also sought Calhoun's advice. Since Alabama had agitated for neither a state nor a southern convention, Chapman expressed "some fears that the suggestion of either might have a bad effect." But at the same time he assured Calhoun that the people were "sound on the subject." When the legislature met in November, Chapman recommended a provision for calling an immediate state convention, should Congress pass the Wilmot Proviso or a similar measure. He further suggested inviting other southern states to unite with Alabama in a convention to consult upon the general state of the Union and the best means of preserving southern rights.[11] But the new governor, H. W. Collier, in his inaugural address of 17 December 1849, made no recommendation regarding a gathering. He declared of the proposed Nashville meeting, however, "When that convention shall assemble, Alabama will be there. Some of her chosen sons shall give utterance to the united sentiment of her people—with her persecuted sisters, she will present an unbroken front to insult and usurpation."

A few days later, Collier transmitted to the legislature a communication from the Alabama congressional delegation regarding the crisis over the failure to elect a Speaker of the House. He declared, "The time for decided action has arrived" and recommended that the General Assembly "announce the ultimatum of Alabama upon the grave question which now convulses the Union."[12] Both the Alabama house and senate drafted resolutions in response, but neither set ever passed both houses. Each favored a convention should Congress pass any overt acts against slavery, but the house recommended a state meeting, the senate, a southern convocation. Collier was, therefore, left in doubt regarding Nashville. On 25 January he inquired whether the General Assembly could properly adopt or advise any course relative to the convention. Four days later, Leroy Pope Walker, Speaker of the Alabama House, introduced a bill approving the Nashville Convention and providing for the selection of delegates, four for the state at large to be chosen by the legislature, and two from each congressional district to be chosen by the voters of the respective districts. The house referred the bill to a select committee whose chairman was Thomas H. Watts, a prominent Whig of the Montgomery District. The committee report embodied the view of some of the leading Whigs that no convention should be held unless and until Congress adopted the contemplated antislavery measures, and then it should be only a state convention.

Since steps toward the Nashville Convention were blocked in the regular meetings of the legislature, members of both houses met in an extralegal "legislative convention" in the hall of the House of Representatives on the evenings of 6 and 7 February and selected delegates to represent the state at Nashville. They chose eight for the state at large and four for each congressional district, dividing the number equally between Whigs and Democrats. Among the most prominent leaders chosen for the state at large were former Senator Benjamin Fitzpatrick, Judge John A. Campbell, and Leroy Pope Walker. Alabama Democrats did not give wholehearted approval to the manner in which the legislature selected the delegates, but they generally supported the convention with enthusiasm.[13] The editor of the Montgomery *Advertiser and State Gazette* stated that on the whole he was pleased with the result, for Alabama was where she ought to be. Yet the legislative assumption of authority appears to have angered North Alabama, for the Huntsville *Democrat*, a leading paper, denounced the "legislative convention," which acted without the slightest authority from the people and chose five out of eight delegates at large from the General Assembly. This is not surprising, however, for the results of the state election the previous year had indicated that north Alabama was becoming more unified for conservatism and that south Alabama was becoming more unified against northern aggression; these tendencies would continue throughout 1850 and 1851. But the southern rights element, led by Clement C. Clay, Jr., urged the necessity of the Nashville Convention in meetings at Huntsville where they were outnumbered two to one. Whig journals that were especially partisan also opposed the action of the legislature. Throughout the period, however, the Montgomery *Alabama Journal*, the most widely circulated Whig paper in the state, favored the convention.[14]

In Mississippi, the editor of the Vicksburg *Whig* was optimistic over the southern movement that his state had initiated. He may have overemphasized its influence, however, when he wrote, "It is evident that the new Southern movement started by Mississippi has produced more effect at the North than everything else which has been in reference to the slavery question." On 7 January retiring Governor Joseph W. Matthews recommended calling a state convention in case Congress passed any "obnoxious" legislation, including the admission of California. Although his successor, John A. Quitman, made no special recommendation, he declared the South would not submit its constitutional rights and observed that the people of Mississippi had taken their stand; he had no doubts that their representatives would maintain it by providing means to meet every probable contingency.[15]

In February, Governor Quitman received and transmitted to the legislature a letter from the Mississippi delegation in Congress announcing the probability that California would be admitted as a free state. They regarded such a proposition "as an attempt to adopt the Wilmot Proviso in another form," and the congressmen requested an expression of opinion from their constituency. In his special message Quitman recommended firm remonstrance against the admission of California with slavery restricted there. The Nashville Convention, to whose deliberations this question might be safely submitted, afforded the opportunity for such action.[16] Regarding this suggestion as an attack on President Taylor's position, the Whig legislators adopted resolutions denying that the admission of California was an attempt to adopt the Wilmot Proviso in another form. This action, combined with other factors, brought about a party struggle in the legislature concerning the Nashville Convention. Since the Whigs favored popular election of delegates, they attempted to cancel the selections of the October Convention; one group of Whigs even attempted to prevent representation at all. But the legislature adopted a plan whereby the body in joint session would choose new delegates, a procedure the Whigs considered even more disagreeable. They attacked it as unconstitutional and illegal, and many refused to participate in the selection of a new slate of delegates on 6 March. Twenty-seven representatives, all except three of whom were Whigs, signed and submitted a protest for entry upon the journal. The Whigs also objected to the legislature's appropriation of $20,000 to defray the expenses of delegates to Nashville and to the passage of a set of resolutions referring the admission of California to the Nashville Convention, to be considered with other grievances. Editorials in the Whig press declared that the legislature had no more right to insert this issue, disavowed by the October Convention, than to usurp the people's rights by appointing delegates to the Convention.[17]

Florida Senator David Levy Yulee was considered a key

man in gaining his state's support for the convention and Calhoun had written to him approximately two weeks after the Mississippi Convention adjourned and enclosed a copy of the proceedings. Calhoun urged Yulee to use his best efforts to induce both parties in his state to unite in support of the Mississippi resolutions and to appoint delegates to the Nashville Convention. If the Whigs refused to cooperate, the Democrats should act alone. Calhoun asserted that Mississippi's course was the only one that afforded "any prospect of saving the Union, or if that should fail of certainly saving" the South. His hope for the future would be strong if all of the southern states responded favorably. But his hope would be "faint indeed" if the movement failed. "Concert thereafter, I fear, would be impossible; but without it, nothing can be done."[18]

The Florida legislature had, in January 1849, endorsed in general terms a southern convention at some future time. All three Florida congressmen favored a sectional meeting and undoubtedly regarded the legislature's action as an endorsement of the Nashville gathering.[19] On 6 February 1850 United States Senators Yulee and Jackson Morton and Representative E. C. Cabell (Whigs) addressed a letter to Governor Thomas Brown, urging him to assume leadership in devising a method for appointing delegates in conformity with the spirit of the preceding year's resolutions. In addition, Cabell wrote a separate letter to Brown, defending his personal stand. Cabell explained that he had abandoned his previous opposition to a convention, because the Nashville meeting would be an advisory body "to define the position of the South" and to propose methods of redress; he warned of the danger of waiting for aggressive action before calling a convention. Governor Brown, a "forthright old Union Whig," replied that he believed he lacked the authority to appoint such delegates or cause them to be elected, and he regarded the convention "as revolutionary in its tendency, and directly against the spirit if not the letter of the Constitution." Moreover, he regretted that such a move had been made before any overt act against southern rights had occurred; the convention would be useless and could result in more harm than good. Senator Morton resented the governor's attitude and carried on a heated newspaper correspondence with him. One letter stated that Morton did not consider Brown's attitude toward the Nashville Convention appropriate for his position as chief executive of a slave state or with the views of the people of Florida. He attempted to make Brown realize that the object of the Nashville Convention would be to maintain the Union if possible but certainly to preserve the South. Brown, who resented Morton's criticism, reiterated his stand by replying that the convention would be "wholly impotent" to impress the North.[20] The Whig press opposed the Nashville Convention and approved Brown's course, while the Democratic press, almost unanimously, followed the opposite policy.[21]

The southern movement was a sectional as well as a party issue in Virginia. The Richmond *Whig* declared it had heard of only one paper west of the mountains that had expressed an opinion favorable to a southern convention of any kind. At this time, leading citizens in western Virginia were trying to devise means to rid themselves of Negro slavery. But the Richmond *Enquirer*, organ of the conservative wing of the Democratic party in Virginia, declared that the Nashville meeting offered the best means for saving the Union and preserving southern rights. The Richmond *Whig* opposed submission, but the editor believed a southern convention would have value only if Congress passed the objectionable acts; then the people, not the politicians, should call the convention. David Campbell, a leading Whig and former governor, also believed that citizens should instigate such a movement. He declared that Virginia should not commit herself by participation in the assemblage and requested a friend to use his influence against sending delegates.[22]

The Old Dominion also had a small group of southern extremists, including Edmund Ruffin, M. R. H. Garnett, and Senator James M. Mason. The most outstanding of these, however, was Nathaniel Beverley Tucker, who wrote to James Henry Hammond and William Gilmore Simms urging them to lead South Carolina on; Virginia would follow from necessity. On 27 January 1850 Tucker wrote Hammond that he had spent several days at Richmond trying to influence some members of the legislature. He met with some success: many with whom he conversed had begun to calculate the value of the Union; even Governor John B. Floyd agreed with him. Garnett reviewed the "alarming situation" in a pamphlet published in 1850 entitled *The South and the Union.* Since the South desired to preserve the Union as it was, it must insist upon sufficient guarantees for future political equality, or dissolve a Union which no longer possessed its original character.[23]

Governor Floyd declared to the legislature that "the time has already passed for the discussion of the question between us" and recommended sending delegates to Nashville. In the House of Delegates, J. H. Claiborne offered a resolution calling for a committee on Federal affairs, which was amended to provide for the appointment of delegates to Nashville. The House referred Claiborne's amended report to a joint committee, which recommended more moderate resolutions. The original plan provided for a method of delegate selection very similar to that used in Georgia and state funding of all expenses. The joint committee resolutions, formally adopted by the legislature, only "recommended" the selection of representatives to the congressional district conventions, and advised that these meetings elect delegates from each party to the Nashville Convention. Whig leaders, who considered the whole idea useless but needed to satisfy their eastern constituents, were responsible for the change as well as the legislature's indefinite postponement of resolutions for subsidy of the delegates. A member of the House of Delegates, however, wrote Congressman Paulus Powell that getting delegates to attend the convention and bear their own expenses would be difficult.[24]

The North Carolina press gave little attention to Mississippi's call in the autumn of 1849. Only William W. Holden's Democratic *North Carolina Standard*, self-appointed defender of southern rights, expressed approval of the idea. Holden declared that if the other southern states elected delegates, Governor Charles Manly should convene the legislature in special session to assure North Carolina's representation. Early in the following year, however, the Nashville Convention became a subject of contention in the state. The Democratic press generally favored participation, while the Whig press, at first hesistant to condemn it, soon began openly to refer to the movement as a scheme of the disunionists. But there were exceptions among the Whig journals, notably the Charlotte *Hornet's Nest*, which led the campaign for the convention in the western part of the state. On 25 January the Democratic Wilmington *Journal* asked, "Shall not North Carolina be represented there? She ought to be, and we believe she will be." A convention representing the united South would convince the North that the South was in earnest. On the other hand, the Raleigh *Register*, leading Whig paper in the state, expressed a desire to see North Carolina cooperate with the other southern states in any judicious movement, but advised the state to hesitate a long time before committing itself to a convention of doubtful objectives.[25]

Edward Stanly, North Carolina Whig congressman, became alarmed at the excitement in the South and determined to keep his state out of the southern movement if possible. He declared in Congress, "If that convention meets, and a proposition is made to consider even whether the Union ought not to be dissolved, I hope the citizens of Nashville will drive every traitor of them into the Cumberland River." Stanly thought the western part of the state should lead in opposing the convention and urged a friend to try to arrange for the papers in the west to "denounce the dissolution efforts of the chivalry destructionists of the South." In order to prevent the people of Jones and adjacent counties near the coast from supporting the convention, Stanly urged his friends in that area to oppose any attempts at southern rights meetings. Another prominent Whig, E. J. Hale of Fayetteville, feared that the Whig party would suffer from a neutral or hostile position on the convention question. But he also felt that that consideration should not be weighed against disunion, as true patriotism required standing by the Union at the hazard of party supremacy.[26]

Governor Manly opposed the Nashville Convention throughout the entire period and refused to call a special session of the legislature.[27] The response to Mississippi's call in North Carolina, therefore, took the form of numerous southern rights meetings of both Whigs and Democrats; these were much more prevalent near the coast than in the uplands. On the whole, the meetings adopted firm yet moderate resolutions that expressed love for the Union but a determination to resist northern aggression. These gatherings usually approved the Nashville Convention and often appointed delegates to a district convention. W. H. Haywood, Jr., prominent Democrat of Raleigh, reported, however, that "not a county meeting (where resistance was offered) has voted for the detestable scheme."[28]

Only two congressional districts in North Carolina chose delegates to Nashville. On 11 and 12 March some 104 delegates representing every county in the district held a southern rights district convention at Wilmington. The convention elected Robert Strange, Democrat, and Griffith J. McRee, Whig. In the west, an especially strong movement in favor of the convention existed in Mecklenburg County, where some 275 leading citizens of both parties signed a call for a convention at Charlotte in April. This meeting chose Walter L. Steele, Whig, and Green W. Caldwell, Democrat, to represent Mecklenburg District.[29]

News traveled slowly to Arkansas because of inadequate mail facilities. Not until January 1850 did the editor of the state administration-controlled *Arkansas Banner* note the "fearful state of affairs in Washington City" and suggest taking steps toward sending delegates to the convention. The *Arkansas State Gazette and Democrat*, the other Democratic journal at the capital, declared that there was no cause for alarm and opposed such action. Apparently, the general population worried little at first about southern rights and the Nashville Convention, although a public meeting at Van Buren in Crawford County on 4 February passed resolutions proclaiming love and devotion to the Union, so long as the North respected southern rights and interests and kept the Constitution "inviolable"; it also appointed eight county delegates to the Nashville Convention. The press reports no other such meetings during the early part of the year.[30]

The *Arkansas Banner* published Congressman Robert W. Johnson's "Address to the People of Arkansas" about the middle of February. Johnson, a devout follower of John C. Calhoun, issued a clarion call for Arkansas to cooperate with the other southern states and outlined a plan to mobilize the people. He recommended that each county take steps between then and June to ensure Arkansas full and able representation at Nashville. In announcing the purpose of the convention, he declared, "The South will present to the world one united brotherhood, and will move in one column under a banner—Equality or Independence, our rights under the Constitution within or without the Union!!" Evidently Johnson believed the danger to southern rights was great enough to justify secession. In an address a few days later to the "Corps Editorial," he declared that he did not believe the North would force the South to separate from the Union, but the North would use its power to take all the territories if the South would submit.[31]

Meanwhile, Johnson had written Albert Pike, one of the best known men in Arkansas, and asked him to represent the state at the Nashville Convention. Pike, a prominent Whig and well respected lawyer, refused and clearly defined his position. He agreed with Johnson that the North was primarily responsible for the crisis, that slaveholders had the right to take their property to new territories, and that Congress had no right to prohibit slavery in any territory, for this would destroy state and sectional equality. But the South itself was responsible for some of its difficulties, and other problems resulted from natural causes. The South would always be a minority; its power in the national government would continue to decrease. Disunion was not the remedy, however, as it would only result in war. Pike recommended the formation of a new southern party, composed of Whigs and conservative Democrats, who would meet on "a conservative middle ground," vote as a unit, and force the North to act justly toward the South. "*There must be one party in the South*, if the South intends to assert its rights," declared Pike. Why, then, did Pike oppose the Nashville Convention whose very purpose was to create a united South? Pike believed that the convention would lack a "conservative middle ground"; it would comprise many "hot-headed" men, who would increase rather than allay the excitement. He also opposed using small groups of politicians or the legislature to select delegates, for the people should control the selection. If he attended the convention, he would have no legal power to speak for the state. Furthermore, the convention was not only unnecessary but dangerous.[32]

Johnson's views provoked sharp criticism, debate, and a newspaper war. The *Banner* supported him, but the *Gazette and Democrat*, as well as the Whig press, abhorred the suggestion that the Union might be dissolved. The Washington (Arkansas) *Telegraph* insisted that the whole idea of a southern convention was premature. The Helena *Southern Shield* denounced the convention as being "unwise and inexpedient," because of its sectional nature and "revolutionary" character.[33]

A few scattered county meetings took place in response to Johnson's plea. During the month of March, public meetings to consider the sectional crisis occurred at Batesville, Princeton, and North Fork, in Independence, Dallas, and Izard Counties, respectively. All three meetings passed resolutions condemning the Wilmot Proviso, affirming the rights of the South to the territories, commending the actions of Arkansas congressmen, and recommending a state convention at Little Rock to select delegates to the Nashville Convention. Izard County chose four representatives to attend any state convention that would meet, Independence County three. Dallas County selected eleven delegates to the Nashville Convention.[34]

William Conway B.,[35] member of a very prominent family, part of the Johnson-Conway faction in state politics and associate justice of the Arkansas Supreme Court, assumed leadership in the Batesville meeting. He offered the resolutions that were adopted and was one of the three representatives chosen to attend a possible state convention. The judge favored a southern assemblage, and wrote his North Carolina sweetheart, Miss Lucy Williams, that he planned to attend the Nashville Convention and assured her "a joyous time" if she would meet him there. If Judge Conway attended the meeting, his role was that of a spectator. Actually, social events and the prospect of seeing Miss Williams, a beautiful and talented socialite, may have attracted the judge more than the infringement of southern rights.[36]

In his final annual message to the legislature, Louisiana Governor Isaac Johnson advised the adoption of proper measures to send delegates to the convention and stated, "I feel a proud assurance that Louisiana will support with courage and dignity any measures the convention may adopt." Governor William Walker, inaugurated in February 1850, expressed a love for the Union but a preference for dissolution to the Wilmot Proviso. Of a similar nature were his recommendations that Louisiana act with Mississippi to repel the encroachments of the antislavery interests. The New Orleans *Daily Crescent*, however, expressed regret that the governor advised the legislature to send delegates to the "unnecessary" Nashville Convention. "We should be mortified to find Louisiana dangling on the tail of any such movement," declared the editor. A "dignified, moderate and firm course" would be more valuable than "all the cheap patriotism of convention resolutions and addresses." The New Orleans *Bulletin*, a leading Whig journal, also immediately opposed the governor's recommendation, as the convention would increase sectional antagonism. The New Orleans *Bee* described Walker's views as "a rehash of the extravagancies of the South Carolina school, with its 'quioxotic' remedy of a Southern Convention."[37]

On the other hand, the editor of the New Orleans *Courier* regretted such opposition to a convention "highly conservative in nature" that was "perhaps the best . . . mode of preserving the Union and the Constitution." He assured his readers that the gathering was for deliberation only. The influential New Orleans *Picayune* presumed the legislature would accede in the governor's recommendations. The editor believed that protest would be destructive, as unanimity of sentiment and action were "particularly requisite" in the present crisis, and confessed to some confusion as to the object of the meeting. A convention of men of "proper character" of the whole South could lend "greater dignity" to southern sentiments and might be beneficial. Although some no doubt proposed to use the Nashville Convention as an "entering wedge" to dissolution of the Union, but he did not think the meeting would do anything to impair the integrity of the Union.[38] Other journals expressed the opinion that Louisiana should be represented so that her influence, if necessary, could bolster the cause of the Union.

Former Democratic Congressman John Slidell of New Orleans, whose hostility toward Senator Soulé continued, declared his own hostility to a southern convention, but appeared somewhat equivocal. While an attack on slavery in the District of Columbia would justify a firm stand, passage of the Wilmot Proviso would not be sufficient provocation for disunion. Yet perhaps the time had already arrived when it was necessary "for Southern men to pass the true line of resistance to secure themselves from further aggression."[39]

On 20 February the decidedly Democratic Louisiana Senate voted 26-1 to adopt the so-called Slavery Resolutions, which recommended that each parish send a representative to the Nashville Convention and empowered the governor to convene the legislature to discuss appropriate action should Congress pass the Wilmot Proviso or abolish slavery in the District of Columbia. But some of the most influential legislators, both Whig and Democrat, opposed sending delegates, and the house, containing a large Whig majority, never voted on these senate resolutions. After two or three days' debates, in which the measures encountered strong opposition, the house postponed them, and all efforts at reconsideration failed. Louisiana, therefore, took no official action in response to Mississippi's call for a southern convention.[40]

In Texas, the Nashville Convention faced almost insurmountable obstacles, which included the opposition of both Senators and a large majority of the state's newspapers. Senator Sam Houston ridiculed the idea, asserting in a speech at Knoxville, Tennessee, that the convention instigators contemplated a dissolution of the Union; "Every d——d rascal who attends it, or advocates it, ought to be hung with a d——d great rough halter." Nevertheless, the southern rights movement had some strong supporters in the Lone Star State. Although retiring Governor George T. Wood made no specific mention of the convention itself, his message to the legislature stated that the South should "make common course" against the impending danger to her security. Newly inaugurated Governor Peter Bell also failed to advocate representation at the Nashville Convention specifically, but he did recommend the Virginia Resolutions as a model for a "firm, but temperate stand." On 30 January the legislature adopted strong proslavery resolutions committing Texas to Calhoun's position on southern rights and promising common cause with the South in defense of slavery. Throughout the legislative session the editor of the *Texas Republican* at Marshall urged the legislature to insure Texas representation at Nashville.[41]

Shortly before adjournment, the Texas legislature passed a joint resolution recommending that the people choose representatives to the convention on the same day, the first Monday in March, that they would select a permanent site for a capital. Each of the two congressional districts would elect four delegates. A joint resolution instructing the delegates to ignore any plans that might lead to a dissolution of the Union failed to pass. Several of the newspapers of the state denounced the legislative resolutions. The Whig Galveston *Journal* indicated that the people did not consider the emergency serious enough to warrant the action recommended by the "ill-timed" resolution. The editor of the influential Houston *Weekly Telegraph* thought the Nashville Convention would likely "prove as abortive if not as odious as the Hartford Convention." Some editors mentioned the impossibility of obtaining a fair vote of the whole state in the short time between legislative action and election.[42]

Legislative members and interested citizens of the two congressional districts met in separate meetings at Austin and nominated four delegates for each district, but accurate results of the election are unavailable. The Austin *Texas Gazette* declared that not one man in a hundred voting for the seat of government cast a ballot for the nominees. Had the convention met before the present session of Congress it might have served to embody southern sentiment and systematize its public action, but that goal was now unattainable. The people's indifference toward the election did not arise because the men were unacceptable, but because the people distrusted the plan, if not the purpose. J. Pinckney Henderson, the only prominent person chosen, was the sole Texas delegate to attend the convention.[43]

The border slave states' response to the convention call matched their earlier position in the sectional crisis. Though the governor of Maryland made no specific reference to the Nashville Convention in his annual message, he indicated that the preservation of the republic "must now rest upon the firm, united, temperate, but determined action of the Southern states." Maryland's representatives must, therefore, reflect the sentiments of their constituents by a solemn declaration of an unalterable determination of the states to make common cause with the South, in the event of the passage of the Wilmot Proviso or any similar scheme. During the impending session, the legislature adopted unanimously a series of resolutions in line with these recommendations, but made no decision in favor of the southern convention. Nor did the people of any county make any move toward electing delegates.[44]

In Missouri, the St. Louis *Reveille* stated in an editorial that the political affinities of the editors regulated the tone of the press toward the southern convention in both Missouri and Kentucky. Those in favor of the Wilmot Proviso or similar measures were strongly inclined to denounce the South as plotting treason; those who thought the North had wantonly invaded the rights of the South expressed confidence that nothing inconsistent with the security of the Union was contemplated. The editor concluded that the politicians and newspapers were playing upon public prejudices to advance their personal interests. Moreover, he believed disunion sentiment undoubtedly originated in the North with the abolitionists, but the South was at fault in permitting feelings to control judgment by acting on suggestions of demagogues.

The question at issue in the Missouri election of 1850 was invariably union or disunion, with the voters divided into three groups: Democrats, Whigs, and disunionists. In almost every county except St. Louis, leading Democratic politicians opposed the reelection of Senator Thomas Hart Benton, a strong Unionist. A Union meeting at St. Louis on 18 March declared both the Wilmot Proviso and the Nashville Convention "inexpedient" and favored a compromise on the slavery question. The Missouri legislature represented this same divided sentiment in adopting very strong resolutions but making no mention of the Nashville Convention. Apparently, the people manifested no desire for representation there.[45]

Kentucky Governor John J. Crittenden took a firm stand for the Union in his annual message, declaring that Kentucky "deprecates disunion as the greatest calamity; she can see *no remedy* in it—none certainly for any grievance as yet complained of or to be apprehended."[46] Henry Clay's correspondence reveals concern that his state would cooperate in a "disunion" movement. Before the end of 1849, he asked his friend General Leslie Combs[47] to organize, if possible, "large powerful" meetings of both parties at various places to express determination to stand by the Union. He hoped to see a similar expression of opinion from the legislature and enclosed some resolutions that he desired to see adopted. About a month later he wrote again to Combs, "I am awaiting with anxiety for popular expression in Kentucky in favor of the Union, let what come that may." He feared delay, as the "contagion of disunion" might attack his state. Finally, on 6 March he reported to his son James that the Kentucky legislature had given him no instructions, passed moderate resolutions, and refused representation at the Nashville Convention, and he concluded, "All this is well." A few days before Clay's letter, the state senate had killed a proposition supporting the convention by a vote of 26 to 9.[48]

Meanwhile in Tennessee the desire to be hospitable somewhat offset intense partisanship. The state press initially approved the call for the Nashville Convention.[49] Even the Nashville *Republican Banner*, leading Whig paper and organ of John Bell, could see no harm in a southern meeting. Shortly after the Mississippi Convention, the *Banner* expressed the hope that the forthcoming convention would be fully represented and extended the delegates a cordial welcome on behalf of the citizens of the state. The editor's attitude changed in early 1850, however, and the *Banner* began to oppose the gathering as "a desecration to the capital of the state." The Nashville *Union* (Democrat) attributed the *Banner's* "miraculous summerset" to the influence of the "potential voice" of Bell. When the *Union* charged inconsistency, the Whig *Banner* claimed that no voices called for disunion in October, but now the situation had changed.[50] All the Whig papers, with the exception of the Memphis *Enquirer* and later the Trenton *Banner*, soon unanimously opposed the convention. On the other hand, the Democratic press favored the assemblage and urged Tennessee's participation.[51] The editor of the *Union* believed that the citizens of Tennessee approved the convention and thought that the selection of her capital as the meeting place brought honor to the state.[52]

Tennessee Democrats, led by their newly inaugurated governor, William Trousdale, planned to provide by law or resolution for executive appointment of delegates. The Democratic-controlled House of Representatives entertained a resolution requesting the governor to appoint two delegates from the state at large and two from each congressional district, irrespective of party. The resolution, which also recommended that the people of each county appoint one or more to attend the convention, passed the house 34 to 28, with only one Democrat opposing it. In the senate, the Whig committee on resolutions reported that organizing a southern convention was not a part of their duty. If the people desired such a meeting, they should act in their primary assemblies, for neither the General Assembly nor the governor possessed this authority. The senate rejected Democratic effort to pass a resolution requesting the people of the state to adopt the suggested course by a vote of 11 to 9.[53] Cave Johnson, a prominent Democratic politician and former postmaster general, reported these proceedings and remarked, "The proposed convention at Nashville alarms me." But W. F. Cooper, later secretary of the Nashville Convention, stated that most Tennesseans, at the opening of Congress, favored a southern convention and believed that the

South must show an "unbroken front." He pointed out that the press of both parties had expressed approval, whereas "not a solitary voice in Tennessee" would have approved if disunion were an objective. Cooper and the other moderates desired representation from all southern states, particularly Tennessee and Kentucky. They wanted some "cool heads and compromising spirits to keep the hotspurs in check."[54]

Developments in Congress, in the meantime, tended to affect the southern movement. Undoubtedly, the introduction and progress of the compromise resolutions instilled hope in many southerners that a settlement would be reached in Congress, hence obviating the necessity of a southern convention. Although Whig sentiment in favor of the convention diminished, the change was not altogether partisan.

# 5

# *A Change in Sentiment*

The southern movement reached a peak around the end of February. In Washington southern radicals countered more moderate Whigs and Democrats, and many feared that the impasse would lead to conflict that would eventually destroy the Union. Webster's conciliatory speech on 7 March, then, did much to reassure moderates on both sides that compromise was not an impossibility. The effect of this speech on the southern movement is difficult to ascertain, however. Herbert D. Foster has indicated that the steadily growing agitation for secession in the South until March 1850 constituted a serious danger to the Union, but Webster's conciliatory policy inspired such confidence in southerners that the southern convention movement proved relatively harmless by June.[1] Certainly, Webster, like Clay, had more influence in the country at large than he had in Washington, and his oration received favorable approval in the South as a whole. But Foster errs in assuming that Webster's influence served to restrain the radical purposes of the Nashville Convention, since the motives of the convention were never entirely radical.

Indeed, a change was already under way in the South even before Webster spoke to the Senate. On 4 March, three days before the speech, the editor of the Mobile *Daily Register*

(Democrat) asked, "Shall the Southern Convention be held? This has become an important practical question." He observed that a few weeks previously the thoughtful men of both parties of the South had apparently assented in the necessity of the convention, but recently a countercurrent of sentiment had developed. Some had denounced the convention as "iniquitous in its purposes, and treasonable in its designs—having in view nothing less than a dismemberment of the Union, and an overthrow of the Federal Constitution." Assuring his readers that the purposes of the convention were "to defend and protect," and "not to encroach or destroy," the editor expressed the opinion that such an assemblage was more necessary now than it had ever been before. The only alternatives were a southern convention or unqualified submission. Because of the Tennessee legislature's disapproval of the convention, he suggested another meeting place, preferably Washington City.

Webster's speech received applause in most southern papers, while many condemned Calhoun's remedy as impracticable.[2] The New Orleans *Picayune* gave the highest compliments to Webster's oration and declared that no other man had brought to the side of conciliation "so much grandeur of intellect and power of position." The editor thought the reception of Calhoun's speech indicated few southern supporters for his ultraism. Equally laudatory was the New Orleans *Bee*, which called Webster's speech a "colossal product of intellectual greatness." The Washington correspondent of the Baltimore *Sun* named it a "historical event" and declared that Webster had "most effectively killed Calhounism and peaceable secession," as well as "the Wilmot Proviso and the free-soilers." In Mississippi, the Jackson *Southron* praised the speech and reported that it "extorted the universal praise" of every southern paper noted. Even the radical Charleston *Mercury* described the address as "emphatically a great speech, noble in language, generous and conciliating in tone," but the editor disagreed with those who thought the danger was over.[3] The *Daily Constitutionalist* (Augusta) asked, "But what produced Webster's speech? It was Southern agitation." The New Orleans *Courier* went so far as to credit the southern movement and the Virginia Resolutions for Webster's speech, the appointment of the Committee of Thirteen, and the peaceful spirit now prevailing in Congress.[4]

While some southern leaders were equally complimentary of Webster's speech, others believed the oration had injured the South by causing hesitation. On the one hand, Governor Charles Manly of North Carolina expressed appreciation to Webster "in the most unqualified admiration of the conservative temper, the lofty eloquence, the patriotic fervor, and above all . . . the self-sacrificing boldness" of his "matchless" oratory. He intended to file Webster's speech among his valuable papers as a "rich legacy" to his children. Another North Carolinian, James Graham, said that Webster's address did more to avert the Proviso than any other speech. Yet he gave Webster less credit in promotion of a settlement than he gave to some of his contemporaries, although Webster had gone "further than any Northern man dare go." W. F. Cooper of Nashville considered Webster's spirit and tone even greater than his argument and oratory.[5] On the other hand, William O. Goode, leading Virginia Democrat, declared that the message had "given courage to all who wavered in their resolution, or who were secretly opposed" to the convention. An unidentified correspondent wrote the Mobile *Register* that Webster's speech had damaged the southern cause more severely than anything that had occurred that winter. It had induced the people of the South to suppose the danger had passed and consequently to let down. Yet the writer did believe that the southern movement had apparently forced the North to abandon the Wilmot Proviso.[6]

The intense press partisanship of that time makes it more difficult today to determine change in journalistic attitude toward the Nashville Convention. The editor of the New Orleans *Bee* (Whig) declared that public opinion on the one hand, and the probability of an early and honorable settlement on the other, had united to destroy whatever popularity the meeting might once have enjoyed. Yet the Richmond *Enquirer* (Democrat) stated that the favorable effect of Webster's speech on the South had been "much cooled down by his revelations" that he would vote for the immediate admission of California as a separate bill, independent of other issues of importance to the South. This, together with Seward's speech a few days later, led the editor to conclude that the South could expect little from an adjustment in Congress. He also intimated that the President intended to establish a military police over the proceedings at Nashville. The Richmond editor was, therefore, convinced more strongly than ever that only the Nashville Convention could save the South from "utter degradation" and the Union from dissolution. Other influential Democratic papers and leaders tried to check the increasing Union sentiment and urge the convention forward.[7]

On 21 March the New York *Herald* observed that its office received perhaps two-thirds of the southern newspapers, and out of a hundred journals, taken indiscriminately, about seventy-five favored the convention; the remainder were either neutral or moderately opposed it. All of the Democratic journals and probably two-thirds of the Whig papers more or less strongly favored such a meeting to consult on the present crisis. The *Herald* divided southern opinion into three main parts: a small element that desired secession sooner or later; a much larger body favoring compromise; and a third group that wished to continue the present excitement for the purpose of using the proceedings of the Nashville Convention to create a new party. The *Herald* conceded that undoubtedly "a speck of disunion was apparent." About three weeks later the same paper reported that the Whig organ in Washington, the *National Intelligencer,* received 300 southern and southwestern papers; of these only about fifty percent supported the Nashville Convention, and a number of this group were backing out. The *Herald* editor feared that the southern people lacked "unanimity, more energy and determination," particularly since the death of Calhoun, the only man who could lead the South in the protection of its rights. The Nashville Convention would be an "irresponsible" body, facing great opposition even in the South, and therefore provided no hope.[8]

After Calhoun's death, some southerners consulted Jefferson Davis about the convention. Davis expressed the view that it should meet for preventive purposes, and that it was necessary to begin an organization of the South—for union and cointelligence were essential. He believed that a postponement would result in abandonment of the southern convention and the accusation hereafter as "disunionists who were arrested in their purpose."[9]

Specific developments in various southern states indicate a change toward the convention. The Alabama legislature, stung by public criticism of the manner of selecting delegates, authorized the governor to call conventions in all counties to approve or disapprove its action, and the proposed convention was discussed at spring meetings. Although the southern rights group tried to influence the delegates toward an aggressive defense, public opinion as a whole leaned toward conservatism. Though a few counties advocated secession, most failed to call meetings; others did not assemble. The Montgomery *Alabama Journal* attributed this apparent apathy, not to hostility to the convention, but to the belief that movements toward a satisfactory adjustment were in progress. Opinion was divided, not over whether to hold a convention, but when it should assemble. Some desired to await congressional action; others believed that an immediate gathering might influence events in Washington.

Alabama Whigs reflected a change that was fairly common throughout the party in the South. The *Journal* indicated that the vast portion of the Whig party, "the planters, its bone and sinew," approved. Alabama delegates should attend the convention not only to help unite the South, but also to prevent possible mischief.[10] Although twenty-seven Mobile Whigs upbraided Mayor C. C. Langdon, editor of the Mobile *Advertiser*, for his opposition to the convention, Representative Henry W. Hilliard, one of the most prominent Whigs in the state, still opposed the gathering. He believed that no meeting should precede aggression and advised all Whigs to spurn the movement.[11] William H. Murphy, Whig delegate at large, indicated that he planned to attend the convention; if its object were dissolution of the Union, a situation he did not anticipate, he would be needed to prevent such a move. George P. Bierne, delegate-elect from the sixth congressional district, conferred with Senator Berrien of Georgia about the convention and later at a Huntsville meeting led Whig and Unionist elements in opposition to the meeting. After this local convention adopted Bierne's resolutions two to one, most of the group left, whereupon the southern rights faction adopted new resolutions and chose Reuben Chapman (Democrat) as a delegate.[12]

The Georgia legislature provided for preliminary county meetings to be held early in March to choose delegates to congressional district conventions. These would nominate one or more candidates from each party for popular selection as delegates on 2 April. In spite of urging by the southern rights press, very few of these meetings took place. The Savannah *Republican* reported no more than a dozen, and perhaps 1000 voters out of some 95,000 participated. In the Cherokee Superior Court Circuit citizens of several counties met without party distinction and disapproved of the legislature's support of the Nashville Convention. Monroe County (Forsyth), one of the most populous and wealthy in the state, attempted to hold a meeting, but failed to interest enough people to accomplish anything. Similar failures occurred in Clarke County (Athens) and Bibb County (Macon). Although attendance at the district conventions was light, nominees were chosen for each of the eight districts. In the eighteen-county first district, Chatham County (Savannah) took the matter in hand and selected delegates. At Columbus a meeting that called itself "bipartisan" chose the delegates to represent the second district. Only four out of nine counties sent representatives to the sixth congressional (Howell Cobb's) district convention at Gainesville. On 30 March, the editor of the Augusta *Chronicle* (Whig) wrote: "It cannot be denied that the whole movement is an entire failure, a miserable abortion . . . . The pretended meetings have been like Angels visits 'few and far between' and not one of them in any section of the state have [*sic*] been even *respectable* in point of numbers."[13] Before the elections occurred three days later, the Democrats were admitting the truth of the Whigs' allegations, but blamed the lack of interest on the influence of the Whig press and the belief that Congress would make an equitable adjustment by the time of the Nashville Convention. Indeed, the opposition of the Whig press had become bolder, while the Democratic press reflected no change.[14]

The real test of Georgia's sentiment toward the Nashville Convention came on 2 April, when the people went to the polls. Only slightly more than 3,700 citizens—roughly four percent of the state's electorate—voted. Many counties held no election. In Muscogee County (Columbus) the candidates received 113 votes, but ninety-eight persons cast ballots for "No Convention," and seventy-eight for "No Disunion." Only two people in the city of Athens cast ballots. Democratic indifference contributed almost as much as that of the Whigs to the insignificance of the vote. Indeed, Whig counties of coastal Georgia cast votes in higher proportions than did other sections. But the election was a dismal failure; the great mass of both parties had ignored it. Even some of the states' rights papers joined the opposition press in considering the movement dead in Georgia and declaring that the convention should be canceled or at least that no representative from Georgia should attend.[15]

What is the explanation for this public apathy in Georgia, Alabama, and most other states? Why was there a change in sentiment? In the first place, the masses were never as alarmed as the politicians, who originated both the southern congressional caucus and the Nashville Convention. Generally, the people had little or no opportunity for participation, in most cases not until the final phase. By that time there was a belief that Congress would make a satisfactory adjustment, which largely accounts for the change of sentiment among both people and leaders. There was a general misunderstanding of motives for the convention; many feared it was a disunion movement. No sectional meeting should be held before Congress had actually enacted some objectionable legislation. Public reaction is certain proof that the southern people in general wanted to maintain the Union in 1850. In addition, many people cared little whether slavery went to the new territories or not; they had other more important things on their minds. Naturally, the decline in sentiment for the convention was more common among the Whigs, many of whom had opposed the entire southern movement from the beginning. The Whigs were essentially conservative and they abhored sectional strife. Economically, many southern Whig planters (and many planters were Whigs) must have reasoned that they had more to lose than to gain through agitation of the territorial issue. Some Whigs finally approved the convention because of their disappointment in Taylor. Clay's proposals and Webster's speech restored their confidence and they drew back. Some approved the convention merely to try to control it, as they had previously done in the congressional caucus. Prospects of a congressional settlement also affected the Democrats since it promoted the cause of the Union faction. But some Democrats continued to approve the meeting in order to prevent extreme action. It is impossible to determine the effect of Calhoun's death, but in any event the convention proponents had lost their leader.

Reflecting the divergent views of the convention expressed by southern newspapers, the reactions of convention delegates elected in Georgia varied. Former Governor George Troup and Henry L. Benning, the most prominent (both were well known for public service) men elected, agreed to serve. But several of the chosen delegates refused to go, and Governor Towns had to fill the resultant vacancies. James A. Meriweather, longtime Putnam County Whig, declined his election in the seventh congressional district; he believed the people disapproved of the convention and therefore its capacity to do good no longer existed. In the third congressional district, Judge James Scarborough stated in a letter of resignation to the press that he would never support a disunion movement. Both delegates in the sixth district, Judge John Billups and Junius Hillyer, declined to serve. Henry G. Lamar, appointed to fill the vacancy of Hillyer, also refused. He felt that his hearty approval of the convention and firm measures would cause him to misrepresent his constituents whose views were different. On the other hand, Judge Walter T. Colquitt, state delegate-at-large, declared the "Nashville Convention must be held."[16]

Other leading Georgia politicians expressed their opinions. On 25 April Iverson Harris wrote Senator Berrien that he was mistaken in thinking that Georgia was "fully aroused."

Few persons beyond the circle of Calhoun's friends in the Democratic party were willing to endanger the Union for an instant over the admission of California. The great mass of Democrats, as well as Whigs, would agree to her admission if Congress approved the other provisions of the suggested compromise. Charles Jenkins reported to Berrien on 15 May that very little excitement existed in Georgia. He believed that a large majority would acquiesce cheerfully in the report of the Committee of Thirteen. But another of Berrien's correspondents, C. B. Strong, believed the convention was essential, not to dissolve but to save the Union, if this could be done properly and honor preserved. More significant was a letter from J. H. Howard: "The Nashville Convention *will* assemble and though some partisans may be in attendance, the spirit which will control that convention will give tone to the South at all hazards." He urged Berrien to offer the extension of the Missouri Compromise line as a substitute for the report of the Committee of Thirteen.[17] A few weeks earlier, Hiram Warner, Union Democrat, had written Cobb that the question should be settled if possible before the Nashville Convention and thereby obviate the necessity of the meeting. He feared that the convention might do less good than was hoped; it might even be harmful. Warner also believed that a settlement based on the Missouri Compromise would be satisfactory.[18]

Despite Governor Thomas Brown's refusal to cooperate, Florida chose delegates for Nashville. A meeting at Quincy in Gadsden County on 23 February heartily approved the call for a southern convention and recommended the method later used to select delegates. Members of both parties participated in county meetings to choose representatives to judicial district conventions. Besides Gadsden, the press reported meetings in Madison, Duval, Marion, Leon, Jefferson, and Jackson Counties. A convention in each of the state's judicial districts then appointed the delegates on the basis of population—two from the Western District, two from the Middle, and one each from the East and South. These district conventions also made an effort toward bipartisan action.

Joseph M. Hernandez, delegate-elect, addressed a letter to

the Eastern District meeting at St. Augustine. Formerly, wrote Hernandez, he had had faith in Congress to remedy southern grievances and had been inclined to regard the Nashville Convention "as premature and urged more for political effect than any other." But after reading Seward's speech and noting how Congress had failed to heed the views of Webster and others, he had become convinced that the South would finally have to adopt measures for its own safety. Hernandez did not, however, attend the Nashville Convention because of illness.

The *Florida Sentinel* reported that neither Governor Brown nor his followers attempted in any way "to discourage or thwart the action of the friends of the Nashville Convention." The editor supposed, however, that no advocate of the convention would contend that a tenth of the people of Florida had attended the meetings for the selection of delegates.[19]

As the Compromise measures in Congress progressed, North Carolina's sentiment in favor of the Nashville Convention diminished. By the first of April, the *Newberrian* stated, "The Nashville Convention, we take it is pretty nearly on its last legs in North Carolina." W. H. Haywood, Jr., leading Democratic critic of the convention, explained the disunionists' failure to break up the Union by the simple fact that the people were not willing. The Wilmington *Journal* suggested in an editorial on 10 May that postponing the convention might be best: "All chances of its usefulness are gone. Were it to meet tomorrow, it would have the moral power of a party convention." The people would not act as long as they entertained any hope of a fair settlement in Congress, although action would be the best means of securing a settlement.[20] Near the end of the month, even the *North Carolina Standard* rarely mentioned the convention. William W. Holden, editor of the *Standard*, said, "In regard to the Nashville Convention, that is a dead question. In going for it I but yielded to the will of the majority, and did not dream of proscribing anyone." He also indicated that Robert Strange, recently chosen delegate, now thought the meeting was inexpedient. The announcement of Strange and Griffith J. McRee, the delegates from the Wilmington District, that they would not attend the meeting was "the finishing stroke" to the convention in North Carolina. Strange and McRee feared that any resolutions the convention might adopt would affect the compromise proceedings adversely, and they and a majority of the people in their district doubted the wisdom of a meeting at that time. The delegates from Mecklenburg District, where interest had been high, also failed to attend. Green W. Caldwell was ill, and important business kept Walter L. Steele at home. Consequently, no representative from North Carolina was in Nashville on 3 June 1850.[21]

Although the southern movement in Virginia was never strong, legislative action further weakened it, and Webster's speech and the possibility of compromise seriously thwarted election attempts. Webster's speech increased the impression that the controversy could be satisfactorily adjusted. Mayo Cabell, local politician, declared that the people were "calm and deliberate" and he had no doubt everything could be settled in a satisfactory manner. Disheartened by the thought of compromise, Beverley Tucker made a similar report to James Henry Hammond on 13 March, and about two weeks later wrote, "Our politicians have gone over to the compromisers." He had lost hope in everyone except South Carolina: southern leaders had betrayed their section. Another Virginian, Richard K. Crallé, thought it was highly important "to sustain the southern convention as a *means of* preserving the Union." Only this could be its legitimate purpose. Unfortunately, those who favored the convention had not sufficiently presented this view, and on 9 April the editor of the Richmond *Whig* observed, "The thing is dead for all mischief and the Virginia legislature killed it."[22]

In spite of official indifference, though, three county meetings were held in Virginia in February; others took place in late March and April. On 20 April, William O. Goode, who would later be chosen a delegate, wrote Senator R. M. T. Hunter requesting him to urge the Virginia delegation in Congress to stimulate their friends in their respective districts to participate in the elections. In spite of this urging, less than half the counties in eastern Virginia finally elected representatives to the district conferences. Primaries were mostly confined to the regions between the James and the York, south of the James, and along the Rappahannock, with scattered meetings in the Charlottesville, Portsmouth, and Mecklenburg districts. In several of the counties that took no official action, the ultras held extralegal "primaries" and elected representatives to the district conferences. Some county meetings instructed the delegates not to attend if the compromise measures passed Congress before the Nashville Convention met. Other meetings opposed the appointment of delegates. The most notable of these met at Richmond. Assembling for the third time within a month, this "primary" group at the capital finally voted down the convention 214 to 105. The resolutions adopted did not disapprove of the convention *per se,* but opposed it only at the present time and on account of the Compromise.[23]

West of the Blue Ridge only Jefferson County, the home of Senator James M. Mason, elected delegates to a congressional district conference. But many of the western counties held bipartisan mass meetings to protest against secession and endorse the action of opponents of the convention. The editor of the Leesburg *Washingtonian* regarded the gathering as more dangerous to the Union than almost anything then agitating the country. According to Charles Ambler, the historian of sectionalism in Virginia, "Had secession come in 1850, there can be little doubt that this part of Virginia was then ready to take the same step it took in 1861."[24]

When the district conferences met in May, seven out of the fifteen Virginia congressional districts chose fourteen delegates. Only six of the fourteen elected actually went to Nashville. Neither delegate from the Richmond District attended, and Congressman T. H. Haymond from the western part of the state told the United States House of Representatives on 21 May that his section would send no representatives and that the effort to send delegates to the Nashville Convention had been almost an entire failure in Virginia. Haymond assured his listeners that the friends of the Union "need have no fear of Virginia."[25]

W. F. Cooper succinctly described the situation in Tennessee. By the first of April he had come to the conclusion that the convention, "if not a humbug," would prove a failure as far as his state was concerned. The people exhibited "scarcely any interest"—certainly no enthusiasm—for the gathering. The able efforts of Clay and Webster had changed the scene since Mississippi had proposed a southern convention, and a final adjustment was a distinct possibility. Although Cooper sincerely trusted the meeting was unnecessary, he believed that Tennesseans were in a dilemma. They had sanctioned the plan and invited the convention to sit in Nashville; therefore how could they honorably refuse to act with other southern delegates? Although the times favored an amicable settlement, a continuance was not assured. The South could ill afford to "cease to do battle," and if Congress should settle the crisis satisfactorily, the convention would doubtless govern its action accordingly. Cooper and other Middle Tennesseans who favored the meeting desired to see the delegates adopt a set of mild and conciliatory resolutions expressing southern gratification for the change and southern attachment to the Union. They favored primary meetings that would appoint delegates who would ensure full representation from Tennessee and proper action at the convention. Moreover, the Democrats must not allow the "treacherous cry of the Whigs" to alter their position, as this would ruin the party for "years and years" in Tennessee and be a direct admission that the object of the convention was disunion.[26]

Other prominent leaders in the Volunteer State expressed opinions for and against the convention. Former Democratic Governor Aaron V. Brown strongly pleaded for the convention in a letter in the *Union*, declaring, "Those who have sanctioned and advocated this convention cannot and will not recede." If the Whigs would not unite with the Democrats, the Democrats alone must do the "difficult work." Also supporting the convention, Democrat Senator Hopkins L. Turney believed that the people of Tennessee would supply every possible facility and send delegates to the convention. On the other hand, Senator John Bell (Whig), an important Nashville businessman, proclaimed to the Senate that he did not countenance the southern convention. If it should produce any good, he would take no credit; if any evil should ensue from its deliberations, he would not be responsible.[27] Another leading Nashville Whig, Boyd McNairy, wrote of his decided disapproval of the convention to Governor Crittenden of Kentucky. McNairy believed, however, that it would meet unless a satisfactory adjustment should be made in Congress, and that it would produce much evil, with shame and disgrace reflected upon the participants. McNairy told Crittenden that another Whig politician, Ephraim Foster, thought the movement would "resolve itself an abortion."[28]

After the Tennessee legislature failed to provide for the election of delegates, several counties held meetings for this purpose. On 13 April the Nashville *Union* called for such a meeting in Davidson County, appealing to voters irrespective of party but limited to "friends of the convention." The Whigs outnumbered their opposition in the Nashville District, but Democrat Andrew H. Ewing represented Davidson County in Congress. A few days later Ewing told the House that he believed a majority of Nashvillians considered the convention "unwise and inopportune," but they also deeply sympathized in the feeling of alarm which had caused their southern brethren to adopt "this ulterior motive." In reply to some who had prophesied ill will for the convention in Nashville, he declared that under no circumstances would the people of Nashville "treat with rudeness and indecorum a reputable body of their fellow citizens" who had assembled at their city for the discussion of such "grave and solemn interests."[29]

When the Davidson County meeting occurred, the Whigs construed the call as an invitation to discuss the propriety of choosing delegates instead of a call to elect them. More Whigs than Democrats were present at the opening of the meeting. In an attempt to make the convention a party matter and convey the impression that only the Democrats favored the meeting, the Whigs proposed and passed an amendment that appointment of delegates was inexpedient. This accomplished, the meeting adjourned and the Whigs retired. The friends of the convention remained, however, immediately reorganized, and passed resolutions drawn up by the presiding officer, Andrew

Jackson Donelson, nephew of Andrew Jackson, who believed that Tennessee should be represented regardless of the object. The *Union* reported that this rump session appointed twenty-nine of "the best men in the county."[30]

Similar meetings occurred in the Middle Tennessee counties of Maury, Lincoln, Sumner, Giles, Bedford, Cannon, Smith, Franklin, Marshall, Lawrence, and Montgomery. The *Union* declared that half of the fifty Giles County delegates were Whigs and that Whigs were also among the most active in securing appointment of Bedford County delegates. Generally speaking, however, Democrats favored the election of delegates, while Whigs opposed it.[31] Yet leading Montgomery County Democrat Cave Johnson wrote James Buchanan from Clarksville, expressing his fears of what the southern hotheads might do but indicating that he felt no anxiety for the Union. In spite of overtures to serve as a delegate from his district, Johnson rejected any connection with the convention. Furthermore, he urged friends at Nashville and elsewhere to delay the meeting until October, after Congress had acted. If a convention then seemed necessary at least "our Southern blood would not be so hot under the October sun." He wrote to Donelson in a similar tone approximately a month later expressing especial fears about the effect of the convention on the Democrats in the next election, for the Whigs desired to make the question an issue. Johnson urged Donelson, a delegate-elect, to use his influence "with excitable men that will be there to keep them cool and prevent as far as possible any harsh expressions," which might be useful to the Whigs.[32]

Divided sentiment prevailed in West Tennessee, where even fewer meetings occurred than in the middle section. Only Hardeman, Weakley, Lauderdale, Tipton, Fayette, Henry, Benton, and Shelby (Memphis) counties were reported to have held meetings. A gathering of Shelby Countians appointed eleven delegates at Raleigh, but none of them attended.[33] Two congressmen representing this section expressed opposing opinions. Frederick P. Stanton, Democrat and Representative from the Memphis District, had signed the Southern Address the previous year; he now opposed the admission of California and favored the Nashville Convention. Another West Tennessee Congressman, Christopher H. Williams (Whig), who favored the admission of California, expressed his opposition to the convention in a speech before a congressional committee. Williams believed the call was "ill-timed and unnecessary" and opposed it: the plan proposed a remedy for a contingent evil, outside the Constitution, and there would be sufficient time for action after Congress passed unsatisfactory legislation. He advised the young and talented of both parties to stay away from the convention and "to leave it to old men, and to political cripples . . . for nothing is more clear to my mind, than that it will prove a political winding-sheet, to all those who trust to its embrace."

In East Tennessee William G. Brownlow, editor of the Knoxville *Whig*, heartily agreed with convention opponents, regarding the "ungodly assemblage" as "a mischief making affair." The most outspoken of critics, Brownlow wrote, "Crimsoned with shame be our cheeks . . . palsied be our right arm . . . detested be our name and memory when with the mad zealots of our native South we call for a Southern Convention at Nashville." He declared no East Tennessee politician was "willing to hazard his reputation by being made a cat's paw for certain ambitious leaders in an unholy crusade against the Union." Sensible men knew that if they participated in that convention they could never "shake off the odium" which would be brought upon them—a handicap that Brownlow predicted would continue into the third and fourth generations. Moreover, he thought the people of Tennessee should prohibit such a meeting in the state. In case Tennesseans were unwilling to take a stand, Brownlow recommended that President Taylor issue a proclamation forbidding such a convention anywhere in the United States and order General Winfield Scott to Nashville with power to call upon the entire land force to prevent the meeting.[34]

In spite of Brownlow's opposition, Knox County Democrats, a weak minority, held a meeting at the courthouse and chose twenty-two delegates, several of them Whigs, but none attended. The most widely-known among these delegates was the physician-historian Dr. James G. M. Ramsey.[35] Little sentiment for the convention existed elsewhere in East Tennessee. Marion County (Jasper) appointed six delegates, but apparently no other East Tennessee meetings occurred. The Greenville *Spy*, Andrew Johnson's home organ, finally took a firm and decided position in favor of the convention. In a long article urging support from both parties, the editor declared that the Nashville Convention contemplated no evil to the Union. Its only object was to unite the South, and thereby save its institutions from further aggression.[36]

A series of county meetings in favor of the Compromise report began in Tennessee around 22 May. Both the *Union* and *Banner* came out in favor of the Compromise. The latter alleged that the "conventionists" were basing their scheme on the idea that if the Compromise passed, the Democrats might claim the credit.[37]

The progress of the Compromise measures also stimulated a heated discussion in Arkansas. To Congressman Robert Johnson the Compromise was a total surrender of the most vital contention of the South, and Whigs were traitors to that cause. The *Arkansas Banner* continued to support Johnson and cited the opposition of every Whig paper in the state on the southern question. The Whigs, according to the *Banner*, opposed the Nashville Convention because they feared it would weaken the national strength of their party. Albert Pike, who believed Clay's proposal was a wise and sincere effort to solve the dispute, boldly opposed Johnson's position and sent a copy of his earlier reply to Johnson to the *Arkansas Gazette and Democrat*. The publication of his letter on 22 March launched Pike on an active campaign against the Nashville Convention and in favor of the Compromise. As the head of the Whig party in the state, he spoke and wrote with influence. As the convention drew nearer, Pike increased the tempo of his activity. On 15 April, in a widely publicized debate at El Dorado in Union County, he "utterly repudiated" the Nashville Convention, declaring that it could "do no good" and was "almost sure to do injury." Through the able and vigorous support of the powerful *Gazette and Democrat*, Pike and his Whig followers gained the allegiance of many Democrats. Thus he achieved notable success, even though no Whig paper existed at the capital in 1850.[38]

Arkansas held other county meetings in May. Chicot County chose one, and Jefferson County appointed eight delegates to the convention. Judge Sam C. Roane, candidate for the state senate and brother of Governor John S. Roane, was the most prominent person selected from Jefferson County; he was one of the two delegates to attend the convention. Voters at a meeting in Fulton County declared that without a national adjustment soon, the Nashville Convention was the only remedy, and chose fifteen delegates. Few persons showed up at a second meeting in Helena, but an enthusiastic gathering on national affairs, irrespective of party, took place in Desha County on the very day the convention assembled in Nashville. The meeting expressed confidence in an amicable adjustment and recommended canceling the convention.[39]

According to Cleo Hearon, only Mississippi and South Carolina demonstrated continued public sentiment for the convention. Even in Mississippi, as opinion in favor of the Compromise developed, the Whig support for the gathering began to decrease. The editor of the *Southron* (Whig) noted that although the convention had at one time represented the spontaneous movement of the people of the state, irrespective of parties, it had become almost exclusively a party affair. But the Vicksburg *Sentinel* (Democrat) reminded its readers that the prospect for an honorable adjustment in Congress would never have existed without the resolute stand of the southern states and the emphatic declarations of southern congressmen. "To abandon now would be an exhibition of weakness and vacillation," continued the editor. Generally, the Democrats continued to approve the convention.[40]

The Compromise measures also divided the opinions of Mississippi's leaders on the advisability of holding a convention. Since Senator Henry Foote's name had been connected with the origin of the movement, his position at this time is significant. Because he supported the Compromise and had disagreed with Calhoun, Foote was accused of opposing the convention. He wrote to the *Mississippian* on 29 April, thanking the editor for repelling false charges that Foote was or ever had been hostile to the convention. Judge Sharkey, who had served as president of the October Convention, used the developments at Washington and the report of the Compromise committee as public proof of the necessity of holding the convention. A few days after the Nashville assemblage adjourned, however, Sharkey revealed that he had been convinced before it met that "the convention movement would result in a total failure." Congressman Albert Gallatin Brown believed with Senator Jefferson Davis that the convention should meet in order to warn the North against further aggression toward the South. Brown desired to see the convention stand firmly for the Missouri Compromise line, since he, like all of his state's congressional delegation except Foote, opposed the Compromise.[41]

Although the introduction of Clay's Compromise plan and the prospect of a satisfactory adjustment somewhat lessened the support for a southern convention in most of the other southern states, sentiment had not changed in South Carolina.[42] W. N. DeSaussure, Columbia politician, reported that there was no excitement, but a "calm determination to see the game out." The North thought the southern movement was "all a game of brag" and the Nashville Convention would never meet. "It will meet and when met *must act*," declared DeSaussure. Otherwise, it would be better not to meet at all. On 7 May a former resident of North Carolina wrote to his parents that the abolition question ran "high" in South Carolina and the people in the state were very much agitated.[43] South Carolinians almost unanimously condemned the proposed Compromise. They attacked Clay's resolutions as unacceptable in the South because the concessions were not reciprocal. The Charleston *Mercury* declared, "It is the growing conviction that his scheme is a snare." In other words, the North would make a few minor concessions only to prepare the way for greater aggression. The editor of the *Spartan* (Spartanburg) expressed his distrust of the committee, especially when "the great compromiser" became the chairman. The South could never obtain its rights by appealing to northern magnanimity or pleading before Compromise committees. When the Charleston *Courier* and a few Charleston Whigs supported the Compromise, the *Spartan* severely assailed them as being "willing to swallow that villainous concoction of Northern depravity and scoundrelism called a compromise."[44]

Although a traveler to South Carolina reported to Judge Beverley Tucker in Virginia that while there he saw "no man who did not seem ripe for disunion," some few Unionists still had not been converted. Joel R. Poinsett favored Clay's Compromise and preferred it to the Missouri Compromise; Benjamin F. Perry also believed Clay's measure should be adopted. "But the whole state of South Carolina is opposed to it and a large portion of the state for disunion *per se*!!" he declared. The faculty of South Carolina College included at least two Unionists, Matthew J. Williams and the leading political scientist, Francis Lieber. While Williams thought more on the subject than he spoke or wrote, Lieber spoke out fearlessly for the Union.[45]

The day after Calhoun's Senate speech, Hammond wrote to him averring that his ideas were "the only safe and sound ones." A few days later, however, he confided in his diary that since realization of Calhoun's plan for the restoration of equilibrium was impossible, disunion would be the result. At that time, Hammond was inclined to believe that Congress would "enter into another fatal truce"; if so, the Nashville Convention would probably not meet. Still later, he wrote William Gilmore Simms that "The Nashville Convention if it meets will sink into a mere presidential caucus." Unless things took a turn for the better, he probably would not even go.[46]

Meanwhile, during March and April public meetings in the districts and parishes were choosing representatives to attend conventions in the various congressional districts for the purpose of selecting delegates to Nashville. Although these primary meetings gave the delegates no instructions on what course they should follow at the convention, the resolutions did declare that southern rights should be protected and guaranteed or a dissolution of the Union ought to be effected.[47]

Shortly after Mississippi issued the call for the convention,

William Gilmore Simms, editor of the *Southern Quarterly Review*, expressed a desire to be chosen as a delegate. He also wrote Hammond that he had counseled the amateur writer David F. Jamison to run as a delegate; if all three went, they would carry some strength which might be important to the issues.[48]

Apparently, in some instances at least, the leaders sounded out a possible delegate's availability and his opinion on the all-important questions before the congressional district conventions. In fact the leaders secretly insisted on candidates who would not hesitate, should disunion prove necessary. The chairman of electoral votes for Abbeville addressed one such inquiry to Benjamin C. Yancey, who declared his convictions in a rather lengthy reply. Although Yancey indicated that he would accept "so distinguished an appointment," he felt others must be far more capable of discharging it.[49] In order to present an undivided front on southern rights, the leaders invited Joel R. Poinsett, recognized Union Democrat party leader of the state, to run for delegate. The provision attached to Poinsett's invitation was that he would attempt to preserve the Union, if practicable, but would assert and maintain, in any event, the constitutional equality of the southern states. Although Poinsett did not recommend a southern convention at this time, he indicated that he would serve as delegate, provided the object of the convention did not imply a dissolution of the Union, an alternative he would never sanction. Some of the Charleston leaders desired his conservative influence at the convention to offset the hotspurs, but they decided that a public avowal of all the sentiments expressed in Poinsett's letter would preclude his election. His friend Richard Yeadon, former editor of the Charleston *Courier*, wrote that he feared that Poinsett's reservations would render his election utterly hopeless. Poinsett replied that he had come to the same conclusion, because he had long been aware that both the district and the state were prepared for the extremity. As he conscientiously believed such a measure would lead to immediate civil war that would probably end in defeat for the South, he considered it wrong to yield to public opinion and by any act on his part to aid in the perpetuation of destruction. But if the revolution came—for there could be no peaceable secession—he was ready to take his hopeless stand for the South.[50]

Before the congressional district conventions even met, General James Hamilton, the president of the Nullification Convention of 1832 and former governor of South Carolina, addressed a letter to the Charleston *Courier* declining to serve as a delegate if elected. He said he was hopeful that an adjustment would soon be made upon terms of honor and safety to the South, and that Webster's speech was only the beginning of a change in northern opinion. But Hamilton was a Texas bondholder, an attorney for owners of over half the bonds, and an indefatigable pro-Compromise lobbyist connected with William W. Corcoran, wealthy banker and Texas bondholder, and other lobbyists, Though he claimed to keep southern rights steadily in mind, some southerners doubted his sincerity.[51] One change occurred in the group of delegates-at-large selected by the state legislature. Franklin H. Elmore, who was appointed to fill Calhoun's vacancy in the Senate, resigned as a delegate-at-large to Nashville, and Governor Seabrook appointed J. W. Hayne of Charleston to the vacancy. Although Hayne questioned the right of the governor to make the appointment, he wrote that he must accept, as "it was a post no decent man would seek and which no good citizen could decline."[52] Hayne did not, however, attend the convention, and apparently the governor appointed no one else.

The meetings of the primary-elected representatives in their respective congressional districts took place on 6 May. Contenting themselves with the election of the Nashville delegates, they refrained from adopting the customary reports. Each of the seven congressional districts chose two delegates, among whom were such prominent men as R. F. W. Allston, Robert Barnwell Rhett, and Francis W. Pickens. All of this group attended, leaving only one vacancy in the South Carolina delegation at Nashville, the best record by far of any state represented.[53]

Even as some delegates were already traveling toward Nashville, Simms told Tucker that he was confident that the people of South Carolina were "ripe for the better system" and although he doubted the will of North Carolina, Georgia, Kentucky, and Tennessee, he believed that Alabama, Mississippi, and Louisiana would "come manfully to the scratch." Unquestionably, he believed that Tucker would find at Nashville "many choice spirits" who would agree with him and Hammond on the important issues.[54] An analysis of the delegates reveals the number of "choice spirits" present, as well as the type of men chosen in response to Mississippi's call for a southern convention.

# 6

# *The Delegates: Unionists and "Choice Spirits"*

If the North failed to exhibit a spirit of moderation before the Nashville Convention met, observed Virginia delegate-elect William O. Goode in March 1850, "no human sagacity" could foresee the consequences. "That body will consist of men for the *most part anxious to preserve the Union*, but firmly resolved to save the South. The safety of the South is the leading, the prevailing object, and the predominant idea." William Gilmore Simms felt that "the South was particularly fortunate" in selecting so many delegates who were men of experience as well as thought. W. F. Cooper, convention secretary, declared that he had never seen a finer group of men assembled together—"the talent of the South." The delegates were not merely politicians, but men of "thought and character"—judges, lawyers, professors, writers, and wealthy and educated planters. Soon after the convention began, William F. Gordon, another Virginia delegate, reported "a great deal of talent" among the members.[1] Modern historians, however, have differed from these contemporary observers in discussing a few "notable" figures, while implying that the unmentioned majority lacked prominence in southern affairs.

This chapter will analyze the delegates' personal, economic, geographic, and political backgrounds; their views on the convention and related topics; and their participation in activities leading to its assemblage. The typical delegate who traveled to Nashville in the late spring of 1850 was a man in his mid-forties who could seek advice from several older cohorts at the same time that he gave a little counsel of his own to the younger men in the convention hall. If he came from an older seaboard southern state, he could probably boast of his state nativity. But if he hailed from the new Southwest, he more than likely claimed some other southern state as his birthplace. His education had not been neglected; reading law may have attracted him. Chances are he was a Democrat, but he might have been a Whig, sensitive to southern rights and northern aggression. Though he loved the Union and desired to see the crisis resolved—exceptions allowed—he was fast approaching the conclusion that the South, sooner or later, must set forth the ultimatum "Thus far shalt thou go and no farther." He may have held local or state office; perhaps congressional membership was or would be listed on his record for posterity. More than likely he combined his public service with certain agrarian pursuits. Usually he owned some land and some slaves. If he owned more than a hundred, or very few or none—Tennessee excepted—he was in the minority.[2]

The southern rights movement that culminated in the Nashville Convention was more significant in the lower South, where cotton and slaves were of greatest importance. South Carolina, the most radical of the nine states represented, sent seventeen delegates, who turned out to be the most representative group, geographically and politically. Mississippi, where the call for the convention had been issued, followed close behind with eleven delegates, only one short of a full delegation. Georgia's eleven representatives spoke out as clearly for southern rights as any of the delegations, even though the masses had been apathetic in the election of delegates. The young state of Florida showed her interest in the sectional issues by sending four delegates. Texas, more concerned with the maintenance of her boundary than with southern rights, supplied only one representative. The largest delegation among the states in the lower South came from Alabama, which may be regarded as a state transitional in attitude from the lower to the upper South. Though her twenty-two delegates comprised a few ardent states' righters, the group as a whole wielded a conservative influence. Louisiana was missing from the roster, as the legislature had refused to provide for the selection of delegates, and no unofficial meetings had occurred. A rumor circulated that representatives from the Pelican State had ascended the Mississippi to Memphis and turned back, as they believed the convention was doomed to failure.[3]

The state of South Carolina as a whole was well represented at the convention. Although the three delegates-at-large who attended the convention were all from the seventh congressional district, the remainder were well distributed geographically, with two delegates representing each of the seven districts. The delegates were almost equally divided among low, middle, and upper country. The South Carolina delegates, whose ages ranged from 35 to 74, with a median age of 46, were fairly typical of the general representation. The eldest of the group, Langdon Cheves, celebrated orator in Congress during the War of 1812 and second president of the United States Bank, was still vigorous enough at 74 to cross the mountains to defend southern rights. The two youngest, Maxcy Gregg and James Chesnut, Jr., later served as brigadier generals in the Confederate army; Gregg died defending the southern cause. The delegates had strikingly similar backgrounds. All but one were native-born sons. Approximately two-thirds of the group had gone beyond secondary school; at least eight were college graduates, and one other delegate probably attended college. Thirteen studied law, were admitted to the bar and practiced.[4] Cooper said of the Carolinians, "as finished gentlemen, as intellectual statesmen, as polished speakers, they stood a head higher than their compeers." Another observer commented that South Carolina had "sent her jewels" there, and considered the Carolinians perhaps the most talented, Mississippi alone excepted.

All except two of the South Carolina delegates engaged in agriculture, even though they might not have personally directed their estates.[5] Nine of these men had enough slaves to be classified as large planters, three as small planters, and two as farmers.[6] Almost all of the Carolinians combined farming with other occupations or professions. George A. Trenholm was a financier and merchant as well as planter. Cheves was a planter, lawyer, and financier, David Jamison, another planter-lawyer, was also a history scholar and writer. Robert Barnwell was a planter, lawyer, and educator. The remaining two delegates, not engaged in agriculture, were classified as lawyers.

The Palmetto State delegates also occupied a fairly high economic rank for the time. Of fifteen delegates located on the census record, only one owned no real estate. Chesnut had real estate valued at $108,000 followed by James H. Hammond with $100,000. R. F. W. Allston, a rice planter, with $130,000 in real estate and 401 slaves, was the wealthiest of the group in 1850. Robert Barnwell Rhett owned 306 slaves and Francis W. Pickens 299, while Cheves and Hammond each held more than 200 slaves. John A. Bradley, with only six slaves, was the smallest slaveholder, and it can be safely assumed that not more than two of the delegates held no slaves at all.

Almost all of these seventeen delegates had some sort of public service careers. Thirteen were at some time in the state legislature, and Barnwell, Hammond, Pickens, and Cheves had served in the United States House of Representatives prior to their selection as delegates. Cheves had been Speaker of the House during the Thirteenth Congress. Barnwell was appointed to the United States Senate on 4 June (the second day of the convention) to succeed Franklin H. Elmore. Rhett succeeded Barnwell, who did not seek election in December 1850, by defeating Hammond, who was later elected to the Senate. Hammond had also served as governor of the state. Allston later became governor, as did Pickens, who was serving when secession occurred in 1860.

All of the Carolina delegates were probably Democrats; Whigs had always constituted a small minority in the state. It is also safe to conclude that none of the Palmetto State delegates would have hesitated at disunion in 1850 if they were assured of southern cooperation. At least seven had participated in the nullification controversy. Pickens had gained distinction by replying to President Jackson's nullification ordinance and by writing the "Hampdon" articles, which supported state sovereignty. Hammond had advocated the nullification convention through his newspaper, had been an unsuccessful candidate for the convention, and had assisted in military preparations. Between 1830 and 1832, Cheves, while rejecting nullification, had unqualifiedly accepted secession. He also rejected separate state action and advocated cooperation among the southern states. Allston, who was made colonel of the militia during the nullification episode, also preferred cooperation to separate state action. Rhett, Barnwell, and William DuBose were members of the nullification convention and signed the nullification ordinance. Of the entire group, Rhett was the most ardent states' righter in declaring for "downright resistance." As early as 1835, Pickens had predicted an inevitable conflict with the "Goths and Vandals" in defense of the peculiar institution. "Why should we delude ourselves with the false and visionary hopes that we shall be able to avoid this contest?"[7]

The specific views of some of the delegates indicate something of their mood. Rhett had taken little part in the activities leading to the convention, but by the time it met he had begun "to assume the air of the prophet justified." In 1849 he had expressed sorrow that the Wilmot Proviso or the abolition of slavery in the District of Columbia had no chance of passage. "Would to God they [Congress] would do both, and let us have the contest, and end it once and forever," he declared. "It would then accomplish our emancipation instead of that of our slaves." But he did not think northern statesmen would commit any "such blunder."[8] Jamison argued that slavery was the indispensable basis for a successful republic, and that the abolition campaign and the excesses of northern democracy made separation as necessary as it was desirable.[9]

Hammond favored disunion beyond a doubt. The theme of southern nationalism continues throughout his extensive correspondence for this period. In various letters and in his diary he formulated his views. He declared that the convention must open the way to dissolution; if it did not, he preferred that it never meet—he had no faith in amendments, nor in pledges and guarantees. Moreover, he adamantly opposed any address to the North and believed another southern address was unnecessary. "A very short preamble and a couple of resolutions"—which he confided he had already drawn up—would be sufficient. The substance of these resolutions was that the slave states should immediately call conventions to send delegates to a General Congress, which should be empowered to dissolve the Union, write a new Constitution, organize a new government, and in the meantime appoint a provisional government until the Constitution could become operative. Circumstances would govern whether he proposed such resolutions at Nashville, as he had no intention of making a fool of himself or acting prematurely. If he found the South "unprepared," he would say little; if he found "them ready" he would go into the matter "heart and soul." He would not give "a snap of his finger" for any constitutional amendments unless they gave the South equal votes at all times in both houses of Congress and the electoral college. If he found a movement favorable to actual resistance, he would join it regardless of how mild it was initially. On the eve of his departure for the convention, Hammond confided to his diary, "I am loth [*sic*] to go believing nothing will be done to repay the trouble. But as something important may be done it is my duty to go."[10]

In contrast with his associates, Pickens, who advocated defending southern rights and preserving the Union, was not as ultra as some at Nashville, according to Benjamin F. Perry, a leading Unionist. Pickens had told Perry that Cheves and Hammond were very bitter against the Union, but he believed that no one should look to disunion or desire it *per se*; it should be avoided if possible. He also opposed separate state action and thought the whole South should act together. In his diary, Perry related a conversation with Robert Barnwell in which Barnwell had said that he believed the House would defeat the Compromise, but "if it passed he thought it would suspend all action on the part of the South."[11]

When the second session of the convention met on 11

November 1850, sixteen delegates represented South Carolina. Only Allston and Hammond of the original group were missing.[12] Most of the delegates remained active in southern affairs thereafter. DuBose, Cheves, William J. Hanna, and Drayton Nance died before secession and war. Of the remaining thirteen, Barnwell, Chesnut, Gregg, Jamison, Rhett, Henry C. Young, and J. N. Whitner became members of the Secession Convention of 1860. Jamison served as president of the Secession Convention. Rhett, Chesnut, and Barnwell, members of the Montgomery Convention of 1861, helped to frame the Confederate Constitutions; in fact, Rhett was one of the principal architects.[13] Trenholm not only served the Confederacy as Secretary of the Treasury during the last year of the war, but a branch of his company became financial agents for ship construction, purchase of arms, and other material.[14]

Of the eleven delegates representing Mississippi at Nashville, William L. Sharkey, Joseph W. Matthews, Alexander M. Clayton, and Thomas J. Word had been selected both by the October Convention and the legislature. The October Convention had chosen E. C. Wilkinson, and the legislature had appointed the six remaining delegates. Three delegates were from North Mississippi, three from the extreme southwestern part of the state, and the remainder from the central portion. All of the delegates selected by the legislature to represent the state at large attended, as well as those from the first and fourth congressional districts. One legislative delegate attended from the second, while one delegate selected by the legislature and one selected by the October Convention represented the third.

The Mississippi delegation comprised some of the most prominent men of the state, whose ages ranged from 35 to 51, with a median age of 43, slightly below that of the South Carolina group. The Mississippi representatives, with the possible exception of one, were not native sons. Two each were born in Virginia and North Carolina, four in Tennessee, and one in faraway Maine. The birthplaces of two of the delegates remain uncertain: Joseph W. Matthews was born in either Tennessee, Alabama, or North Carolina, while the census record gives the birthplace of C. P. Smith as the Natchez District, Mississippi, but another source lists South Carolina as his place of birth.[15]

Almost three-fourths of the Mississippi delegates had been trained in the law. Only one delegate, John J. McRae, is known to be a college graduate, but S. S. Boyd was, according to description, "highly educated." Matthews' education was simply described as "limited."

Eight of the Mississippi delegates practiced law. At least four of the eight lawyers, as well as the remaining three delegates, engaged in agriculture; four were major planters. The Mississippi delegates were not as wealthy as their compeers from South Carolina, nor did they hold as many slaves. Clayton, both a lawyer and a large planter, was the wealthiest delegate, with real estate worth $28,000. T. Jones Stewart was the largest slaveholder with 184 slaves. Three delegates besides Clayton possessed real estate valued at more than $20,000, but no delegate besides Stewart owned as many as 100 slaves; Boyd, Clayton, and Wilkinson owned more than 50 slaves. Two delegates owned no slaves and another only one.

Members of the Mississippi delegation had rather extensive public careers, especially within the state. Seven served in the Mississippi legislature, and Word had been a member of the North Carolina House of Representatives. Word served in Congress before 1850; J. J. McRae was a congressman during the following decade. Clayton, Sharkey, Smith, and Wilkinson had judicial careers. All except Wilkinson served at some time on the High Court of Errors and Appeals for Mississippi, with Sharkey acting as Chief Justice. Matthews was governor when the state issued the call for the Nashville Convention. McRae served as governor in the succeeding decade and John J. Pettus during the secession crisis and the war, while Sharkey acted as provisional governor from June until October 1865. The delegates were also quite active in civic and educational pursuits in the state. Clayton, Matthews, and Wilkinson served as members of the Board of Trustees for the University of Mississippi; Clayton, one of the founders of the university, was president of the board in 1850. Smith was a member of the executive committee of the first Mississippi Historical Society, and Matthews had a prominent part in the establishment of the Mississippi Blind Institute and Insane Asylum.

Sharkey, Word, Boyd, and Stewart were Whigs. Wilkinson's party beliefs are uncertain, but he was probably a Whig. The remaining six were Democrats; however, Smith had at one time been a Whig. Since the delegation was designed to represent each party equally, the Democrats had supplied their full share. According to the editor of the *Southron*, the same individuals who had supported nullification most actively in 1833 were the most ultra advocates of the Nashville Convention; many of them were delegates to the convention. With a few exceptions, this applied to the minority of Whigs who supported the convention, as well as the Democrats. Practically all of the Democrats in the delegation had rather strong states' rights views. Former Governor Matthews who had served as president of the May Convention in Mississippi, as vice president and member of the resolutions committee of the October meeting, advocated firmness in any northern attempt to invade constitutional rights regarding slavery in the territories. In his judgment, the Wilmot Proviso was the most "impolitic and unjust measure" ever presented. Popular orator and newspaper editor McRae, called by one observer "the most talented and active member of the Mississippi delegation," played a leading role for the states' rights Democracy during this period. He denied, however, that the purpose of the Nashville Convention was the dissolution of the Union and drew up resolutions, which Mississippi presented at Nashville, declaring that preservation of the Union was the aim of the meeting.[16] In an address to the people on 10 December 1850 McRae, Clayton, and other members of the States Rights Committee expressed a desire to save the Union, if it could be restored to its "pristine purity," but conceded the right of secession to every state. Clayton's views followed those of McRae, and Smith was also a member of the states' rights group. He was in favor of southern state conventions to secure certain constitutional changes that would provide ample security for the South. Because of southern interest in Cuba, it is significant that Smith was connected with the movement for the liberation of the island in 1850.[17] Pettus also held states' rights views at this time; he was an unqualified disunionist by the latter part of the decade.

The views of the Mississippi Whig delegates varied somewhat from those of the Democrats. When questioned about his proposed attendance, Word skillfully defended the convention against the charge of disunion. He said, "The principal objective of the Nashville Convention, as I have understood is to call our erring brethren of the North *back into the Union*." The northern states had failed to observe the portion of the Constitution regarding fugitive slaves, and therefore had "as to that subject seceded and dissolved the Union." Through united and concerted action, the South might resist all dangerous departures from the Union and "prevent the calamities of secession and disunion." At a Union festival the following year, Boyd, a Unionist Whig, reported that he had attended the convention with the determination to "allay all unnecessary heat and excitement" and secure a united and just exposition of southern rights under the Constitution.[18]

The views of Judge Sharkey, who served as president of the Nashville Convention, are especially important. The editor of the Vicksburg *Sentinel* reported that Sharkey, "a very decided Whig" and "a man of great ability," had not participated in party politics for years beyond casting his vote and expressing his opinions in private conversation. But as president of the October Convention, he had probably written and certainly endorsed, the address to the southern states. He had defended the Mississippi Convention in correspondence with the *National Intelligencer* editors and attempted to vindicate himself and others from the charge of unfriendliness to the Union; he claimed that every member of the convention was a friend of the Union. As late as 24 May he had advocated the Nashville Convention as a meeting which "originated in the desire to preserve the Union by preventing a blow which might prove fatal to its existence."[19] On the eve of the assemblage, however, Sharkey was doubtful about the results of the convention. In the meantime, he expressed his approval of the Compromise in a letter to Foote. He advised Foote to support the Compromise in the Senate and assured him that the mass of the southern people would be content with this settlement. If the Compromise could be adopted, southern honor would at least be "safe." In a second letter to Foote, Sharkey again endorsed the Compromise with two exceptions—the number of representatives accorded to California and the lack of a provision to create two states out of that territory. Although the *Washington Union* had published extracts of this correspondence prior to the convention, the delegates probably knew nothing about it; in fact it is very likely that if they had known, they would not have chosen Sharkey to preside over the convention. Even so, one of the delegates later revealed that Sharkey had remarked "that even after reaching Memphis I was poised between the backward and forward steps."[20]

Sharkey's inconsistencies and vacillations did not cease, even after the convention ended. A few days after adjournment, he wrote to the editor of the *Southron* explaining his correspondence with Foote. He had believed that any prospect of a "creditable" convention was unlikely, because of the impossibility of uniting the South in vindication of its rights and the "advices from Washington City," and a failure would tend to encourage aggressions on the South. The Compromise had few friends in the convention, and he had supported the 36°30′ line, his preference even before the meeting. The Mississippian was indeed a Unionist. "From such an advisor or leader, in these times of peril good Lord deliver us and the South," wrote the editor of the Vicksburg *Sentinel*. On the other hand, President Fillmore was so impressed with Sharkey's great service to the Union cause while presiding over the convention that he invited Sharkey to become Secretary of War. Sharkey refused the post,[21] however, and he also declined to call the second session of the Nashville Convention in the fall of 1850.[22]

Wilkinson had also played a significant role in the proceedings leading to the Nashville Convention, having served as chairman of the resolutions committee of the October Convention and as a member of the committee to prepare the address. At this meeting he had delivered an address described as "a well reasoned and sensible protest" against the condition of the South.[23]

Several of the delegates were later prominent during

secession and the war. Clayton served on the committee to prepare the ordinance of secession at the Mississippi Secession Convention[24] and for approximately three months was a member of the Montgomery Convention or Provisional Confederate Congress. During the war he acted as Confederate judge for the state and aided the war effort in various ways. McRae was a representative in the first Confederate Congress. Sharkey continued to oppose secession and establishment of a Southern Confederacy, although he remained loyal to his state. At least one Mississippi delegate, G. F. Neil, served in the Confederate Army.[25]

Georgia Whigs questioned whether the state should send delegates to Nashville because of the insignificant vote in April; some Democratic delegates even declined to go. Eleven representatives, including two delegates-at-large, attended the convention. Only five of the sixteen delegates chosen in April were in this group. Governor George Towns appointed the remaining four to fill vacancies of those who declined. Geographically, the delegates were unevenly distributed. Former Governor George Troup from the first district (lower Georgia) could not attend because of illness in his family. His Whig colleague, James H. Cooper, refused to go. As no successor was appointed in either instance, the first district, as well as the sixth (Howell Cobb's), lacked representation at Nashville.[26] The second, fourth, and eighth districts sent two delegates each, while only one delegate represented each of the third, fifth and seventh. The two delegates from Richmond County on the coast provided the only representation for eastern Georgia; the Putnam County delegate was the only one from the central part of the state. All of the remaining delegates came from the western or northwestern part of the state. Three lived in Muscogee County on the Alabama line; one came from Harris County, also bordering Alabama; and one each from nearby Upson and Meriwether Counties. Floyd and Cobb Counties in northwest Georgia sent one delegate each.

At 29 James N. Ramsey was the youngest of the Georgia delegates; Jacob G. McWhertor, 61, was the oldest. With a median age of 42, the representation from the Empire State of the South was younger than either the South Carolina or Mississippi delegation. Five of the eleven delegates are identifiable as natives of Georgia; two were born in South Carolina and one each in Virginia and Kentucky. The birthplace of Walter T. Colquitt was either Halifax County, Virginia, or Georgia, while that of Obediah Warner remains unknown.[27]

The delegation was an educated group. The four most prominent men, Henry L. Benning, Walter T. Colquitt, Martin J. Crawford, and Charles J. McDonald, had attended college and studied law; at least two graduated. Five more representatives were professional men.[28] Eight were lawyers, and at least five, possibly six, also engaged in agrarian pursuits. Three of them had sufficient slaveholdings to classify them as planters. The remaining three delegates included a major planter, a doctor-farmer combination, and a newspaper editor.

Half of the eight slaveholders in the group owned fewer than twenty slaves; two held more than twenty slaves, but fewer than fifty. Benning and Robert Bledsoe, the two largest slaveholders, held sixty and fifty-seven slaves respectively. McDonald, the wealthiest delegate, with real estate valued at $38,500, owned only eighteen slaves. Two delegates owned no real estate, and three had less than $10,000.

Benning, Colquitt, Crawford, McDonald, and Obediah Warner had judicial experience, all having served as district or circuit judges; Benning, McDonald, and Crawford were also Associate Justices of the Georgia Supreme Court after 1850. All five men were members of the Georgia legislature at some time, as were James N. Ramsey and Obediah Gibson. Colquitt had served in both houses of Congress before 1850, while Crawford was a congressman during the following decade. McDonald had been governor of Georgia from 1839 to 1843. Colquitt, McDonald, and Bledsoe had been brigadier generals in the Georgia State Militia, Bledsoe for eleven years; Ramsey had served as captain. Simpson Fouche had attended the Memphis Railroad Convention as a delegate the previous year, which left only two Georgia representatives, Jacob G. McWhertor and Andrew H. Dawson, lacking public service records.

The Georgia delegation, led by the secessionists Benning and McDonald, consisted of eight southern rights Democrats and three Whigs. Neither of the Whig delegates that the legislature chose to represent the state at large attended. Of the eight Whigs originally elected in April, only Crawford of the second district attended; the other seven resigned or failed to appear. Governor Towns had appointed both of the remaining Whig delegates who attended, Ramsey and Bledsoe from the fourth and seventh districts respectively, as well as Democrats Dawson and McWhertor from the eighth district. Since the legislature chose two additional Democratic delegates, only half of the eight Democrats elected in April actually attended. One has to conclude, therefore, that the Georgia delegation to the convention was largely unrepresentative of the people who had nominally chosen the members.

The Georgia group, as a whole, was quite radical. Though the specific views of the Whig delegates are not as well known as those of the Democrats, they were also concerned about southern rights. Both Crawford and Ramsey spoke to southern rights meetings during the summer, and the simple fact that Governor Towns appointed Ramsey and Bledsoe indicates that their views were undoubtedly acceptable and probably similar to his. Benning, an ardent secessionist, was the most outspoken of the delegates. In July 1849 he had boldly stated, "The only safety of the South from the abolition universal is to be found in an *early* dissolution of the Union." He had no doubt that the North would abolish slavery as soon as possible "without too much cost." Even dissolution and a Southern Confederacy were not sufficient remedy inasmuch as some states of the Upper South were getting rid of their slaves. Benning's solution was "a *consolidated* Republic of the Southern states," that would put slavery "*under the control of those most interested in it.*" He expressed these views again the following year. Since the North had the will to abolish slavery and was rapidly acquiring the power to execute its desire, abolition was inevitable unless something were done to change the North's attitude, or stop its acquisition of power. "If there is a remedy *within* the Union embrace it by all means, if not, do not hesitate to go beyond for one. A remedy at any cost," continued Benning. Noninterference would not stop northern acquisition of power, but the extension of the Missouri Compromise line would retard it. Every southern congressman must stand up for the rights of the South and make no humiliating compromise with the North. The doctrine of states' rights would be the only security for slavery.[29] Publicly, Benning declared that the Nashville Convention should provide "a remedy for the coming evil," that is, devise some means to obviate the North's determination to abolish slavery or, if that were impossible, to arrest the acquisition of power by the North to abolish slavery.

McDonald vindicated the necessity of the convention in a public letter accepting his apointment. The southern states would not complain "if the Constitution were administered according to its letter and spirit"; but if anything violated the fundamental rights of the South, "the aggrieved States must consult and adopt some measure of safety for themselves" with dispassionate calmness and firmness. In another public letter McDonald suggested that the motto for the convention should be, "The Union, with the Constitution; no Union without it." Judge Colquitt, the second Democratic delegate-at-large, set forth his views in a lengthy, six-column letter in the *Federal Union*. The importance of the crisis compelled him to accept the appointment as delegate, and the results of the April election increased his commitment. Colquitt thought the South must hold the convention and adopt and carry out decisive measures. He had no fear for the Union; the only danger was that fear of dissolution would cause "an unjust and dishonorable sacrifice" of southern rights. Manly resistance might produce civil war, but he did not think it likely. "We *must* maintain our *rights* at all hazards," observed Gibson when he accepted the nomination as delegate. He had believed this for many years. Proceedings of the convention and accounts of the southern rights meetings later reveal that Dawson, Fouche, and McWhertor held similar views. One of Cobb's correspondents accused "Fouche, Colquitt and all that class of men" as desiring dissolution of the Union *per se*.[30]

Only McDonald, Bledsoe, Benning, and McWhertor returned to Nashville in November for the second session of the convention, at which McDonald presided. Colquitt and McDonald died before secession and war. Benning, Fouche, and Ramsey were members of the secession convention of 1861, and Benning served as a brigadier general in the Confederate Army. Crawford served the southern nation as representative in the Confederate Provisional Congress, as special commissioner to the United States government, and as a member of the Confederate armed forces.

Although the masses of Florida had also shown little interest in delegate selection, four of six representatives chosen by judicial districts attended the convention. Illness kept away Whig Joseph M. Hernandez, the only representative elected from the Eastern District, and congressional duties apparently prevented the attendance of E. C. Cabell, the Whig delegate elected from the Western District.[31] Thus only James F. McClellan, a Democrat, represented this district. Both Middle Florida delegates, Democrat Charles H. DuPont and Whig Arthur J. Forman were present at Nashville, as was Bird M. Pearson, a Democrat representing southern Florida. Thus three Democrats and one Whig represented Florida, with all districts of the state except the East accounted for.

All of the delegates were in their forties except McClellan, who was twenty-six. DuPont and Pearson were natives of South Carolina; Forman was born in Maryland and McClellan in Tennessee.

Evidently all except Forman, who engaged solely in agriculture, had studied law; McClellan was the only lawyer who did not also farm. DuPont's 73 slaves gave him status as a major planter; Pearson, with 30, had a medium-sized operation. Forman had 100 slaves, more than any other Florida delegate; McClellan owned none. DuPont was the wealthiest, with real estate valued at $37,000.

All of the Florida delegates except Forman had public service experience, primarily in a judicial capacity. Both DuPont and Pearson served as justices of the Florida Supreme Court; DuPont was Chief Justice at one time. Pearson had been state's attorney in South Carolina before moving to Florida.

McClellan served as judge of the Circuit Court and was author of the second digest of the laws of Florida. All three were original members of the Florida Historical Society, organized in 1856.[32]

One report states that DuPont and Forman were the first men in Florida "to put the convention in motion." Forman carried around the first paper for signatures to call a meeting in Gadsden County, and DuPont, as chairman of the committee, prepared the Gadsden resolutions recommending a full representation of the southern states at the Nashville Convention. Forman presided at the Tallahassee district convention until a president was selected, and DuPont served as chairman of the committee on credentials. It is not surprising that these men were unanimously elected delegates from the district, though they were both residents of Quincy in Gadsden County.[33] Newspaper accounts do not mention activity of either of the other delegates in preconvention proceedings.

Very little is known about the specific views of the Floridians. DuPont was connected with the conservative group in 1840, but by 1842 this group was disintegrating and appeared to be leaning toward support of Calhoun. As DuPont refused to support the Whigs that year, he probably returned to the Democratic party about that time.[34] Evidently, Forman was a conservative in 1850, as he voted against Barnwell Rhett's radical address at the convention.

DuPont was the only one of the group who returned to Nashville for the second session. None of the delegates participated in the Secession Convention of 1861; no record of Confederate service has been noted.

Although Texas had elected eight delegates to the Nashville Convention, J. Pinckney Henderson alone represented the Lone Star state. A native of North Carolina, Henderson was educated at Lincoln Academy and the University of North Carolina, although he withdrew before graduating to read law. Only 42 years of age, he had already experienced a colorful career. He fought in the Texas War for Independence and served the Republic as attorney general, secretary of state, and diplomat to England and France. He was a delegate to the constitutional convention when annexation occurred and became the first governor of the state. He had served in the Mexican War as a brigadier general. In 1850 he was a resident of San Augustine County, owned $30,000 worth of real estate and nine slaves, and was a Democrat. Before the convention, Henderson, with Louis T. Wigfall, had made fiery speeches in the state. Like all Texans, he was most concerned about the boundary dispute with New Mexico. After the convention, he and Wigfall continued to address several public meetings in volcanic terms. Seven years later Henderson was elected to the United States Senate, where he served until his death in 1859.[35] Texas sent no delegates to the second session of the Nashville Convention.

Only nineteen of the thirty-six delegates chosen by the Alabama legislature attended the convention. The three representatives elected at county meetings augmented the state delegation to twenty-two members. Seven delegates came from North Alabama, thirteen from the Black Belt, and two from Mobile. All of the delegates selected from the state at large attended. Only the second (Montgomery) congressional district sent a full delegation. None of the delegates chosen by the legislature for the third and sixth districts attended, but John Hunter and Reuben Chapman, selected in county meetings, represented these districts. William Byrd, who was also chosen by a county meeting, served the first district. The delegates ranged in age from 32 to 69, with a median age of 42, the same as Georgia's. Only two members of the Alabama delegation were native sons. Six delegates each were born in Virginia and Georgia and five in South Carolina. The remaining three delegates were born in North Carolina, Massachusetts, and either Mississippi or Tennessee.

Eleven of the delegates attended college, some graduating; one attended an academy and one a military school. Eighteen delegates had read or studied law.[36] Almost forty percent of the Alabama delegation was the frequent lawyer-planter combination; nine of the lawyer delegates had slaveholdings large enough to classify them as planters. Five more of the lawyers were probably engaged in agriculture; one of them was also a minister. Only three practiced law alone. The four remaining delegates were large planters. One of these was also a merchant; another was a physician.

James Abercrombie was the wealthiest, with $50,000; almost three-fourths of the delegates had real estate valued at $10,000 or more. Every Alabama delegate held slaves. G. S. Walden and Leroy Pope Walker had only four slaves each. John S. Hunter was the largest slaveholder with 201 slaves, but five other delegates owned more than 100 slaves. Thus almost half of the delegates owned more than fifty slaves.

Practically all of the Alabama delegates had public service records. Thirteen delegates served at some time in the state legislature. Reuben C. Shorter had served in both houses of the Georgia legislature before moving to Alabama. Abercrombie, Reuben Chapman, Benjamin Fitzpatrick, and George Goldthwaite all spent time in Congress, and seven delegates, almost one-third, had had state judicial careers. Fitzpatrick had served two terms as governor. Chapman had left the executive office the year before, and John A. Winston became governor five years later.

At least seven, possibly eight, of the Alabama representatives were Whigs; the remainder were Democrats. On the whole the delegation represented the more conservative sentiment in the state, although a few ardent states' righters were present. The editor of the *Alabama Journal* reported that the great majority did not desire disunion, but wanted to check the causes that were rapidly promoting dissolution. These men asked nothing more than the rights to which the Constitution entitled them. Apparently, many attended in order to prevent extreme action. Thomas J. Judge, who moved to strike out the clause condemning the Compromise in the Nashville Convention address, was one of the most outstanding Whig delegates. Significantly, the Alabama delegation sustained Judge, indicating their general conservatism.[37] Two other leading Whigs were the "old patriotic veteran" James Abercrombie and William Murphy, both of whom may be designated as Unionists.

Former Governor Chapman's position as a moderate

states' righter was typical of the Democrats. He hoped that a firm yet temperate exposition of rights and grievances expressed with unified sentiment through a southern convention might lead the North to pause in its aggression and agree to abide by the Constitution. Burwell Boykin, a Mobile Democrat, referred to the convention as a "deliberate and advisory assembly" of the southern people, the results of which would be referred to them for consideration.[38]

Judge John A. Campbell, Democrat, author of the resolutions that the convention adopted with some modifications, was by far the most outstanding Alabama delegate. In 1847 he had written his first article proposing a plan to secure equal treatment for the South in any acquired territory. He recommended the formation of a southern sectional party whose main purpose would be the defense of southern rights under the Constitution. To achieve this result he advocated election of men devoted to the cause of the South and above subservience to a national party. Yet at the same time Campbell's views on slavery were advanced, even radical, for his time. He stated clearly his own personal distaste for the institution and advocated several vital changes in the relation of master and slave. A few years later, he voluntarily liberated all his slaves. Campbell also encouraged emigration of white wage-earners to the South and advocated the stimulation of industrial activities. While he opposed secession as a remedy for the existing evils, he clearly recognized the wrongs inflicted upon the South. This was uniformly his position from the close of the Mexican War to the outbreak of the Civil War. The Compromise measures did not satisfy his sense of justice.[39]

William L. Yancey, Alabama's foremost states' rights leader, did not participate in the Nashville Convention. He based his refusal upon his opposition to the policy of moderation to which the convention was supposedly committed.[40] Goldthwaite, one of the most ardent states' righters in the delegation and paradoxically a native of Massachusetts, had indicated in an address at Montgomery shortly before the convention that if the slavery controversy were ultimately to end in disunion, this was the time.[41] Leroy Pope Walker, as leader of the southern rights group in the legislature, had demanded that the state send an official delegation to Nashville. In time he would become, next to Yancey, Alabama's leading secessionist. Jefferson Buford was also a relatively strong states' righter, and John A. Winston's views were growing more radical over the years.[42]

At the second session of the Nashville Convention Alabama's delegation was reduced to five; Chapman and Buford were the only members of the original group to return. Three years later Campbell became an associate justice of the United States Supreme Court, where he remained until the war began; thus he was a member of the Court at the time of the Dred Scott decision. Buford is best known for his unsuccessful attempt to settle proslavery advocates in Kansas during the decade following the convention. In 1860 John L. Erwin presided over the bolting wing of the Charleston Democratic Convention that met in Richmond. During the secession crisis, Campbell and Fitzpatrick, then a United States Senator, made unsuccessful public declarations in an attempt to restrain the surge toward secession. Goldthwaite was a member of the committee to confer with Governor Albert Moore regarding the secession convention, and Buford and Nicholas Davis, Sr., served in the convention.[43] William Cooper was appointed as a commissioner to Missouri to address the cooperationists in the legislature who favored the South. Chapman represented the Confederacy in France. Walker served as Secretary of War in the Confederate Cabinet, became a brigadier general in the Confederate Army, and for the last three years of the war was judge of a military court. In addition to Confederate military service, Thomas J. Judge of the Fourteenth Alabama Regiment was a judge in the Confederate Alabama Military Court.

In the upper South, North Carolina delegates declined to attend the convention, and Missouri, Kentucky, Maryland, and Delaware had selected no delegates. Six of Virginia's fourteen elected representatives attended, and Arkansas, demonstrating little interest in the southern movement, sent only two delegates, Tennessee, with 101 representatives, had by far the largest delegation at the convention. Since Nashville was the site of the convention, this was only natural, as the journey in 1850 for the out-of-state delegates was certainly long and tiresome. Although the large Tennessee delegation was as a whole the most conservative group at the convention, any similar conclusion drawn for the upper South would have to be qualified. In fact, one observer remarked that the Virginia delegation was "if possible more ultra than any of the rest."[44] Actually, as in some lower southern states, the delegates from the upper South varied from extreme fire-eaters to pro-unionists.

The Virginia delegation lacked geographical balance. No delegate was present from the western part of the state; Albermarle County, the only interior county represented, was also the farthest west. Three delegates were from the coast or tidewater area, while the remaining two were from the area bordering North Carolina.

The oldest person of Virginia's six-member delegation was 66, the youngest, 33; the median age was 50. All of the Virginia delegates were native-born. Three of the delegates had graduated from college, while four had studied law and were admitted to the bar.[45] Four delegates were planters; two of these were also lawyers. Another lawyer combined business with his law career, while the remaining delegate was a lawyer, a professor of law, and a writer.

William O. Goode, whose real estate was valued at $52,285, was the wealthiest delegate from the Old Dominion; R. H. Claybrook, with $10,000, possessed the least. With eighty-six slaves, Willoughby Newton was the largest slaveholder, followed by William F. Gordon with fifty-four. Apparently, two delegates held no slaves. Thus it appears that one-third of Virginia's delegates owned no slaves, another third belonged in the small-planter category, while the remaining third were large planters.

Claybrook was the only representative who did not have a public career. The editor of the Richmond *Enquirer* described him, however, as "a gentleman of a high order of talents, increasing professional reputation." Goode and Gordon served in the state legislature and the United States House of Representatives; Newton also served a term in the House. Gordon had been a member of the State Constitutional Convention of 1829-30. Thomas S. Gholson and Beverley Tucker had judicial careers.

Claybrook, Newton, and Gholson, who was strongly pro-union, were Whigs. Newton was an extreme states' rights man, but he thought in 1850 that southern rights could be preserved within the Union. Although Claybrook's views are little known, the Richmond *Whig* reported that he delivered a "beautiful tribute to Southern rights" in an address to a Northumberland County meeting. Goode was a states' rights Democrat, who favored southern protection in the Union if possible. His strong states' rights speech at the Lawrenceville second district convention did not advocate secession, but some considered it too radical.[46] Gordon, an extreme state's right Democrat, had "hob-nobbed" with the nullifiers in Washington and became a Whig in protest against President Jackson. In 1837, however, he had followed his idol, Calhoun, in a return to the Democratic party.

Beverley Tucker, whose writings were nearly all devoted to an exposition of extreme states' rights, was one of the most ardent defenders of southern rights in Virginia and at the Nashville Convention. As early as 1820 he had expressed himself boldly in favor of secession and he maintained this view with inflexible consistency for the remainder of his life. Outraged by the nullification controversy and the Force Bill, he wrote his novel, *The Partisan Leader*, with a single purpose: to popularize the doctrine of secession and encourage Virginia to act upon it. Though the background of his political thinking was clearly Jeffersonian, Tucker could not condone Jacksonian democracy. He was not interested in partisan politics and never sought public office. In 1850 he felt that many southern leaders were traitors to their section. He upbraided the Democrats, with whom he associated himself, for attempting to restore old party lines and for rejecting Whig cooperation in an attempt to create an all-southern party. A few weeks before the convention met, Tucker declared that he "would give $1,000 for six hours on the floor of the Senate, to say what no man has dared to say." A bold stand for southern nationalism by an eloquent speaker "would scare the robbers from their prey, and rouse the South to a fixed determination to resist."[47]

The participation of the Virginia delegates in the preconvention proceedings and their views concerning the assemblage had a decided effect on the temper of the meeting. Claybrook had participated in the Northumberland County meeting and served as a delegate at the first congressional district convention at Hampton. Newton had played a prominent role in the Westmoreland County meeting, where he had been appointed to attend the eighth district convention at Tappahannock. Gordon, one of the twelve delegates elected extralegally from Albermarle County, had served as a representative to the fifth district conference at Charlottesville. Goode had also been a district delegate, but evidently neither Gholson nor Tucker had participated in these meetings.[48] On 7 May Tucker reported that he had been chosen as a delegate to the Nashville Convention without going out of his house or even being known in half the counties of the district. "I have been elected . . . only on the ground of my being one prepared to 'set my foot as far as who goes farthest,' " he declared. Newton strongly opposed the admission of California, taking the extreme southern viewpoint that it was only a substitute for the Wilmot Proviso. Gordon wrote that the proposed admission of California and New Mexico and the rejection of the Missouri Compromise line "fills our cup of humiliation to the brim." He regarded such action as "a designed insult and indignity to the whole slave holding states," was prepared to resist if the Compromise should pass, and hoped the entire South would be of a similar mind. Goode believed that even the extension of 36°30′ to the Pacific "was almost disgraceful" to the South, but public opinion must be consulted and concessions made for peace and tranquility. If 36°30′ could not be achieved, he suggested to the Virginia senators that a line a little farther south might be a good idea. Goode also indicated that Clay's Compromise would be destructive to the South, but he was willing to accept a compromise approved and recommended by the southern congressmen. A few weeks before the convention the pro-union Gholson advised the postponement of the meeting until a later date, when it was highly probably that the whole South would be represented in council.[49]

In January 1850 Tucker suggested that the Nashville Convention recommend to the southern legislatures the adoption of constitutional amendments to secure all the rights of the South, and until a sufficient number of states adopted the amendments the convention must "be kept up by new delegations." A short time later, he proposed to Hammond that they write under a common signature a series of articles to be published in various southern cities—articles designed to prepare the Nashville Convention for what it should do and to prepare southern minds to receive it. Tucker also outlined a nine-point plan anticipating the dissolution of the Union and the formation of a Southern Confederacy, but he did not believe the public mind was prepared for such action in 1850. Moreover, the northern states would be unwilling to ratify the suggested amendments. A renewal of the Nashville Convention would thus keep the thing "simmering" until the next presidential election, when he hoped the South could prevent the election of any person, withdraw its representation, and therefore might "leave the Union . . . *dissolved de facto*." Toward the last of March Tucker wrote his nephew that some of his letters on secession would be published in pamphlet form and distributed among the delegates of the Nashville Convention, and would "give their colors to the acts of that body." Later, he set forth a three-point program for the convention, including an address to the southern people indicating the rights and remedies leading to the alternative of constitutional safeguards or disunion; an address to the people of the North, temperate but firm, warning them of the consequences of pushing the South too far; and a recommendation for a renewal of the convention by a full deputation of every southern state.[50]

Gordon was the only Virginia delegate to attend the second session of the Nashville Convention. Tucker, Gordon, and Goode died during the following decade. Of the remaining delegates, Newton became a strong proponent of secession in the latter fifties. Even Gholson served in the second Confederate States Congress.

Samuel Calhoun Roane and J. H. Powell, who remains unidentified, represented Arkansas at Nashville. Roane, one of Arkansas's most prominent citizens, has been described as the "greatest jurist of territorial days" and his life "in many respects the most remarkable of the state's history." A resident of Jefferson County in 1850 and brother of Governor John Seldon Roane, he was 46 years of age, a native of North Carolina who had migrated to Arkansas from Tennessee. A planter, he owned real estate worth $15,000 and eighty-six slaves. Nothing specific is known concerning his education, except that it was "not neglected." A Democratic lawyer, Roane had been quite active in territorial days as United States District Attorney for the area, president of the legislative council and judge of the first territorial court. He was a member of the constitutional convention and the first state senate, serving as president of that body and frequently acting as governor during the absence of that executive.[51]

Although the Tennessee legislature had failed to provide for the selection of delegates, 101 men, most of whom had been selected in county meetings, represented the Volunteer State at the convention. Perhaps fewer than a dozen of these delegates were even known outside Tennessee. Several were prominent within the state, but many others were leading citizens only in their respective counties. Almost a third of the delegates were Davidson County residents whose responsibility it was to welcome the out-of-state delegates and to help provide for their comfort, as well as make plans for the convention. Because of the manner of selection and the lack of prominence, identification of some of these Tennessee delegates has been impossible; in other cases only probable identification has been established.[52]

Most of the delegates were from Middle Tennessee, with seven from West Tennessee. Only one delegate, Thomas Hopkins of Jasper in Marion County, was from the eastern division of the state. Davidson County send the largest number of delegates, twenty-nine more than any state. Maury County, home of former President Polk, ranked second among the counties represented, with twelve delegates.

Tennessee sent both the youngest and the oldest delegate to the convention. Two young lawyers, Sam H. Whitthorne and Edward Gantt, both age 22, were the youngest. Former Governor William Hall, age 75, was the oldest. With a median age of 47, the Tennessee delegation was a fairly representative group.

Thirty-five of the ninety delegates whose birthplace could be determined were native Tennesseans. Twenty-four were born in Virginia, fifteen in North Carolina. Kentucky was the native state for six, while three were born in South Carolina. A single delegate was born in Illinois, New Hampshire, Georgia, Maryland, Alabama, New York, and Pennsylvania.

Information on education of the Tennessee delegates is rather sparse.[53] Approximately one-fourth of them at least studied law or medicine. Two delegates attended West Point, one was a Harvard graduate, and at least twelve had been enrolled at southern colleges or universities. The Tennessee group was most diversified as to vocation. Agriculture was the leading occupation, with thirty-five delegates pursuing it alone, while eight lawyers also farmed. Fifteen lawyers devoted themselves exclusively to the practice of law, but six others followed some other activity—four lawyer-writers, one lawyer-teacher, and one lawyer-physician-editor-writer. Eight doctors, four merchants, three clerks, two military men, and one each of other miscellaneous occupations, including the keeper of the state penitentiary and the superintendent of the city cemetery in Nashville, composed the rest of the delegation.

James H. Hammond reported that Tennessee "sent up a mass of yeomanry" who "were honest in the main."[54] The census records verify this statement to a great extent, although several wealthy men are noted. The value of real estate for nineteen men was under $5,000; twenty-two possessed no landed property. Eight more delegates owned real estate worth as much as $30,000, but less than $100,000. William G. Harding, owner of Belle Meade plantation near Nashville, was the wealthiest delegate, with property valued at $170,000. Gideon J. Pillow and James Walker of Maury County and Willoughby Williams of Davidson County all had real estate valued at $100,000 or more. Only fifty-six delegates held slaves; twenty-eight of this number had fewer than twenty slaves, sixteen less than ten. Seven delegates owned more than fifty, but fewer than 100; only two delegates—Andrew Jackson, Jr., adopted son of former President Jackson, who lived at the Hermitage, with 137 and Willoughby Williams of Davidson County with 111 slaves—owned more than 100 slaves.

Almost half of the Tennessee delegates show no record of public service, which further indicates their lack of prominence within the state and even their counties. Twenty-nine served at some time in the General Assembly. William Hall and Aaron V. Brown had been Tennessee governors, while William B. Bate served many years later. Daniel Graham and John E. R. Ray each held the position of Secretary of State for Tennessee at one time. Bate, Brown, Washington Barrow, Thomas Claiborne, A. O. P. Nicholson, and James M. Quarles were congressmen during their careers. Nicholson, Quarles, Westly Humphreys, and William Williams had judicial service to their credit. Among the delegates were three former diplomats—Barrow, Donelson, and Robert Armstrong.

Practically all the Tennessee delegates were Democrats. The Whigs, for the most part, had denounced the convention and blocked the selection of delegates in the legislature. Barrow and Quarles were probably Whigs; there might have been others.

As a whole the Tennessee delegation was a conservative group, a majority of whom were willing to accept the Compromise measures pending in Congress. Cave Johnson reported the Tennesseans preferred the 36°30′ line, except for the fact that they believed it would be defeated and the question left open for agitation. They feared that some of the delegates planned to defeat the Compromise bill by supporting the 36°30′ line.[55]

Donelson, Brown, and Nicholson played the most significant roles in connection with the convention and at the meeting. The rump session of the Davidson County meeting had accepted Donelson's resolutions when he was advised it was the duty of Tennessee to send delegates, although he thought the convention unnecessary and hoped the Committee of Thirteen would succeed. Even if the convention were disunionist in nature, delegates should still be appointed. "Would it not be better policy for us to join our influence with the sound portion of the convention," Donelson asked, "and thus nip in the bud the attempt to dissolve the Union?" Brown had published a letter strongly supporting the convention. Though mild and temperate, it was a firm defense of the motives of the assemblage. Later Nicholson revealed that he had attended the convention with aspirations to check the extremists and to produce unity of sentiment among southerners. Both Brown and Nicholson tended to look with some favor on the Compromise measures.[56]

Because the Tennessee delegates supported the proceedings, the Whigs bitterly criticized their course at the convention. Rhett described the Tennesseans as being "wheeled into line." Hammond related that the ultra-southern group took the Tennessee delegates away from their leaders, and finally captured the leaders themselves except the brother of the late President, William H. Polk, "a poor devil."[57] Evidently, the Tennessee group faced a dilemma at the convention. Though the delegates were aware public opinion in Tennessee was quite different from that of the lower South, pro-southern sentiment strongly affected them. As a result, their views and actions sometimes appeared inconsistent.

Tennessee sent only fourteen delegates to the second session in November; all except two had attended in June. Those returning included Brown, Nicholson, Donelson, Harding, Polk, Pillow, J. B. Clements, Thomas Claiborne, Dr. John Esselman, Frank McGavock, T. D. Moseley, and L. P. Cheatham. All these men were from Davidson County except Pillow and Polk of Maury County. Though Tennessee held no secession convention in 1861, three former delegates of the Nashville Convention, Barrow, T. J. Kennedy, and W. C. Whitthorne, were members of the secession legislature. Several of the delegates served in the Confederate Armed Forces.[58]

Thus a majority of the delegates to the convention were in the prime of life with a scattering of venerable figures and young politicians—men who had often achieved prominence within their states through some kind of public service. Most of them combined public service with agrarian pursuits, as they usually owned both land and slaves. Whig or Democrat, the delegates were, on the whole, concerned both for the maintenance of southern rights and the preservation of the Union; extremists were in the minority. The men who assembled at Nashville, a decade before the South established its own nation, were destined in many instances to play a role within the Southern Confederacy.

While some of the Tennessee delegation were still busy with preparations for the convention at their capital city near the end of May, the out-of-state delegates were already arriving. They were invited to register at the Nashville *Union* office on Cherry Street near the post office, where a subcommittee of the Tennessee delegation was constantly in attendance. Along with the 175 delegates came others attracted by sheer curiosity to the convention, and a lively atmosphere prevailed in the little city of Nashville, as it welcomed the many guests. One visitor found that Tennessee's capital in June 1850 presented "the most charming aspect to the approacher of any inland town in the Union."[59]

# 7

# *The First Session: A Wait-and-See Attitude*

The selection of Nashville as the meeting place of the Southern Convention showed its increasing importance in the South and Southwest. With a total population of 10,165 in 1850, the city stood on the threshold of a decade of achievement.[1] Signs of improvement and progress were everywhere, although Tennessee's capital remained a semirural city. "The Town of Nashville is a very handsome Town," wrote Virginia delegate William F. Gordon to his wife. "The public and Private edifaces are on a scale of Magnificence, everything shews the prosperity of the Country." Symbolic of the progress of both city and state was the imposing half-finished state capitol, construction of which had begun five years before.[2] The Nashville Gas Light Company had been chartered the preceding November, but the oil lamps that had lighted the city since 1821 would not be replaced until February of the following year. On 20 January the arrival of the elegant side-wheel steamer "City of Nashville" had created much excitement, indicating the progress the West was making in supplying transportation for freight and passengers. Less than two weeks before the delegates assembled, workmen stretched the first wire across the Cumberland River for the suspension bridge, which was near completion by the last of June.[3] A meeting of the directors of the

Nashville and Chattanooga Railroad was held in the city on Friday preceding the convention to discuss plans to hasten the construction of the railroad between these two cities and thence to Charleston.

By 1850, Nashville was widely known as the "Athens of the South," in recognition of its cultural characteristics. Its fame as an educational center was due largely to the Nashville Female Academy and the University of Nashville. Plans for new buildings and the organization of a medical school as a department of the university were in progress. William K. Blake opened an English and classical school for boys on 13 May 1850 and during that year a few interested citizens set plans in motion to establish a public school system. Tennessee's capital had no western rival for medical prestige, boasting a number of nationally prominent doctors and an internationally circulated medical journal. A number of impressive churches, representing most of the major religious groups, added to the beauty as well as the religious life of the city. The Protestant Orphan Asylum built in 1850 was a combined effort of several churches. Five daily papers, two Democratic and three Whig, kept residents well informed; this also meant good press coverage for the convention. The city's display of fashion and luxury greatly impressed visitors, one of whom commented that Nashville was as fashionable as New York.[4]

The citizens of Nashville maintained its reputation as "a courtly city," showing true southern hospitality in their reception of the delegates. This countered some dire forecasts that the city would not even permit the convention to assemble there. Residents who had most doubted the propriety of holding the convention were among the most courteous to the strangers in their midst, according to a report in the Nashville *Union.* One eminent Whig jurist, though he opposed the gathering, opened the largest and best rooms of his house to the delegates, remarking that visitors should be received with kindness and civility, and he could never forget the laws of hospitality.[5]

The convention assembled for the first session in the three-year old Odd Fellows Hall. When this building proved too small to accommodate the delegates and the large number of visitors, the trustees of McKendree Methodist Church offered the use of their building, which could accommodate 1,500 people. The delegates gratefully accepted. This historic church, organized in 1787 by the Rev. Benjamin Ogden, was the mother church of Middle Tennessee Methodism. The small stone-and-wood structure that housed the first congregation was reputedly the first church building in Nashville; James Robertson, founder of the city, served as a steward there for many years. Two other buildings, in different locations, had preceded the large parallelogram-shaped building on Spring Street (later Church Street) where the delegates assembled. Dedicated by Bishop William McKendree in 1833, it had served as the site of President James K. Polk's funeral in 1849. The church possessed the largest room for public worship of any Methodist Society in the United States and was the nation's second largest American Methodist church building. In 1850 the pastor was Joseph Cross, and the membership comprised 361 whites. So large a group as the convention could be expected to cause some damage, and at adjournment the Charleston delegation presented the church a new carpet to replace the one that had been injured by those in attendance.[6]

Former Governor Aaron V. Brown of Tennessee called to order the first session on Monday, 3 June. He gave the report of the organization committee, which recommended William L. Sharkey of Mississippi as president and Charles J. McDonald of Georgia as vice president. The committee also advised that the assemblage vote by delegations, with each state casting one vote, and that William F. Cooper, prominent Tennessee politician, and E. G. Eastman, editor of the Nashville *Union*, be chosen as secretaries.[7] The delegates unanimously voted in favor of the recommended officers. Sharkey thanked the delegates in "a brief but animated speech" and asserted that the Constitution's guarantee of universal equal rights had been violated. The object of the convention was twofold: to perpetuate the Union and to protect southern rights and property. Following the speech the delegates appointed a credentials committee, consisting of one delegate from each state, with General Gideon J. Pillow of Tennessee as chairman.[8]

After an opening prayer by one of the visiting clergymen, a practice that continued each day, the delegates devoted the morning session of the second day almost entirely to the manner of voting. Francis Pickens of South Carolina moved adoption of the committee's recommendation, but John Erwin of Alabama objected. He argued that, while some of the delegates represented their states at large, others had been chosen by congressional districts and had no authority to speak for the state as a whole. Such representatives were entitled to a separate vote. William O. Goode of Virginia and J. J. McRae of Mississippi offered amendments providing for separate votes. Several delegates participated in the long and spirited debate that followed. Pickens emphasized sovereign state equality in "a very animated manner," shouting "Equality now and forever or independence" at the end. Both amendments were defeated, and the convention adopted the committee's recommendation. Only Alabama voted "no."

That afternoon, Brown moved to appoint a resolutions committee consisting of two members selected by each state delegation. Debate on the resolutions would be withheld until the committee reported them. Beverley Tucker of Virginia spoke against the motion, Andrew H. Dawson of Georgia replied, and the delegates approved the measure.[9]

Numerous spectators attended the convention. The main body of the church was reserved for the delegates, clergymen, and ladies; other visitors filled the galleries. One interested witness was Cave Johnson of Clarksville, Tennessee, an advocate of the Compromise who had declined to be a delegate. He made a two day visit early in the assemblage and found the members "less restive and factious" than he had expected. He believed the delegates would make 36°30′ their ultimatum, but the Tennessee representatives would withdraw or enter a protest against this policy and stake themselves on the Compromise, which in Tennessee was "exceedingly popular with both parties.[10]

Johnson's surmise was not all conjecture. Beginning around 22 May a series of pro-Compromise meetings had occurred throughout Tennessee. On 1 June, just two days before the convention, large turnouts from both political parties had attended a Compromise meeting in Nashville. Though certain convention delegates were doubtless present, neither Aaron V. Brown nor A. O. P. Nicholson attended.[11] Some of the Maury County delegates had also participated in a Compromise meeting held on 2 June, the eve of the convention.[12]

The press also assessed the sentiments of the delegates. The special correspondent of the Charleston *Mercury* reported that the Tennessee delegation as a group would sustain no measure of resistance. The Tennesseans were satisfied with Clay's Compromise and would not object to its endorsement by the convention. Only "a few stray delegates from Alabama, Georgia, and perhaps one from Virginia" would, however, approve such a move. With these exceptions, the reporter was confident that the convention would favor strong measures in opposition to the Compromise bill and any other compromise unfair to the South. Another special correspondent, J. W. Clay, junior editor of the Huntsville *Democrat*, referred to the delegates as a "dignified and intellectual body," who were "all for the Union, but a constitutional Union." They would only adopt disunion "as a last sad alternative."[13]

Not all of the commentators were journalists or politicians, however. One unique reporter was a young governess who described herself as "Yankee girl" and wrote under the assumed name of Kate Conynham. She attended the convention at the invitation of her host, a "colonel" who lived at "Overton Park," three hours from Nashville. She described the seating of the delegates: South Carolina and Mississippi in the front pews on either side of the broad aisle; Virginia filling two pews on Mississippi's right; Florida on the left of Carolina. The Alabama group sat behind Carolina, while Georgia's representatives were back of Mississippi. The Tennessee delegates occupied the side pew on the pulpit's left. Editors and reporters worked at "a dozen little green tables" on a carpeted platform in front of the pulpit. Sharkey, "a dignified Andrew Jackson-looking" man, McDonald, and the two secretaries sat before the center desk. To the governess "the whole scene was imposing and solemn in the extreme . . . dignified in its character, calm and deliberate in its debates," as if the delegates fully realized the solemnity of the occasion. The convention appeared to her, for the time being, as "the *true* Congress of the country," for the national Congress "seemed to be suspended in action . . . as if waiting for the result" at Nashville. She overheard comments that "the whole tone and temper" of the gathering was not unworthy of the United States Senate.[14]

On Wednesday morning, 5 June, the state delegations reported their selections and the resolutions committee was organized. John A. Campbell then offered a series of sixteen resolutions, which were referred without action to the committee. These resolutions dealt essentially with equal rights in the territories and denied congressional authority to exclude slavery from the Mexican Cession. They did express, however, a willingness to acquiesce in the division of the territories, by an extension of the 36°30′ line to the Pacific, and offered no suitable means of resistance to any law violating southern constitutional rights. Erwin of Alabama next introduced a resolution declaring that congressional reception or consideration of antislavery memorials perverted the constitutional right of petition and would lead to most dangerous consequences. Dawson of Georgia requested that the convention recommend to the people of the slaveholding states that they support the southern press soon to be established in Washington.

The introduction of two lengthy sets of resolutions by McRae of Mississippi and Henry L. Benning of Georgia, respectively, occupied most of the remainder of the third day. McRae's first resolution stated that the aim of the convention was to "preserve unimpaired the Union" by the "preservation inviolate of the Constitution . . . which made the Union." He restated the compact theory and the policy of congressional noninterference with property in the territories. His eleventh resolution declared southern willingness to meet the North in carrying out the Missouri Compromise by extending the 36°36′ line to the Pacific, while the last recommended stopping commercial intercourse with those nonslaveholding states that rejected reasonable terms and continued to agitate the slavery question.

Benning's resolutions were much stronger than McRae's. Beginning "the United States are a Confederacy, in which the several states are equal and sovereign," he cited the principle of equal territorial rights. The North had practically destroyed some southern rights and was attempting to eradicate the remainder. Either the hostile purposes of the nonslaveholding states must be changed, or the South must keep them from securing the power to carry out their objectives. Benning also recommended the extension of the Missouri Compromise line: "the South ought to submit to this but nothing else."[15] He upheld the Texas claims in the boundary dispute and recommended that southerners drop the old party distinctions and judge candidates simply by which one would do the most for the South. Finally he proposed that the convention reassemble if Congress passed the questionable legislation.

Early on Thursday, Beverley Tucker of Virginia offered a series of twenty-one "incontestable" propositions centering around congressional power in the territories and declaring that any federal attempt to exercise the right of empire over a territory was a usurpation of power. The inhabitants of a territory such as California possessed the right to establish law and order over the area, but inhabitants did not include "sojourners and intruders." The South's obligation to resist such a violation of the inhabitants' rights was equally as serious as its duty to resist the Wilmot Proviso. Although Tucker claimed part of the Virginia delegation had approved his proposition, both R. H. Claybrook and Thomas Gholson remarked that they had not seen the proposals. Erwin, one of the most active Alabama delegates, followed Tucker and introduced additional resolutions, many repeating principles already asserted. The first one declared, however, the constitutional guarantee to the southern states for the restoration of fugitive slaves.

Three of the four Florida delegates also spoke on Thursday. Charles H. DuPont spoke about states' rights, recommending a declaration of equality among the states and an assertion of the right to determine violations of such equality. Upon congressional infringement of its rights, the aggrieved state should call a convention of the slaveholding states to determine the mode of redress. As soon as nine states concurred in the call, the convention should meet. Bird M. Pearson introduced an additional series of resolutions that had been adopted at a public meeting in East Florida. James F. McClellan submitted a declaration specifying that certain congressional actions—prohibition of slavery in the District of Columbia, inhibition of the interstate slave trade, conversion of slave territory into free territory, and rejection of a state for admission because of its adoption of slavery—would warrant a southern convention. William H. Polk, representative of Tennessee's conservative sentiments, presented the last resolution at this session. Should the proposed partition on the 36°30′ line fail, the convention should not be deemed antagonistic to the plan of the Committee of Thirteen, provided the amendments thereto conformed to the views of southern senators. Initially, Polk offered his resolution as an amendment to Campbell's fourteenth statement. A motion to table by Walker of Alabama, however, caused Polk to submit his resolution separately.[16]

During the deliberations, "the galleries thundered applause, and the ladies smiled approbation." The people in the lobbies and galleries sometimes applauded rather "vehemently" and were too much disposed to participate, thought the *Mercury* reporter. Had the president been a man of any authority, he could have stopped this intrusion, but, according to the journalist, Sharkey acted like a novice. The applause was no real criterion of opinion, as Kate Conynham heard acclamation for a suggestion of "non-intercourse" one hour and for a defense of the Union in the next.[17]

The spectators provided a welcome diversion to the members, however, who whiled away the tedium of the resolutions through conversations with the ladies, who enclosed the delegates on each side "like borders of flowers."[18] Nashville was noted for the beauty and fashionable dress of its women. The husband of the famous singer Jenny Lind is quoted as having said that there was "more female loveliness in Nashville than you will find in any other city in the Union." William F. Gordon of Virginia, chairman of the resolutions committee, wrote his wife on 6 June that he was very busy—that convention affairs occupied "almost every moment"—and he was in "too great a whirl" at Nashville to write her much. A "spirit of conciliation and much unanimity" had prevailed so far, and he was glad that he had come.[19]

More resolutions, some repetitious, others original, dominated Friday's sessions. Two Alabamians began. Daniel Coleman declared that northern state laws obstructing the return of fugitive slaves violated the Constitution and trespassed on southern rights. Antislavery resolutions of northern legislatures disregarded the obligations one section owed to another and provided proof of a desire to excite the slaves. Jefferson Buford's statements expressed a willingness to "accept and abide by any reasonable compromise" that would end this agitation. For several reasons Buford considered President Taylor's policy in regard to the territories better for the South than the Compromise plan. Abolition agitation had produced both plans, as well as popular sovereignty; if the South permitted this fanaticism to warp national policy and legislation, it would no longer have strength left to oppose the ulterior measures beyond those to which the South had already yielded. E. C. Wilkinson of Mississippi declared that government perversion of the purpose of the Union as stated in the preamble would give each state "the undoubted right to withdraw peaceably from it, without any opposition, complaint, or question from any quarter; and even without partial expression of a reason for such a withdrawal." But he also proposed a resolution stating that the convention refrained from advising such withdrawal at present; it fervently hoped that such an eventuality might never happen and that the Union might be perpetual.

J. Pinckney Henderson, sole delegate from Texas, offered resolutions asserting the "rightful boundary of Texas" as claimed since independence from Mexico, admonishing the southern states of their duty to stand firmly by Texas, and urging members of the convention to pledge themselves and their constituents that the territory should not be taken from Texas without its consent. Goode of Virginia followed, setting forth the specific boundaries. He added that Congress had no constitutional right to assume the payment of state debts contracted after admission but suggested that the Texas debt acquired before annexation might be paid from duties collected at its ports. Tucker added that the whole South was obliged to oppose northern attempts to seize any territory rightfully belonging to Texas; but the southern states also had a right to expect that Texas would not "accept any sum of money as a consideration for admitting an enemy within the gates."

The last resolutions on Friday, offered by Simpson Fouche of Georgia, dealt mainly with the relationship between the states and federal government. One specifically stated that "the right to alter or abolish governments belongs to the people of the several states." Thus a delegate had now added the right of revolution to the compact theory and the right of secession. Fouche also proposed that the convention recommend that southern congressmen insist upon a division of the Mexican Cession at the Missouri Compromise line, and that failure to secure this settlement would be grounds for the convention to reassemble to consider and recommend more effective measures of defense.[20]

By Saturday, the report of the resolutions committee was ready. Campbell read the thirteen resolutions approved by the committee, and Reuben Chapman of Alabama moved for an immediate vote for adoption. His colleague Erwin, however, requested that the whole subject be tabled until Monday, and his motion carried. This is only one of many instances of disagreement among the Alabama delegates. "These gentlemen seem to be in a perpetual snarl," reported the *Mercury* correspondent; whether their differences were personal or political, they had divided on every question and he predicted they would lack unanimity in the final convention proceedings. Chairman Gordon also reported an address to the people of the southern states to accompany the resolutions. Campbell read the address, which the convention voted to table until Monday, and ordered it printed. A. O. P. Nicholson of Tennessee gave the minority report of the committee: the minority concurred with the majority in favor of the resolutions, but they could not fully agree to the address. The minority report, signed by Nicholson and Brown of Tennessee, William M. Murphy of Alabama, Arthur J. Forman of Florida, and Sam C. Roane of Arkansas, was also deferred until Monday.[21]

Additional resolutions consumed the remainder of the day. DuPont offered a substitute for the committee's thirteenth resolution, which offered no means of resistance to congressional laws that might dishonor the South. Should Congress enact a law violative of southern constitutional rights or refuse to adjust the controversy upon terms satisfactory to a majority of the slaveholding states, the convention should propose that the states through their legislatures adopt measures to organize a general convention authorized to prescribe the mode and measures of redress. Burwell Boykin of Alabama declared that any law passed by Congress abolishing slavery in the District of Columbia or prohibiting the interstate slave trade demanded "the strongest counter-acting measures." Obediah Gibson of Georgia offered lengthy resolutions presenting the southern defense of slavery as an institution, pointing out the physical and mental inferiority of the Negro. The opinion that slavery could be abolished was "wholly false in theory." The resolutions of William M. Byrd had been adopted previously in Marengo County, Alabama. Most significantly, they recommended that southern congressmen "sustain any fair and reasonable plan" that was not inconsistent with the spirit of the Constitution, nor incompatible with the safety and honor of the South, and further advised the congressmen to remain at their posts until Congress adjourned or until their constituents summoned them home. Once again, Beverley Tucker, apparently a most active delegate, presented a long series of resolutions. Supposedly in order to avert the necessity of resorting "to the last extremity," and to preserve the Union, he offered a plan of adjustment which included a division of territory at 36°30′; establishment of territorial governments in California, New Mexico, and Utah that could not prohibit slavery; and guarantees in regard to fugitive slaves.[22] Tucker asked for more than the North would be willing to give, as Calhoun had done on 4 March.

On Saturday afternoon the convention adjourned until 10

o'clock Monday. Nashville, a city noted for its gaiety, wealth, and sociability, had "turned out" to entertain the visitors, and the best families had opened their richly furnished homes to entertain them. Brilliant parties occurred nearly every evening; dinner parties were especially popular. During the weekend, some of the delegates probably attended the Swiss Bell Ringers' concert at Odd Fellows Hall on Friday or Saturday evening or the weekly concert—"both a musical and intellectual feast"—at the Female Academy. Riding, both in carriages and on horseback, was a popular pastime, and many delegates probably visited the Hermitage a few miles outside the city, now occupied by Andrew Jackson, Jr., a delegate himself. The city remained delightfully excited as long as the convention was in session; perhaps this was the gayest fortnight Nashville had ever experienced.[23]

When the convention resumed proceedings on Monday, 10 June, the states and the individual delegates unanimously adopted the thirteen resolutions which closely resembled those submitted by Campbell. The adoption of fifteen additional resolutions and an amended address occupied the remaining days of the convention. Before discussing the final proceedings, it is significant, however, to note in some detail the twenty-eight resolutions and the address, which represent the work of the convention.

Both contemporaries and historians agree that the address was more radical in nature than the resolutions, which really offered little that was new. The junior editor of the Huntsville *Democrat* described the resolutions as "mild, but firm, temperate but manly, decided, but free from that gasconade and bravado, which so often mar and destroy the moral force of sentiments and actions otherwise praiseworthy." William Cooper described the address as a clear, logical, and effective argument, but its strong attacks on the Compromise bill made it "by no means unobjectionable." Moreover, Cooper suspected the hand of Calhoun in the address, as its composition greatly resembled that of the deceased Carolinian.[24]

The first thirteen resolutions related mostly to the territorial controversy. The territories belonged to the people of the states as common property; therefore Congress had no power to exclude slavery from them. The slaveholding states could not and would not submit to congressional enactment of any law that restrained the rights of slaveholders to move with their chattels into the territories. In case the dominant majority failed to recognize constitutional rights, the convention recommended division of the territories between the sections, and it would acquiesce in the extension of the 36°30′ line to the Pacific Ocean as an extreme concession.

Resolutions fourteen through eighteen dealt with the rights and interests of Texas. Henderson wrote Senator Thomas J. Rusk of Texas immediately after the convention that the states represented had pledged to stand by Texas in the boundary dispute. But Texas promised to support the South by refusing to sell any part of her territory without a provision that any states formed from it south of 36°30′ would be slaveholding. "I thought that but just to the South," declared Henderson.[25]

Samuel S. Boyd of Mississippi claimed credit for resolutions nineteen through twenty-seven,[26] although various other delegates had also introduced many of them, at least in principle. These resolutions partially related to congressional authority; Congress had no right to create or destroy slavery anywhere, to regulate or prohibit internal slave trade, or to consider antislavery memorials. Congress was obliged, however, to enforce the restoration of fugitive slaves. Slavery existed in the United States independent of the Constitution which recognized it on three grounds: as property, as a personal and domestic relation of service under a state law, and as a basis of political power. Foreign laws that ran contrary to the Constitution at the time of territorial transfer could not continue to exist or be adopted by Congress. Some of these resolutions were, therefore, designed "to put to rest" the preposterous idea that Mexican laws prohibiting slavery were still in force in the territories. The final resolution provided for the reassembling of the convention.

Rhett of South Carolina wrote the address, which was directed to the people of the slaveholding states, exclusive of Delaware. It began with a historical review of northern aggression for the past sixteen years. Without disguise the object of congressional petitions was to overthrow slavery in the states. Although the agitation had increased, the southern states had done nothing to vindicate their rights. At the close of the Mexican War, the nonslaveholding states immediately claimed the right to exclude southerners from the newly acquired territory, not merely from a lust of power, but as a further step toward the abolition of slavery. When the southern states set forth their territorial rights through legislative resolutions, the North ignored them. The convention, therefore, assembled "to take counsel as to the course the Southern states should pursue for the maintenance of their rights, liberty and honor."

Rhett then proceeded to discuss the condition of southern states. A review of northern aggression showed that the past southern policy of nonaction and submission to aggression could not bring peace and safety. The South had tamely acquiesced and waited until the Constitution was "in danger of being abolished—or of becoming what the majority in Congress think proper to make it." Yet a minority, by submission, could as effectively betray the Constitution as a majority by aggression. The crucial question was how the South could preserve the Constitution and protect itself.

Through a critical analysis of the measures reported by the Committee of Thirteen, Rhett demonstrated the unacceptability of the Compromise. Admission of California, an area extensive enough for four large states, was virtually an enactment of the Wilmot Proviso. The Texas boundary bill would transfer from the South to the North territory sufficient for two states. Since the land to be surrendered by Texas adjoined Indian country and the Indians would be unable to maintain slavery in their territory, the southern states would be hemmed in by nonslaveholding states on the entire western border. In addition to yielding land, the South would have to yield to the interests and prejudices of the northern people. Any slave brought into the District of Columbia for sale should be "liberated and free"; the next step, abolition in the District, would not be difficult. In return for all of these concessions, the South would receive the new fugitive slave bill, a right it already possessed under the Constitution. This bill usurped the reserved rights of the states under the pretext of granting a great benefit to the South. The slave might sue his master before the courts for freedom, a measure which virtually extended congressional jurisdiction over slavery in the states, "Under the guise of a benefit the bill is useless as a remedy—and worse than useless in its usurpations." Even if these measures were really a compromise, their expediency for the South was doubtful. During the controversy, the South had three times proposed the Missouri Compromise and twice suggested settlement by the courts, only to have these proposals rejected.

Was any compromise acceptable? In Rhett's view, the South might agree to one more adjustment, not because it was fair, but because it had been twice sanctioned in the past. If the North offered the extension of the Missouri Compromise to the Pacific Ocean, the South could not reject it, provided the compromise distinctly recognized the right of slaveholders to the territory south of 36°30′. "We should take this line between the two sections of the Union; and beside this nothing but what the Constitution bestows," he declared. The address concluded with a recommendation and exhortation to send delegates from every county and district in the southern states to the second session of the convention.[27]

Although the delegates eventually reached agreement on the content of the last fifteen resolutions and the address, a great deal of discussion marked the process of acceptance. After the vote on the first thirteen resolutions, Gholson of Virginia expressed approval of the resolutions as a whole but dissented from the modification of the thirteenth in the address. Although the thirteenth resolution stated that the convention had not reached the conclusion that Congress would adjourn without making an adjustment, Rhett had demonstrated in the address the unacceptability of the Compromise. In the interest of harmony, Gideon J. Pillow of Tennessee proposed, with the approval of his state delegation, alterations that removed the "sting and venom" from the address.[28] His amendment stated that the delegates were unanimous in their approval of the resolutions, but they were not completely united in accepting all of the arguments contained in the address, particularly those relating to the Compromise. No delegates, however, favored the Compromise until it was amended to conform with the resolutions, or in such a way as to guarantee to the South its rights. Following his amendments, Pillow urged unanimity among all the southern states. Thomas J. Judge of Alabama moved to strike out the portion of the address relating to the present Compromise plan. Other amendments by Murphy of Alabama, Claybrook of Virginia, Dawson of Georgia, and others were read and referred with the address to the resolutions committee. Another Tennessee delegate, Thomas Claiborne, did not approve Pillow's amendments and entered a very able protest against any sort of concession. He desired to transmit the Constitution unimpaired to posterity.[29]

As the last matter of business, Chairman Gordon read the remaining fifteen resolutions adopted by the committee and recommended their consideration. The last one stated that the convention should reassemble in Marietta, Georgia, on the fourth Monday after congressional adjournment, and that the southern states be advised to fill their delegations forthwith.

Several important speeches and vigorous debates took place on the last two days. Willoughby Newton of Virginia proposed early on Tuesday that the convention adopt the resolution regarding another meeting, while Pillow moved that the convention reassemble at Nashville on the first Monday of the fourth month after congressional adjournment. Gordon explained that the resolutions committee chose Marietta because of its convenience, and Vice President McDonald added that the change should not be construed as dissatisfaction with Nashville. A discussion of location followed, with Nashville's hospitality and Marietta's convenience the main issues. Well pleased with his reception in Nashville, Tucker indicated his willingness to go anywhere. Although someone had said Jackson's bones would turn in his grave if the convention met in Nashville, Tucker believed that Jackson would want to rise from his grave to assist the delegates, for he had always asked only for what was right and submitted to nothing that was wrong. After much discussion, the delegates voted to accept Pillow's amendment, with a change of time. Erwin then moved to strike out "four" and substitute "six," and the resolution passed unanimously. It stated that the convention would reassemble at Nashville on the sixth Monday after congressional adjournment.

Chairman Gordon reported the address with several amendments, and moved that the convention adopt it. When McRae of Mississippi proposed additional modifications, Gordon and Walter Colquitt of Georgia spoke against them. Gordon contended that the phraseology of the address was not too strong, that the speech was the work of a representative committee, and that he opposed any further attempt to modify or soften it. Colquitt's defense of the address was the "most exciting" and the "most violent" delivered during the convention. He rose, jumped from his pew into the broad aisle, shook his head violently, stamped the floor "as if he wanted to go through," sank down almost to the floor, darted forward, and poured "forth a torrent of words . . . now tragic, and now highly humorous." Kate Conynham described the speech: "It was in oratory what a medley would be in a song! It was wild, fierce, terrible, dreadful, mad—yet most wonderful to listen to. It was eloquence tied to the back of a wild horse, Mazeppa-like!"[30]

At the calmer afternoon session, J. S. Hunter of Alabama defended those who opposed the address. He did not approve the Compromise in every detail, but he preferred it to disunion. John Winston, however, protested that Hunter's views were not representative of the state and declared that he valued the Union for the rights it secured him, but a Union that failed to protect those rights was not worth preserving. Burwell Boykin, another Alabamian, rebuked the spirit of discord and urged the delegates to be temperate, firm, and conciliatory, reminding them that union of all slaveholding states was paramount.

Pickens replied to Hunter in a stirring and eloquent attempt to dispel the idea that dissolution was the object of the convention. But the people of fifteen southern states were looking to the assemblage to protect their rights. If all acted together the Union must remain intact; a middle or halfway course might produce disunion. Pickens' speech "surpassed anything in the way of forensic eloquence," that Kate Conynham had ever imagined, and Secretary Cooper reported that his "fiery look and impressive utterance" filled with sarcasm and figures of speech "fairly riddled" his opponent. Others found Pickens' two speeches "among the most powerful and effective" delivered.[31]

Hammond felt differently about his colleague's orations. In spite of the admiration of the "mob" at Nashville, "They were however *stuff* and sickened the delegation save DuBose." Moreover, Hammond was disgusted because the South Carolina delegation had agreed from the beginning to remain quiet, giving the lead to others, and thus dissipate the prejudice against "South Carolina dictation." He confided to his diary that Pickens and Rhett sought visibility by speaking and being active, while he, Cheves, Barnwell, and most of the delegation favored the stated course.

Gholson next supported the conservatives who wished to amend the address. Although he supported every effort "under heaven" to save the Union, he could never agree to a subjugation of the South. Clay's Compromise needed amendments, but the original measures might serve as a basis for a settlement and guarantee the safety of the South. He concluded by asking whether the members would be willing to dissolve the Union in case the Compromise were passed. Newton, the other Virginia Whig delegate, answered in a very partisan speech, stating that five out of six proposals of the Compromise favored the North, party ties were broken, and the leaders must now seek guidance from the people.[32]

Tucker delivered the "most characteristic and racy speech" on the last day. "A brilliant and powerful performance, rich, copious and keen, with a lightning-like sarcasm," the oration was a plea for southern harmony. Tucker contended the "North would not dare to prosecute war" if some of the southern states seceded, because the North needed southern cotton. Moreover, "the united voice of all the civilized world would command the peace," as the southern states were the only cotton-growing country and slave labor was necessary to produce it. All Europe, especially England, would oppose a northern war on the southern states. Tucker pictured the "magnificent future" of a Southern Confederacy. The Union could still be preserved but not through "cheating compromises"; the South had done with them. A Union of "the Giant and the Dwarf," a partnership in which the Giant got all the profits and "the other nothing but dry blows," would not do. Delay only meant further degradation to the South. Cooper found Tucker's speech "original and indiscriminately savage"; another observer said the Virginian "seemed to be armed with a short dagger, with which he hit right and left without respect to person." Kate Conynham described Tucker's speech as "exceedingly bitter and out of temper. It was the only one that was recriminating against the North; for the spirit of forbearance in this direction has peculiarly marked the body." In the spirit and manner of his half-brother, John Randolph, Tucker "let out his bitterness and was sometimes forgetful that ladies were present."[33]

That afternoon Sharkey supported the proposed amendments before the convention. Although he recommended the resolutions, he planned to vote against the address, as it would divide the South. The Compromise bill was indeed a grievance, but taking offense before Congress had acted was premature. Congress did have the power to admit California, even though the address denied it. Moreover, if the evil were in Congress, the convention could not stop it. "The convention sat for a higher purpose," Sharkey contended, "to do that which could not be done by ordinary legislation."

Hammond replied, in words later described as "unpremeditated." He "demolished" Sharkey, expressing astonishment that an able jurist would find it unconstitutional to investigate a measure before Congress. Measures should be discussed as well as principles, and the delegates were the leaders designed "to point the way." The South "had nothing to do but to march forward in one unbroken column to equality in the Union, or independence out of it." Cooper described Hammond's reply as "cool, clear, and weighty . . . the most finished speech" at the convention, deriving power from the force of its logic and exposing the opposition's weakness.[34]

The address, with Pillow's amendment, received the

unanimous approval of the states. James Abercrombie of Alabama, however, asked for a roll call of individual delegates, whereupon Gholson of Virginia, Forman of Florida, Hunter, Byrd, Judge, Murphy, Abercrombie, and Nicholas Davis of Alabama, and Sharkey—all Whigs—voted against adoption. Byrd explained that his constituents had virtually approved the Compromise. Upon the solicitation of friends, Sharkey withdrew his negative vote, but he refused to change it to the affirmative. Gordon again requested consideration of the other resolutions reported by the committee, and the convention accepted them without further discussion. Dawson of Georgia offered resolutions for the establishment of a southern party and for patronage of the *Southern Press* at Washington, but the convention tabled them. After passing resolutions of thanks to various groups and hearing brief valedictories from the president and vice president, the convention adjourned.[35]

Once their labors at Nashville ended, many of the participants made known their opinions of the convention. As one might expect, the South Carolina representatives were particularly outspoken. Before returning home, Hammond wrote to Simms that the results "do not amount to much." Nevertheless, he was optimistic. The South had met, had acted with harmony throughout the nine-day convention, and, most important, had agreed to meet again. Although he hoped the gathering would strengthen the friends of the South in Congress and "kill" some of the traitors, he knew that a great "submission party" was forming. Through his committee work, Hammond had tried to lay the foundation for a future meeting, as well as "save the credit" of this one. He commented on the individual states: his own "succeeded perfectly" in its policy "to show that we were reasonable and ready to go as far back to unite with any party as honor and safety would permit," and he believed South Carolina had established its credibility among the other southern states. Georgia followed close behind South Carolina and Virginia in knowledge and resolution. Florida was "pretty true," but Alabama appeared to be "in a very rotten condition"; even Tennessee outshone Alabama. He made no comment on Mississippi.[36]

R. F. W. Allston, also from the Palmetto state, expressed disappointment that Congress seemed unaffected by "the reasonable suggestions and firm conclusions" of the convention. Pickens hastened to correct public misconceptions about the powers of the convention; he explained that it was a mere consultative body that had no binding powers on the states represented. Since the states had given their delegates no authority to make enactments, the convention had existed purely to suggest measures that would produce harmony. "The Nashville Convention is the first step towards the development of that state power which will give us equality and independence. . . . We cannot—we dare not—submit finally." South Carolina asked no favors and made no threats; she was content to follow the leadership of others.[37]

In an address to the citizens of Spartanburg District, Dr. Samuel Otterson gave cordial approval to all of the convention's actions. The delegates were united in their purpose—to arrest the course of grievances and to save the Constitution and the Union if possible. For the sake of unanimity at home, the delegates thought it was best to go only as far as many southerners were inclined. Although the address and resolutions were important, their content mattered much less than the fact that the meeting had occurred. The South had convened to seek redress, showing that it could and would act. Otterson boldly challenged his constituents, "Are you ready with me, to hurl back defiance to such presumption and injustice? Bid them restore our equality in the Union or we will leave their association, and wrest from them our constitutional rights of equality in the territories purchased by the common blood and common treasure of the country."[38]

On 22 June a Charleston audience listened to two contrasting interpretations of the convention. Trenholm lauded the convention, saying that great things had been achieved in bringing the South together in common counsel and adopting the Missouri Compromise line. Rhett, however, foretold "the beginning of a Revolution," the "grand Drama of the dissolution of the Union." Congress would reject the demand of the Nashville Convention, and the North would continue its agitation. The South, therefore, faced either submission or disunion. In spite of an increased southern desire for equality in the Union or independence out of it, the Nashville Convention offered little hope of unanimity on "ulterior measures." Discarding whatever restraint had bound him at Nashville, Rhett now openly and without reservation declared himself a disunionist. A few days later, Hammond expressed the fear that Rhett's speech would destroy the good effect of South Carolina's policy at Nashville.[39]

Two Virginia delegates echoed Rhett. Gordon wrote Senator R. M. T. Hunter that whenever Congress rejected the convention's recommendation of 36°30′, which would fill the South's "cup of humiliation to the brim," he was ready for resistance. Approximately a month after the convention, Tucker wrote to Hammond, "We said at Nashville 36°30′ and I hope the South will say so to the end. For God's sake make South Carolina plant her foot there and *secede* if it is denied her. Secession must begin somewhere, or absolute subjugation must ensue." Colquitt had told Tucker that Georgia was "much divided, perhaps equally," but opinion was veering toward disunion; she would take no part against a seceding state.[40]

Returning home to Texas on the steamboat "Cincinnatus," Henderson expressed his opinions in a letter to Senator Thomas J. Rusk. He hoped the crisis would be settled on the basis laid down by the convention, as 36°30′ was the only thing that could possibly satisfy the South or save the Union, and even that was questionable. Personally, he had little faith in legislative compromises, because he feared they would not fully arrest abolitionist aggresssions. Henderson expressed general satisfaction with the convention and cited its "salutary effect" on the citizens of Nashville and all those present. The Whigs were "disappointed sadly" and generally confused, but the results satisfied many of them.[41]

Meanwhile, at a great union festival in Jackson, Mississippi, Boyd, a discontented Whig, insisted the public should judge the convention by the resolutions alone, and not by the address. Sharkey agreed with Boyd that many people had misunderstood the convention, representing it as a disunion assembly. The meeting was a conservative body, and no movement toward resistance could be justified on the convention's authority.[42]

Shortly after the convention adjourned, both Brown and Nicholson of Tennessee wrote letters to the Nashville *Union* editor. Like Boyd, Brown considered the resolutions "the real text—authoritative and binding"; the address was a superficial commentary. Defending the assemblage, he stated that "*the very worst*" the convention had done was to support the Missouri Compromise. As a minority, all the Tennessee delegation could then accomplish was to urge the delegates to declare that they would acquiesce in any other equally favorable adjustment. This was achieved, since the Missouri Compromise was not set forth as an ultimatum; nor did the convention necessarily condemn the work of the Committee of Thirteen. The Tennesseans could, therefore, withdraw from the contest over the address and accept it with a declaration that a portion of it did not satisfy them.

Nicholson presented "a keen and discriminating criticism" of the address, making additional remarks on the meeting itself. He regarded the convention as a preliminary or pioneer movement for the preservation of southern rights and the perpetuation of the Union and believed it had dispelled the charges of disunion. Nicholson thought discussion of the Compromise plan was bad policy, as deliberations should have been confined to topics where harmony was possible. He outlined in careful detail his opposition to the attack on the Compromise in the address. The resolutions proposing the Missouri Line explicitly asserted the doctrine of congressional nonintervention that underlay the Compromise itself and should not be construed as an ultimatum. Nicholson, however, yielded reluctantly to the 36°30′ decision, which he believed involved intervention on one side of the line and not on the other.[43]

Since William F. Cooper was secretary of the convention rather than a voting delegate, his remarks bear special significance. He believed most of the Tennessee delegates favored the Compromise; he certainly approved of it himself and thought the South should unite on Clay's proposals. Had he been a delegate, he would have voted against the address, even with the inserted clause. Nevertheless, he considered the action of the convention "satisfactory and as nearly unanimous as could be expected in so large a body." But Cooper believed that the idea of disunion was more prevalent among southern leaders than was generally supposed. Unless the slavery controversy was speedily settled, the subject of peaceable secession could become a public question in the southern states. The convention had convinced him that South Carolina and Georgia were "already decidedly and almost unanimously in favor of a dissolution of the Union and the formation of a Southern Confederacy," and Alabama, Mississippi, and Florida were rapidly moving that way. So far Tennessee, Louisiana, Arkansas, and Texas were "almost to a man in favor of the Union," but these states might also be infected if the agitation continued. Cooper's prophecy was probably correct. Although the convention accomplished little politically, the gathering did no doubt convince northerners, as well as Cooper, that the South was no longer bluffing. Moderate as it was, the Nashville Convention served as a warning to the North.[44]

But the true impact of the meeting comes, not from the opinions of those attending, but from the impressions of the public and the press. Reactions in the lower South are especially important. There, many states held public meetings, where delegates reported upon the convention and exhorted the people to support southern rights. These gatherings nearly always approved the results of the convention.[45]

In Charleston, the editor of the *Mercury* stated that the people were convinced that the conference would have great consequences: "The convention triumphantly accomplished the purpose for which it was realized. It melted down and dissipated the differences among Southern men, and united them on a platform on which the South can rally." The *Mercury's* special correspondent also praised the "deliberation, coolness, and courage" of the proceedings. But he contended that the compromise report did not have a friend at the convention; some tolerated it purely as a basis of settlement and only a few would have regretted a direct attack on it. At times some

Whig delegates had found it difficult to put principle over party; the Alabama group especially suspected every movement as a Democratic plot. Whig delegates from other states, however, were generally firm, and some from Georgia were "noble fellows." In Columbia, the *Telegraph* commended the delegates' unanimous resolution to reassemble, and many newspapers throughout the state announced, as did Senator Andrew P. Butler, that 36°30′ was the southern ultimatum. Simms also referred to the Missouri Line as the convention ultimatum and called the address, as well as the resolutions, "temperate." Although South Carolina would go further if necessary, she would adhere strictly to her guarantees so long as common action through the convention was productive. Simms had no hope, however, for moderation from the North. The old Unionist, Benjamin F. Perry, described the proceedings as "moderate," but lamented the "spirit of disunion" in his own state.[46]

The editor of the *Federal Union* (Democrat) at the Georgia capital had held little hope for benificent results from the convention, but he now stated that the convention had dissipated all apprehensions that it was designed for disunion. He advocated a united acceptance of the recommendations and claimed that not a "press" in the state opposed an adjustment based on the Missouri Compromise. The Augusta *Chronicle,* an outstanding Whig paper, was still critical, commenting that though some delegates had repudiated disunion, others had "illy concealed their feeling to light the flame of civil discord"; the latter were perspicacious enough to realize that the people would promptly denounce any such action.[47] A Whig paper at Athens, however, declared that 36°30′ was the only platform on which the South could stand "without a sacrifice of her honor, her independence, and her interests." The Macon *Telegraph* (Democrat) thought the address "particularly strong and good." In every way the convention had fulfilled "the hopes and expectations of friends of the South, and brought disappointment to its opponents," exclaimed the Columbus *Times* (Democrat).[48]

John H. Lumpkin, a prominent Georgia Union Democrat

who disapproved of the convention, believed the delegates had proposed the Missouri Line because they knew it was impractical and was the best plan to gain southern support in opposition to the Compromise. Division among the Democrats would give the ultras too much power. They would insist on the Nashville Platform—which was doomed to failure—as a ploy. Congress would pass the Compromise, which could then possibly drive the moderates to join the group contemplating resistance and disunion. But Lumpkin believed the Whigs suffered no such disunity.[49]

Highly satisfied with the results, the editor of the *Mississippi Free Trader* (Democrat) considered the convention one of the "great events" of the period. It had vindicated the South without endangering the Union, dealt honestly with the sectional crisis, and proposed a solution that was both moderate and effectual. "The settlement proposed, and the unanimity which prevailed is evidence that the convention was moved by no desire to aggravate the controversy," commented the Vicksburg *Sentinel* (Democrat). If southerners of all parties would unite in approving its action, the great object of the meeting—the preservation of a Union of equality—would be achieved. Like several southern Whig papers, the *Southron* at Jackson criticized the recommendations. In the same accusing tone that had prevailed before the meeting, the editor concluded that the chief element in the Nashville Platform tended directly to the formation of a Southern Confederacy, and therefore to a dissolution of the Union. Some Whig papers contended that the Missouri Line would have the effect of making two free states out of California instead of one, as southerners would not emigrate.[50]

Public opinion in Alabama was divided several ways: some persons withheld their approval because the South disagreed on the address; others had hopes for the Compromise measures; while a few who favored 36°30′ objected to its being made an ultimatum. Predictably, William L. Yancey preferred the address to the resolutions.[51] The junior editor of the Huntsville *Democrat* had reported from Nashville that "quiet, peaceable, dignified action," had won admiration from the convention's most outspoken enemies and silenced the charges of treason and disunion. This north Alabama paper gave bold editorial approval to the recommendations. "Devoted to the Union, more devoted to the South . . . we plant ourselves, this day upon the platform of Southern rights, erected by the Southern Convention, and throw our banner to the breeze, with the inscription: 'Equality in the Union or independence out of it'." The *Alabama Journal* (Whig) at the capital described the general tone of both the address and the resolutions as "excellent and commendable" in most respects. Had there been a full representation, the convention might have settled the whole crisis. Under the title "36°30′ through to the Pacific" in large conspicuous letters, the Eufaula *Democrat* declared, "Let this be the ultimatum of the South. Here, all together let us stand—here too, if need be, all together, let us fall." Yet the Florence *Gazette*, the most independent and outspoken Democratic paper in the state, treated the convention with sovereign contempt. Since its readers cared so little about the actions of that "conclave of grave and reverend seignors," the editor remarked that he would not fill his columns with an extended account of the "sound and fury of some of its tremendous orators." He admitted, however, that the proceedings were milder and more conciliatory than he had supposed possible.[52]

The Tallahassee *Floridian and Journal* (Democrat) commended both resolutions and address. By its moderation, unanimity, and firmness, the assemblage had gratified its friends and "scattered to the wind" the abuse of its enemies. The *Florida Sentinel*, the state's most influential Whig organ, believed the meeting had done nothing to solve—and perhaps something to complicate—sectional differences. Comparing the gathering at Nashville to the Hartford Convention, the editor of the Pensacola *Gazette* (Whig) feared other meetings of a similar nature might endanger the Union. One of Florida's most outstanding citizens, Senator David Yulee, receding from his original uncompromising position, accepted the platform of the Nashville Convention as indicative of the wishes of the southern states.[53]

In Tennessee, the most outspoken approval of the convention came from the *Union* editor, who thought only one object had inspired all the delegates—a desire to unite the entire South upon a common constitutional platform. Because of the salutary effect on the opponents, no furious denunciation was now heard; the convention had "removed all difficulties from the path of the true friends of the South." Although the Whig papers in Nashville praised the dignity and moderation of the gathering, they denounced the doctrines set forth in the address and especially criticized the course of the Tennessee delegation. In an editorial entitled "South Carolina, the Mouthpiece of Tennessee democracy," the editor of the *Republican Banner* exclaimed, "South Carolina has triumphed in the Nashville Convention. . . . The South Carolina set led the rest wherever they chose and this ill-digested address, this bundle of inconsistencies, ultra and untenable is the fruit of their doings." On the other hand, the Memphis *Enquirer* (Whig) declared, "We discover no disunion in their proceedings"; the sentiment to maintain southern rights and the Constitution as the only means of preserving the Union had prevailed.[54]

The resolutions and address received slight attention in Virginia. While the Ritchie Democrats accepted the resolutions, they ignored the part that spoke of disunion and favored the Compromise; in so doing they undoubtedly spoke for a majority in Virginia. The Richmond *Enquirer* (Democrat) believed that true southern unity at Nashville would have aroused the people to a firm stand, but the South remained divided. Not until the Compromise was defeated or the North broke the compact would the whole South be incited to determined action. The editor of the Lynchburg *Virginian* (Whig) commented, "The resolutions contain vague, metaphysical positions," although the South had advanced the theory of nonintervention, "the assumed guardian of Southern rights" had proposed a legislative act in the extension of the Missouri Compromise line.[55]

Judging from "present appearances," the editor of the *Arkansas State Gazette and Democrat* did not believe a second meeting would be necessary. Nor did he think that the South would sustain the position of 36°30′, as the people believed a satisfactory adjustment could be readily achieved on the basis of the Compromise plan.[56]

In North Carolina, the editor of the Raleigh *Register* (Whig) rejoiced that his state had sent no delegates. Time had proven Governor Manly's wisdom in abstaining from any connection with the Nashville Convention. "The scheme is dead, and buried, too, without even the formal honors of a respectable ritual," declared the editor. Since the delegates were empowered to speak for a very small minority of people, the South was in no way committed by their actions, and the people would exercise their own judgment on the merits of the Compromise as independently as if the convention had never assembled.[57]

In contrast to this negativism and its own earlier disapproval, *DeBow's Review* in New Orleans had only complimentary remarks for the personnel and action of the convention. The New Orleans *Bee* (Whig), calling the resolutions the work of "agitators and mischief-mongers," regarded them not as "violent," "only impossible" and predicted that neither the North nor the South would sanction the extension of the Missouri Line. Although the convention resolutions were more moderate than many had expected, the New Orleans *Courier* (Democrat) thought 36°30′ endangered the South more than any plan of adjustment, as it would actually add to the number of free states and its constitutionality remained questionable. But the *Courier* said that all New Orleans papers favored the Compromise plan, and Senator Solomon Downs had recently stated that he did not know of a paper or individual in Louisiana who was not in favor of the Compromise. With incisive cynicism, the Baton Rouge *Gazette* declared that, after all, the recommendation of the convention would have little or no influence on the southern public.[58]

The newly established *Southern Press* at Washington commended the proceedings and spirit prevailing at Nashville. The editor believed that at least three-fourths of the South would support the "able, clear, calm, and firm" address which presented the only ground on which the South could be unified. Moreover, he thought that three-fourths of the northern voters would acquiesce in the adoption of the Missouri Line.

Proceedings of the convention had been telegraphed all over the nation, and the reaction in the border states and the North varied. The Baltimore *Patriot* described the effect of the meeting as "just nothing": the delegates appeared doubtful about their course of action; the public read accounts of the proceedings out of idle curiosity, not because of their importance; the convention should simply be forgotten.[59] A paper at Dayton, Ohio, published Benning's resolutions as evidence of the disunionism in the South, but a Pottsville, Pennsylvania, editor saw the proceedings as characterized throughout "by moderation, good feeling, and a spirit of patriotism."[60] The New York *Commercial Advertiser* scoffed, "The long agony is over; the Nashville Convention has met, talked, voted, adjourned, and the *Union* is not dissolved." Actually, the assembly was a "god send to the cause of peace and Union"; it should teach a lesson. In contrast, the New York *Herald* declared that the proceedings had disappointed the northern politicians, because the delegates acted like "rational, decent, honorable men." The resolutions were quite sensible and the address an "admirable document." The report of a Nashville correspondent for the *Herald* remarked on the "lofty patriotism, glorious devotion to the Constitution, and manly firmness" of the meeting.[61]

At the nation's capital, the *National Intelligencer* reported that the convention had not harmed the country, chiefly because of its impotency. Attempting to promote the Compromise plan, "Father" Ritchie of the Washington *Union* heartily agreed with the principles of the convention, but he could not accept its remedies. He thought it was unfortunate that the convention presented any ultimatum or resolutions and attacked the address for misrepresenting the Compromise. But ignoring its action was impossible, as several distinguished men had attended.[62]

What effect the convention would have on congressional legislation remained to be seen. Approximately a month after the convention adjourned, Webster remarked, "Far be it from me to impute to the South generally the sentiments of the Nashville Convention. The Nashville Address is a studied disunion argument. It goes upon the ground that there must be a separation of the Southern states." Senator William R. King of Alabama disagreed with Webster, believing the southern delegation in Congress would unite in support of the convention's recommendation. Nevertheless, he still thought 36°30′ would fail.[63]

It is ironic that the Nashville Convention proposed the extension of 36°30′, which involved congressional interference north of the line and was absolutely antithetical to Calhoun's platform of noninterference. Surely the results would have disappointed Calhoun: the South remained divided, and the convention had accomplished little. But the results would probably have been the same had Calhoun lived two more months. The oratory may have been more impassioned, the emotions higher, but the basic temperaments and the final action would no doubt have changed little.

Although somewhat ineffectual, the convention was by no means insignificant; it did, however, fail in its most important purpose—to unite the South. Why? Since the Nashville Convention was a movement of the politicians, rather than the people, a major reason for its failure to unite the South was partisan politics—Whigs versus Democrats and Democratic factionalism. Most Whigs and many Democrats distrusted Calhoun and regarded him as a disunionist. The majority of the southern people were never as disturbed as some politicians; only for a very short time were the people aroused to the degree that unification seemed a possibility. Convention proponents were not in total agreement on the purpose of the meeting. Although a majority of them did not propose to use the convention for disunion, the minority who did caused many people to regard the convention as a step toward secession and even war. This misunderstanding of motives was very significant. Southerners tended to have faith in the Union as long as no objectionable legislation had actually been passed. Moreover, most southerners were reluctant to support a sectional meeting once they perceived that the danger to the South might be averted. The belief that a satisfactory adjustment could be achieved in Congress was, therefore, an obstruction for unity through the convention method. The Nashville Platform of 36°30′ itself had several disadvantages, many of which some Democrats even noted. It came too late to serve as a unifying factor; it was impractical and its constitutionality was questionable. But most important the Missouri Compromise line contravened Calhoun's doctrine of congressional noninterference.

Yet in the summer of 1850 the future action of the South remained a moot question. Would the people choose to stand on the platform of the Nashville Convention as an "ultimatum," or would they accept the Compromise measures if they became law? Suppose Congress passed neither the convention recommendation nor the Compromise measure. What then? These vital questions faced the nation as the convention passed into history and the debates on the Senate committee report continued. As summer progressed, Washington felt the heat in more ways than one.

# 8

# *Adjustment and Reaction*

"'The fate of our compromise is uncertain. I think it will pass the Senate," Henry Clay wrote his son Thomas on the last day of May. "The Administration, the abolitionists, the ultra Southern men and the timid Whigs of the North are all combined against it. Against such a combination it will be wonderful if it should succeed." Ten days before, as Taylor showed no intention of yielding, Clay had openly declared war on the Administration. Soon after the Senate debates on the committee's report had begun on 13 May the editor of the administration paper (the *Republic)* who had appeared friendly to the Compromise, had been replaced. The strong opposition of the new editor convinced Clay that Taylor intended to obstruct his plan, and he began a vigorous attack on the President's program. Five bleeding wounds, he said, threatened the nation; the Compromise measures could heal all of them, while Taylor's plan would heal only one. While the southern delegates were traveling and deliberating in Nashville, Clay's opponents in Congress were speaking, amending, obstructing, and maneuvering in every conceivable way to defeat the Committee's plan. Yet Clay had reason to be hopeful; the sentiment of the country was for compromise, and even more important, many Democratic leaders were now giving support.[1]

During June the South's cause appeared to advance somewhat in the Senate. Three of the six successful amendments to the omnibus bill were the work of southerners—John Berrien, David Yulee, and Pierre Soulé. The most important was Berrien's, which changed the clause prohibiting territorial legislatures from acting on the subject of slavery. A bare majority of the Committee of Thirteen had added this legislative restriction to the omnibus bill over Clay's objection. Berrien's amendment substituted the phrase "establishing or prohibiting African slavery," for "in respect to African slavery," thereby empowering territorial legislatures to protect slave property in case a judicial decision should prove favorable to the institution.[2]

In the House, the group led by Toombs and Stephens of Georgia successfully blocked efforts to carry Taylor's separate California bill to a vote before the Senate could act on the Committee's report. Three days after the convention adjourned, Toombs delivered his famous "Hamilcar speech" and produced the greatest sensation in the House that Stephens had ever witnessed. Similar to those given in Nashville, the speech was an able polemic for the South's right to an equal share in the territories. "I claim the right for her to enter them all with her property and security to enjoy it." Toombs declared, "She will divide with you if you wish it, but the right to enter all or divide I shall never surrender." Should Congress deprive the South of this right, he was ready to "strike for independence."[3]

Although the Nashville Convention address had virtually condemned the Compromise and the delegates had recommended 36°30′ instead, the Tennessee proceedings strengthened the moderates who were working for the Compromise. For the time being at least, the ultras had been restrained; the delegates had indicated a willingness to "wait and see" what Congress did. Yet the important fact was that southerners had conferred with one another and had laid plans to meet again after congressional adjournment. Without adopting any "mode of resistance," the convention itself served as a warning. Enough had been said and done at Nashville to indicate what might happen next time, if Congress did not relieve the situation in a manner acceptable to the South.

To complicate matters further for Taylor, things were happening in the Southwest that threatened a military collision between Texas and the Federal government, weakened the President's position, and created a whole new state of affairs in Washington that further entangled the Texas question with the Compromise issue. In keeping with Taylor's plan for the people of New Mexico to frame a constitution and seek admission to the Union, Colonel John Munroe, commander of the national forces in the area, called a convention that sat from 15 to 25 May and within a month the people had approved a constitution that excluded slavery. The act precipitated a crisis in Texas, which regarded the New Mexico boundaries as a gross infringement on its own domain. Governor Peter H. Bell of Texas immediately sent two letters to Washington: to Texas congressmen who were informed of the crisis he vowed to use force to uphold Texas claims; from the President he demanded an explanation and disavowal of Munroe's action. The governor also called a special session of the Texas legislature for 12 August.

Taylor meanwhile, aware of the climate that the Nashville Convention (which had adjourned five days before) had created, sent Congress a special message on New Mexican affairs, in which he denied that he had ordered forcible resistance and declared that the Federal government should maintain possession until the boundary quarrel was settled. When Congress received news of the New Mexico constitution on 25 June southern members began at once to hold caucuses; southern radicals considered the President's proposals an outrage upon Texas, while southern moderates opposed them as a way of blocking the omnibus bill. North Carolina Congressman David Outlaw declared, "If the Administration persists in their present course, they will be left without a corporal's guard in the Southern states."[4] Southern Whig congressmen, at a secret meeting on 1 July, appointed Toombs, Humphrey Marshall, and C. M. Conrad to call upon the President and warn him that persistence in this policy would cause his southern friends to join the opposition. Each apparently called separately, but all three concluded that there was "no longer any hope."[5] When Secretary of War George W. Crawford of Georgia indicated that he could not sign a contemplated order to Colonel Munroe to resist any Texas attempt to exercise jurisdiction in New Mexico, Taylor replied that he would sign it himself. On Independence Day the *National Intelligencer* published a letter from Stephens in which he declared that the first Federal gun that fired against Texans, without the authority of law, would be "the signal for the freemen from the Delaware to the Rio Grande to rally to the rescue. . . . The cause of Texas, in such a conflict, will be the cause of the entire South." An unfinished message lay on the President's desk urging Congress to admit both California and New Mexico, and asserting that he would never permit Texas to seize any part of New Mexico's rightful area. Civil war was doubtless a possibility, but the President never finished his message. He died five days later.[6]

Millard Fillmore of New York now became the chief executive. He had earlier caused southerners to be suspicious of his attitude toward slavery and related topics. Although he had maintained a cautious public silence on the Compromise, he had privately confided in April that he supported Taylor in the sectional battle. Early in July, however, he had called at the White House and informed the President that if the vote on the Compromise bill tied in the Senate and he felt obliged to vote for it, as he might, he would do so to promote the best interests of the country, not out of hostility to the Administration. Two days after Fillmore's inauguration, Webster reported that the new President favored the Compromise, and undoubtedly recent events had increased the probability of its passage. As Secretary of State, Webster became the dominating spirit of the Administration. Before assuming his new duties he made a final appeal on 17 July for the omnibus bill, or at least for separate passage of the various measures. Passage of the bill would benefit the South in several ways: abandonment of the Proviso would appease her "wounded pride" and the bill would provide "an acceptable and satisfactory mode for the reclamation of fugitive slaves" and achieve "the general restoration of peace and harmony."[7]

Texans also anxiously awaited the new President's policy regarding the Texas-New Mexico dispute. J. Pinckney Henderson wrote to Governor Quitman of Mississippi that he hoped that Taylor's successor would be "more cautious," but he desired to know how far Mississippi was prepared to redeem her delegates' Nashville Convention pledge, should Fillmore order United States troops to resist Texas. Henderson presumed the Texas legislature would appeal to the southern states. The Texas-New Mexico dispute and the promise of southern support for Texas from the convention delegates precipitated southern rights meetings endorsing the Nashville Convention in Harrison, Upshur, Panola, Shelby, and San Augustine counties in Texas.[8]

The day after Webster's final oration, Senator Henry Foote gave strong approval to the resolutions adopted at the Nashville Convention and said he thought the address was probably less objectionable than he had heard. Although he believed disunionists were present at Nashville, especially from South Carolina, they were a small minority, and not a single Mississippi delegate could be charged with having disunion sentiments. Foote believed that the convention proceedings deserved great respect, but he wondered why the delegates adopted 36°30′ when better terms could be obtained. He was glad that the delegates did not make the Missouri line an ultimatum.

On 22 July Clay spoke for three or four hours "with a power and animation and eloquence worthy of his palmiest days" in his final plea for the omnibus bill. Patriotism was the dominant note. The majority of the people, said Clay, desired the passage of the Compromise. He showed the South what it had gained and asked the North what it had lost; he stormed at both the southern disunionists and the abolitionists.[9] Maneuvering and countermaneuvering filled the last days of the month. A series of amendments centering mainly about the Texas-New Mexico boundary was suggested in order to gain three or four vital southern votes, and Clay left the Senate on 30 July in a triumphant mood.

The next day, however, brought the wreck of the omnibus. On a 33-32 vote, the Senate eliminated the New Mexico territorial part of the omnibus in its entirety—a move that doomed the plan of the Committee of Thirteen. Following this significant decision, a 29-28 vote struck from the bill everything related to Texas and a 34-25 vote removed California statehood. Only the Utah territorial bill remained; it passed without a roll call on the following day. In his excellent analysis of the 31 July reckoning, Holman Hamilton concludes that "neither sectionalism alone nor partisanship alone can account" for the results. The compromisers' basic error, however, was the attempt of Clay and the Committee of Thirteen to unite the various measures in one bill.[10]

Shortly thereafter Clay left Washington for a rest at the New England shore, and Stephen A. Douglas, chairman of the committee on territories, then assumed leadership of the Compromise forces. Although Douglas regretted very much the failure of the Committee's report, his hopes for its passage had never been high. "By combining the measures into one Bill the Committee united the opponents of each measure instead of securing the friends of each," he wrote on 3 August. Earlier Douglas had in essence written and reported the several bills combined in the omnibus; he now made plans for separate measures. Tennessee Congressman Andrew Ewing agreed with Douglas that separate action on each proposition would be the only hope.[11] California statehood was dearest to Douglas' heart, but the seriousness of the Texas situation and the Administration's influence gave the Texas matter priority. The new Texas boundary bill passed the Senate first on 9 August. According to Douglas, he and James A. Pearce of Maryland prepared this bill, giving Texas $10,000,000 and 33,333 square miles more than the omnibus bill had originally proposed. Under considerable pressure, the Texas senators agreed to support the measure.[12]

Although the boundary bill had been passed in relative concord, the next two weeks saw much impassioned speaking, primarily centering around California statehood. Southern voices rose in protest on the Senate floor. "Now," declared Jefferson Davis, "we are about permanently to destroy the balance of power between the two sections." Jeremiah Clemens of Alabama boldly asserted that if his state resisted the California law by secession or by any means, he was at her side. "If this be treason, I am a traitor—a traitor who glories in the name," he declared.[13] Nine southern Democratic senators and one southern Whig had signed an agreement that they would use any means that a majority of them might determine to prevent the admission of California, unless the southern boundary was reduced to 36°30′.[14] On the other hand, Sam Houston, who favored the Compromise, contended that unless some positive action in derogation of constitutional rights occurred, the South would neither secede nor nullify and asserted that the Nashville Convention was a "surreptitious meeting," whose action was "a piece of flagrant arrogance." How could the South now take a position on 36°30′, which it had formerly repudiated? Robert Barnwell of South Carolina replied that the convention was not a "surreptitious" assemblage but a group "summoned together under very high auspices"; the South's reception of its proceedings represented a "burst of approbation." Convention delegates had never tried to intermeddle or intrude their counsels on any deliberative body. "They claim no authority here; they utter no voice of counsel, much less of threat to this body."[15]

California statehood passed by a majority of sixteen on 13 August; of the southern senators only Houston and John Bell of Tennessee voted for the bill.[16] R. M. T. Hunter of Virginia then introduced a protest, with the request that it be entered on the Senate journal, representing ten southern senators and giving reasons for their dissent. With this protest the struggle of the southern extremists against passage of the Compromise bills in the Senate ended for all practical purposes.[17]

Only two days later the New Mexico bill passed, and the Senate approved the fugitive slave bill on 26 August. Thirteen senators from the slaveholding states did not vote on the New Mexico bill, but no southern senator voted against it. With the virtual end of the Senate struggle, William Alexander Graham, Fillmore's newly appointed Secretary of the Navy, wrote his brother in North Carolina that in ten days tranquility would prevail everywhere except among abolitionists and disunionists.[18] The battle for the Compromise now shifted to the House, but the Senate did approve, on 16 September, the bill restricting slave trade in the District of Columbia. From the slaveholding states only Houston, Benton of Missouri, and the Kentucky and Delaware senators voted in the affirmative; six southern senators did not vote. Houston was the only southern senator who voted for all six bills.

The most significant development in the House began on 28 August, when Linn Boyd of Kentucky offered an amendment combining the Texas boundary and debt bill with the one for New Mexico territory. Again the northern and southern extremists were in coalition, as they had been so often in the Senate. On 5 September Representative Outlaw reported that "things look more gloomy than at any time since Congress assembled. Faction rules the hour, passion has taken the place of reason."[19] The next day, however, the bill passed in a victory for the moderates; more than two-thirds of the southern members voted for it. The House approved California statehood and the Utah bill on 7 September, while the fugitive slave bill received a good majority five days later and the District bill passed on the 17th. President Fillmore, who a few days before had referred to the passage of the Compromise as the "height of my ambition," now signed these five bills—the Compromise of 1850—with the hope that harmony might be restored to the nation.[20]

Washington was jubilant; moderation had prevailed, and the Union was saved. The Nashville Convention had not united southern congressmen in support of 36°30′ as Senator King had predicted. Why not? The extension of the Missouri line violated Calhoun's doctrine of nonintervention and was, he believed, even unconstitutional. Many southern congressmen realized that 36°30′ would not help the South. California was destined to be free soil; extend the line and the nation would have two free states instead of one.

Now the nation faced the important question of whether the South would accept the Compromise measures. Those in favor of resistance placed their hopes in the cotton states, where opposition to the Compromise was greater. Thus the real contest over southern policy took place in these states, especially South Carolina, Georgia, Mississippi, and Alabama. Since the Georgia legislature had earlier in the year instructed the governor to call a convention in case California was admitted to the Union, the Empire State now became the center of attention. Immediately after the defeat of the omnibus bill, Iverson Harris, Georgia politician, had reported to Senator Berrien that not only was the South far from being united but Georgia itself was rent with division. The friends of the Nashville resolutions and the Clay Compromise respectively were doing all they could to widen the differences, concerned more about their ascendancy in the state than the destiny of the South. Although many county meetings had ratified the Nashville proceedings, Harris believed that a very large majority of the people would not only submit but would be satisfied with the Compromise. Benjamin F. Perry, South Carolina Unionist, remarked that if Georgia expected to head a disunion movement he had no doubt that South Carolina would sustain her. But he predicted that the southern states would not unite in such a movement because the feeling of loyalty to the Union was too strong.[21]

Whether those who opposed the Compromise elsewhere in the South would attempt to influence action in Georgia was as significant as the response of the state itself. William Gilmore Simms thought it was important to urge Georgians to "give the tone and impart courage to the Nashville Convention. If Georgia will but wag a single finger in defiance, S. C. will lift her whole hand and the fist shall be doubled. With two states in action, the whole South are enforced." From Washington, Barnwell requested James Hammond to "operate upon Georgia," and later he wrote, "Georgia is the first battlefield and we must fight valiantly there." But Hammond did not think any South Carolinian should attempt to influence directly the Georgia proceedings, and he, therefore, declined invitations to address state meetings, most notably the mass meeting at Macon on 22 August.[22] Robert Rhett, however, had no such reservations. He opened this gathering with a speech of nearly two hours, and was followed by W. L. Yancey. Some 800 "fire-eaters" responded with wild enthusiasm to their appeals that Georgia should "secede temporarily," and to Rhett's assurance that South Carolina would follow wherever Georgia might lead. Although the speeches prompted disunion, L. T. Chapman of the *Journal and Messenger* reported to Stephens, "You may rest assured the people of Georgia are not prepared for any such result."[23] The Democratic press urged that Governor Towns must summon the convention, but the Whig papers did not consider the admission of California enough provocation for a state convention. On 23 September Towns issued the proclamation that a state convention would assemble 10 December, and that elections for convention members would be held on 25 November. As Richard Shryock describes it, "This proclamation was the opening gun in the final battle for secession, both in Georgia and in the lower South as a whole, and it was naturally followed by a volley from both sides."[24]

The passage of the Compromise tended only to increase disunion sentiment in South Carolina and to bring it more into the open. From Washington, Francis Lieber, South Carolina Unionist, reported that when his country was in danger he deeply regretted that he lived in the Palmetto State. He was going home to "a lot of fools" who stopped him at every street corner and poured "patriotism of the sling and 'hailstorm' sort" down his "revolting throat."[25] Governor Seabrook indicated, however, that he would wait for the movement of Georgia and one or two other southern states before committing South Carolina. "A false step on her part, at this time, would ruin her and the causes of the South," he declared. A special session of the legislature before or during the second session of the Nashville Convention would embarrass the proceedings and would be "unwise and impolitic." In the meantime, every district or parish should hold meetings before the regular session of the legislature in late November. Seabrook also sent identical, confidential letters to the governors of Alabama, Virginia, and Mississippi, informing them of Georgia's impending convention, and asking whether their respective states were prepared to adopt any scheme to second Georgia "in her noble effort to preserve unimpaired the Union of '87." He assured them that as soon as the governors of two or more states should assemble their legislatures or furnish some other evidence of determined resistance, South Carolina would call her legislature, unless it was already in session, for resistance measures. Governor Towns reported to Seabrook that the situation in Georgia was critical; although the people were prepared to act decisively, a group of "cunning politicians" was attempting to thwart resistance. The Southern Rights Party could ill afford to lose strength by any premature movement in another state. Any decisive step in South Carolina would contribute largely to the overthrow of the southern party in Georgia and secure an opposition majority in the state convention. He, therefore, suggested that South Carolina make no move before the election of convention delegates.[26]

Mississippi Democrats generally opposed the Compromise, with Governor Quitman at the center of the opposition; the Whigs, with some very notable exceptions, favored it. Felix Huston, a leading politician, urged Quitman from Natchez to follow the policy of separate state secession. He believed another southern convention would result in defeat. "Let Georgia or Mississippi take the lead and secede. . . . Gradually the other states will join." Huston further advised that a special session of the legislature should pass decided resolutions and call a state convention. Barnwell, however, attempted to influence Quitman against separate state action and in favor of united action of all slaveholding states. The first opportunity for the South to unite for common counsel would be the reassembled Nashville Convention, which should take place in Georgia. The resolutions should be able and firm and come from either Mississippi or Georgia, preferably Mississippi, but these states should send new delegates committed to this purpose. Barnwell favored a southern congress to which the question of seceding or demanding guarantees would be submitted, and until its assemblage, he recommended nonintercourse. He did not believe the friends of southern rights in Georgia could carry their convention for decisive measures. Although South Carolina should not move alone, he would favor her secession if any state would sustain her, and thus force a southern congress. But first southerners must counsel in Nashville.[27]

Governor Quitman became convinced that he must follow

his inclination to convene the legislature, and on 25 September he issued a proclamation calling a special session on 18 November to consider "the alarming state of our public affairs . . . that the state may be placed in an attitude to assert her sovereignty, and that the means may be provided to meet any and every emergency which may happen." Three days later Quitman explained his views to Nashville Convention delegate John J. McRae. If he had hesitated in the emergency, he would have violated his trust. No effectual remedy except secession existed, although he was willing to adopt any other measure that would "promise a radical cure of the evils." The legislature should call a popular convention of delegates with the full authority to deal with federal relations. Quitman considered his propositions to be consistent with the Nashville Convention, although he did not believe the convention could do much beyond presenting a plan of joint action for the states. He said that William Sharkey, who now opposed the convention, probably would not call it together, but in the event the meeting took place, the Mississippi legislature would convene the following week, and the two bodies could communicate by telegraph. Quitman expressed similar views to Seabrook, stating that he was obliged to take preparatory steps promptly to invoke the sovereign powers of his state without waiting for the other states. The leaders appeared ready for resistance, regardless of consequences; yet the population, composed of immigrants from other states, was not homogeneous, and its position might be disappointing. Quitman informed his daughter that he had taken and would maintain "bold positions." Even if the legislature decided against him, he could resign with the consolation that at least he had done his duty. "I will not be the instrument of surrendering our birthright of liberty and equality."[28]

After Towns and Quitman issued proclamations, excitement mounted in Charleston, and the city clamored for an immediate convocation of the legislature. But citizens at a meeting in Columbia on 7 October, called at Seabrook's request, resolved against recommending assembly. Believing that most of the population supported secession but feared playing the role of leader, Seabrook wanted to stimulate Mississippi, Alabama, Florida, and Virginia to perform their duty and simultaneously conciliate Georgia. He, therefore, prepared a proclamation convening the legislature on 18 November, the same day as the Mississippi legislature.

Seabrook submitted a copy of this publication to Governor Towns and asked whether it would injure the resistance party in Georgia. Evidently Towns replied unfavorably, as Seabrook did not issue the proclamation. He wrote to Quitman that the universal belief in his state was that primary leadership from South Carolina would be a fatal blow to the great cause, but he repeated that his state was ready to second Mississippi or any other state in the resistance movement. He added that South Carolina leaders desired united action by a southern congress called by any united body, be it the Nashville Convention, the Georgia Convention, or the Mississippi legislature. Such a congress would have full authority on the part of the states represented to secede from the Union forthwith, or to present to the supreme authorities of the nation propositions for a new bargain between the states.[29]

Francis Pickens agreed in the necessity of a southern congress. "Yield everything for concert of action except vital principle. Look steadily to firm resistance in some shape or form," he advised. He believed the South, at least the cotton states, would finally act together, and if so the danger was past. The North would drive the southern states to union by committing aggression after aggression until the South was compelled to act.[30]

Passage of the Compromise measures clearly demarked the lines dividing the public opinion in Alabama. Clarence P. Denman has divided the people of the state into three groups—the southern rights men, the ultra Unionists, and the southern rights Unionists. The southern rights men believed that the Compromise was a one-sided adjustment which had required the South to make all the concessions.[31] Some of them agreed with John A. Campbell, who declared in a letter to Governor Collier, "For one, I made no profession of love to the Union apart from an equal and impartial administration of the Federal government and a rigid adherence by it to the Constitution." The states had the right to withdraw from the Union whenever the people willed it; in fact it was the duty of a people to overthrow a government that arrayed itself against their institutions. Many of this group, however, opposed secession at this time and sponsored other forms of resistance. The ultra Unionists contended the Compromise measures benefitted the South; they supported the Union, right or wrong. Between these two extremes lay the southern rights Unionists, who accepted the Compromise in order to preserve the Union. Henceforth, they felt, the responsibility lay with the northern people, whose failure to abide by the Compromise would force the southern rights Unionists to ally themselves with the secessionists and strike for southern independence. Whig leaders, such as Thomas J. Judge, James Abercrombie, and Representative Henry Hilliard, generally supported this position.[32] Many Democrats also belonged to this group, including Alabama's two senators, W. R. King and Clemens, who upon their return to the state urged the people to accept the Compromise. King especially regretted the effort to identify the Democratic party with immediate secession. Resort to extreme measures would only divide the Democrats and insure an easy victory for the Whigs; the Democrats must free themselves from "the suspicion of being disunionists."[33]

The most outstanding leader in the campaign against the Compromise was William L. Yancey, who strongly advocated the organization of the people in the Southern Rights Associations as a means of preparing the state for the conflict, "Congress had boldly tendered it—submission or secession," he declared. Yancey's cohort was J. J. Siebels, Jr., editor of the Montgomery *Advertiser,* who was in communication with his father and others in South Carolina. The most advanced step toward secession, however, came from the "Eufaula Regency," a group of fire-eaters in southeast Alabama. Through their association they launched a movement for a state convention, and on 22 October they drew up a petition calling upon Governor Henry W. Collier to convene the legislature as soon as possible to begin necessary action to place Alabama in the position demanded by the crisis. Forty-two citizens of Dallas County had sent a similar petition to the governor a month earlier. Although Collier was besieged by other petitions urging that Alabama not lag behind, he refused to call the legislature into special session. In a message to the people he stated that official action should be postponed until after the Nashville Convention had reassembled, and the Georgia Convention and the legislatures of some of the other states had acted. Since no convention was held in Alabama in the fall of 1850, the Compromise controversy was injected into the elections the following year.[34]

The Compromise was the outstanding issue in Florida's election in October 1850. John Beard, Democratic nominee who opposed E. C. Cabell for reelection to Congress, advocated the Nashville platform. Although Beard expressed an affection for the Union, he proclaimed his opposition to the Compromise even to the extent of secession, while Cabell opposed certain sections but upheld the overall Compromise. The election was a rather close victory for Cabell, who carried the wealthy and populous cotton and tobacco counties that had the most to lose by a continued agitation of the slavery issue. The results did not prove that Florida approved the Compromise, nor that all of the 47 percent who voted for Beard were disunionists, but they did show the existence of a strong disunion minority in the state. Immediately after the election, the radicals formed Southern Rights Associations in at least four counties—Gadsden, Leon, Jefferson, and Madison—and probably others. Southern rights advocates comprised 33 percent of the voters in Madison County, sometimes referred to as a "young South Carolina in swaddling clothes."[35]

Public acceptance of the boundary settlement was the important question in Texas. When the special session of the Texas legislature had convened on 12 August Governor Bell advocated seizing Santa Fe first and discussing the title to it afterward. William P. Duval, a leading politician, reported that Texans were "calmly determined" to take possession of the Santa Fe area, and he believed the first hostile gun that was fired in the controversy would dissolve the Union, as every southern state would stand by Texas.[36] On 6 September, however, Webster and Crittenden had rapidly dispatched a message to the Collector of the Port of New Orleans, to be forwarded to Governor Bell by Special Express with the least possible delay. The message announced that the amended Texas bill had passed with all the Texas congressmen voting for it, and it would be sent to Texas by express as soon as the President signed it. Texas Senators Sam Houston and Thomas J. Rusk joined the two cabinet officers in urging the legislature to continue in session until the bill reached them, but the legislature had adjourned on the day the message left Washington, to meet again on the third Monday in November. James Love of Galveston wrote Crittenden that the settlement was "universally acceptable," with the only objection from the "South Carolina school," who could not command a tenth of the vote in the state. When Bell received a copy of the act of 27 September, he issued a proclamation for the people to express their sentiment; the results could serve as a guide to legislative action as required by the law. A majority of the people accepted the new law, and on 25 November the legislature approved an act of acceptance.[37]

In Louisiana all of the Whigs and a majority of Democrats generally and heartily approved the Compromise. Senator Pierre Soulé led the only serious opposition, a faction of the Democratic party recruited partially from South Carolina emigrants. On his return to the state in October, he made a speech against the Compromise and became embroiled with the conservative Democrats, who agreed with Senator Solomon W. Downs. When a group of them interrogated Soulé by letter on 26 October, regarding secession of Louisiana and establishment of a Southern Confederacy because of the Compromise, they considered his answer unsatisfactory and discourteous. Soulé, therefore, failed dismally in making a party question of the controversy. The people as a whole were no more agitated than they had been the preceding spring over the Nashville Convention. Shortly after the passage of the laws, one New Orleans editor had declared that the only possible secessionists in Louisiana were a few South Carolina and Georgia men in the piney woods.[38]

Although some congressmen from the upper South had opposed the Compromise throughout the struggle, these states were expected to acquiesce unless the cotton states forced them into an opposition policy. Most Virginians appeared to reconcile themselves to the distasteful provisions of the settlement. The Democratic Richmond *Enquirer*, edited by the Ritchies, had formerly viewed Clay's proposals as a complete surrender to the North; it now advocated acceptance only as a necessity and not as a fair adjustment. In a similar manner, the Richmond *Whig* had regarded the Compromise as one-sided but now used its influence in favor of adjustment and insisted that all candidates should swear their acquiescence. Only the Hunter faction of the Democratic party and a few pro-southern Whigs continued to oppose the Compromise. They regarded the Ritchie conservatives as traitors to the southern cause.[39] "Would to God there were a man among us to whom we could look," wrote the old disunionist Beverley Tucker to Hammond. "But the politicians of Virginia are the puniest and most paltry that ever disappointed the hopes of the people." Senators James M. Mason and R. M. T. Hunter and Democratic Congressman James A. Seddon were the only men that Tucker considered trustworthy, and even they were "not equal to the occasion." Although Mason later referred to the settlement as a "pseudo compromise" that would prove fatal either to the Union or the institution of slavery, he was forced to declare that he would follow the dictates of Virginia in order to regain his nomination as a candidate for reelection to the Senate in December 1850. Tucker also noted that the geographical division of the state made concert of action impossible, but he assured Hammond of one advantage: "If not for you, Virginia cannot be against you."[40]

Considerable uniformity of sentiment did, however, exist on the fugitive slave law and its reception by the North; many border-state people felt that it would guarantee the safety of their property. Some Virginians advised boycotting northern goods in retaliation for northern hostility to the law. Governor John B. Floyd twice recommended in 1850 a tax on northern goods as the only means to secure redress. From this sentiment developed the Southern Rights Association, whose purpose changed from resistance to advocacy of economic independence as the only hope of the South. Edmund Ruffin, Virginia fire-eater, founded the Prince George County Association, designed specifically to increase southern commerce and manufacturing; and a central association including the counties around Richmond was organized for the same purpose. In its meetings, this association petitioned the legislature to levy a tax on northern goods that could also be obtained through southern manufacturers or direct importation, and advocated steamship lines from Virginia to Europe, the West Indies, and South America.

In spite of these grumblings and dissatisfactions, however, "the mother state" of the South officially accepted the Compromise measures through legislative approval at the 1850-51 session. With only one or two dissenting voices, the assembly indicated that the people of Virginia were unwilling to take any step to destroy the integrity of the Union.[41]

Occasional public meetings in Arkansas indicated sentiment in favor of the Compromise. Democratic Representative Robert W. Johnson, the only steadfast opponent of the Compromise in the Arkansas congressional delegation, remained the most controversial figure in state politics. While the Nashville Convention was in progress, Johnson had made a speech in the House favoring extension of the Missouri Compromise line and pleading for southern unity. In September 1850, however, he announced that he would not be a candidate for reelection to Congress the following year, indicating that he did not desire to carry the anti-Compromise fight before the people of the state. The general feeling was that the Compromise should be given a fair trial and no revolutionary or sectional meetings like the Nashville Convention should be held. In his message to the legislature on 6 November, the new governor, John Seldon Roane, however, asserted state sovereignty and the belief that the Compromise violated the rights of Arkansas and the South. Since he did not wish to see the Union dissolved, he proposed the establishment of a southern nonintercourse system, that is a program of southern nationalism—educating the young men in the South, purchasing supplies from southern merchants, extending southern commerce, and developing a southern consciousness in every conceivable way. The radicals in the legislature accepted the governor's challenge and attempted to pass resolutions repudiating the Compromise, but they failed.[42]

The editor of the Wilmington *Journal* may have expressed the feelings of a majority of North Carolinians when he wrote after the Compromise passage, "It would be both folly and nonsense to say that these measures are all the South had a right to expect . . . but it would also be folly to make a fuss and talk about resistance and all that sort of thing." Almost any plan that promised anything like justice or even the preservation of honor would be willingly accepted.[43] The pro-southern wing of the Democratic party, although forced to acquiesce in the settlement, did not attempt to conceal its dissatisfaction, and a few southern rights meetings condemned the Compromise measures. The *North Carolina Standard* warned the North "to respect and enforce the Fugitive Slave Law as it stands. If not, *we leave you*!" On this point virtual unanimity existed among Whigs and Democrats, conservatives and southern extremists: The fugitive slave law must be enforced. In his legislative meessage in November, Governor Manly declared that North Carolina rejoiced "at the amicable settlement of this distracting controversy," but his state would never surrender its rights even though it cherished a deep devotion to the Union. North Carolina would set a "noble example" by supporting the entire adjustment for the sake of the Union. Several strong southern resolutions introduced in the legislature alarmed the conservative Whigs, and Senator Willie P. Mangum accused the Democrats of making "political capital." Although the Whigs were able to defeat these radical resolutions, they were unable to secure passage of resolutions approving the Compromise.[44]

When news arrived in Tennessee that the last Compromise resolution had passed, the Nashville *Union,* now under the editorship of Henry Watterson, wrote, "What is it we hear? It is the deepest roar of the cannon proclaiming the joy of our citizens without distinction of party that Congress has done its duty and saved the Republic." The *Republican Banner* announced that a "joyful response" came from all quarters, but E. G. Eastman at the *American* office, supporting the Nashville platform, gave an emphatic "no" in response to the question of Tennessee's acquiescence in the Compromise.[45] Tennesseans in general, however, approved the Compromise; newspapers with few exceptions, resolutions of public meetings throughout the state, and expressions of leading men all indicated a willingness to accept congressional action. The state in which the Nashville Convention was scheduled to meet again in six weeks would not resist. On the eve of the gathering, Cave Johnson wrote Buchanan that Compromise support was very strong and he believed it would be politically fatal for any man to voice opposition. Yet in Tennessee, as well as North Carolina and Virginia, the enforcement of the fugitive slave law was an important condition. Johnson said he heard every day that if this law could not be enforced the South should leave the Union.[46]

On 1 October the editor of the *Republican Banner* remarked that the question of most interest to Tennessee was whether the Nashville Convention would meet again. For South Carolina the answer was "yes," for "with fierce intent they are cocking their vizors and getting their lances in readiness, preparatory to an onslaught on the other states." The editor blamed the politicians, called on the people of South Carolina, and urged "abandonment of wild schemes as 'fire-eating' conventions." Nashville, which was planning a banquet for her returning congressmen to sustain them in their support of the Compromise, was no suitable place for such a meeting. A few days later the same editor warned the people of the state "that here in Tennessee is the place where the ball of Revolution is to be set in motion—if possible."[47] Had the passage of the Compromise and the apparent tendency in much of the South to accept the adjustment deprived the Nashville Convention of all *raison d'être*? Would it be, as the editor predicted, a "fire-eating" convention controlled by the radicals? The answer was only weeks away.

# 9

## *Submission or Secession?*

The passage of the Compromise had taken away much of the momentum generated by the first session of the Nashville Convention. Even in South Carolina, the state most interested in reassembly, the cooperationists and the single-state secessionists disagreed. Some regarded the convention as the first step leading to a southern congress with full authority from the states, while others thought a second session would be a waste of time. The *Mercury* stated that the necessity for the convention was urgent. Before the final passage of the Compromise, Robert Barnwell had written James Hammond, "As for Nashville[,] we must go there[;] if South Carolina goes alone she must go, her whole delegation." He urged Hammond to prepare an address and send it to someone in Mississippi for presentation at the next session as South Carolina must remain invisible. Barnwell believed the convention should recommend a congress of the slaveholding states and defend the right of secession. He had asked Charles J. McDonald to urge W. L. Sharkey to transfer the meeting to Georgia, but "old man" McDonald would not cooperate. Sharkey was now a "traitor" who had fallen into Henry Foote's "clutches" and would no doubt undertake any "tricks" Clement Clay, Sr., and Foote asked of him. Barnwell had high regard for Governor Towns, but he observed that the Georgia governor was "evidently looking out for some hole that Georgia may creep out."[1]

By 30 September, however, Hammond had decided that a second session of the convention would be at the least a farce and declared he would not attend. He had actually made this decision when the delegates had voted against meeting in Georgia, and events had strengthened his conviction. He hoped Sharkey would be "fool enough to decline calling it and take the failure on himself," but even if he did issue the call, South Carolina should refuse to attend. A southern congress might accomplish something, but the Nashville Convention could only do harm. Georgia should call the congress, but South Carolina might if Georgia was unwilling. On 18 October Hammond informed Governor Seabrook that his own poor health and illness among his family and slaves would probably keep him away from Nashville. He asked the governor to fill his seat if he felt a full delegation was necessary. Seabrook replied that he lacked the authority to appoint delegates and urged Hammond to attend if possible, while friends unsuccessfully urged him to go. Maxcy Gregg wrote him that he had been the most efficient member of the South Carolina delegation in June and would be able to accomplish more now than any one else. D. F. Jamison and others pointed out that failure to attend would injure him politically in the Senate race, but Hammond remained adamant.[2]

Interest in the second session was slight elsewhere, but fifty-eight or fifty-nine delegates from seven southern states met in Nashville in November. Arkansas and Texas were missing, and more than a third of the delegates had not participated in the June session. The nature of the delegates also differed. Most of the new members, who were apparently chosen in an irregular manner, generally held views more radical than those of the June delegates. The more moderate of the former delegates, who were either content with the Compromise or willing to acquiesce in the unavoidable, did not return.[3] Calhoun's state sent fifteen or sixteen members, the largest and most representative group; Hammond, R. F. W. Allston,

John Bradley and possibly H. C. Young were missing. Dr. James Bradley took Allston's place, and John S. Wilson filled either John Bradley or Young's place.[4]

None of Mississippi's original delegates attended the second session. One source says that Governor Quitman, without authority, appointed three of the eight new delegates, and public meetings in Yazoo, Marshall, and Claiborne counties chose the remainder.[5] William H. Kilpatrick and Thomas J. Wharton, who were lawyers, were probably the most prominent of the new delegates.

In Georgia the governor had the authority to fill vacancies in the delegation. Towns chose Dr. William C. Daniel to replace George Troup from the first congressional district. Troup had written a friend on 1 October, "Finding things every day worse and worse, and particularly after the miscalled pacification by Congress, I resolved, even if able, not to attend the second convention at Nashville." Additional appointees were John P. Snell for Obediah Warner in the fourth district, George R. Hunter for Obediah Gibson in the third, John A. Jones for Simpson Fouche in the fifth, and John C. Sneed for a vacancy.[6] Georgia's eleven representatives included these men, four returning June delegates, and two others. Jones, Hunter, Sneed, and James N. Bethune were lawyers and native Georgians. Jones had written articles denouncing Howell Cobb and other Unionists as traitors to the South. Bethune, Walter Colquitt, and other Columbus extremists in 1850-51 organized the "Coffin Regiment," so called because of Colquitt's declaration that they would march to the Missouri Compromise line with their coffins on their backs and demand the rights for which they were willing to die. They expressed their extreme position in the *Cornerstone* published by Bethune and later received the blame for discrediting the whole southern rights wing of the Democracy.[7]

Only five delegates, three of them new, represented Alabama, compared to twenty-two in June. The most prominent of the new members was Clement Clay, Sr., Democratic lawyer and judge, who had served Alabama in the legislature, supreme court, both houses of Congress, and as governor. A native of Virginia, he grew to manhood and received his education in Tennessee before migrating to Huntsville in 1811. He was active in organizing the Southern Rights Association in Madison County, became its president, and loudly proclaimed the right of any state to secede. He did not, however, favor disunion at the time but urged a rigid system of social and commercial nonintercourse. Another new delegate, George W. Williams, was a native South Carolinian, a lawyer, wealthy planter, and slaveholder. Former probate judge of Henry County and a member of the legislature for thirteen terms, Williams had served as president of a southern meeting at Abbeville in July. A Democrat, he was a strong advocate of secession. The third new delegate was James M. Calhoun, native South Carolinian and a nephew of John C. Calhoun, who was also a Democrat, lawyer, planter, and several times a member of both houses of the state legislature.[8]

One source called the four delegates from Florida "men of little prominence in political affairs"; three had not attended the June meeting. John C. McGehee, a native of South Carolina, was 49, owned 100 slaves, a plantation valued at $25,000, and a sawmill in Madison County. He urged the necessity and rightness of secession and wholly agreed with the more radical southern leaders who desired the South to unite in concerted action. Eleven years later he would serve as president of the Florida state secession convention.[9] P. Woodson White, a thirty-year-old attorney, was a native Georgian, who owned $5,500 worth of real estate.

A meeting in Chicot County, Arkansas, appointed delegates, but none attended, and only two states in the upper South—Tennessee and Virginia—sent delegates to the second session. Tennessee's delegation decreased from 101 to 14 members who, according to reports, gravely debated whether they should participate at all.[10] William F. Gordon was the sole delegate from Virginia. Although North Carolina was not represented at the first session, convention proponents hoped that the Tarheel State would send delegates to Nashville in November. Maxcy Gregg was in communication with political leaders in North Carolina, and on 21 August he wrote John F. Hoke, prominent Democrat of Lincoln County, and urged him to use his influence in his district toward sending a representative. Gregg insisted that North Carolina should not lack representation at a meeting that most of the southern states would probably attend. Approximately a month later, Gregg asked Hoke for numbers and names of delegates and requested that he make efforts by correspondence beyond his own district "towards stirring the people up" to send delegates. A southern rights meeting in October in Mecklenburg County elected two delegates, but they did not attend. Adoption of the Compromise measures had largely checked sentiment for a southern movement.[11]

The Charleston *Mercury* remarked in mid-September that Sharkey probably would not call the convention, but since he seemed uncertain about his allegiance and his opinion, his blessing was not necessary. A short time later, Vice President McDonald wrote a letter, later published in the *Federal Union,* stating that in his opinion the reassembly did not depend on publication of a notice by the president. McDonald said he would be at Nashville, where he hoped to meet a full delegation from the interested states, but in the absence of Sharkey's resignation, he did not think he should issue a notice.[12] True to predictions, Sharkey did not issue a call for the second meeting. Nevertheless, the delegates gathered in Nashville as previously planned.

The environment surrounding the second session was far different from that of the June meeting. The weather was chillier, as was the reception of Nashvillians, who generally gave the representatives "the cold shoulder." Gone were the fetes and parties and the warm demonstrations.[13] Furthermore, some delegates had experienced difficulties in travel; many, in fact, arrived late. The rivers were so low that water travel was impossible, and people crammed all available space on stages from the South and West. Bad roads added to the problems. The special reporter for the Charleston *Mercury* commented that Nashville was one of the most inaccessible places in the South for a general meeting. No doubt many delegates, especially those who wanted to meet somewhere else, must have agreed with him that holding the convention outside the cotton states was a fatal blunder. William F. Gordon, however, reported to his wife that he had reached Nashville "with comparatively little fatigue" after traveling via Charleston and Chattanooga, where some of the delegates had chartered an omnibus.[14]

In spite of the lack of enthusiasm of many of Nashville's citizens, the members of the Christian Church offered their building on Spring Street as a meeting place. It was located about a block from McKendree Methodist Church, though the Christian Church had been established less than a quarter of a century. Visitors again occupied the galleries, but inclement weather kept away a great many natives. One source reported that many of the visitors were Yankee clerks, merchants, and tradesmen who were abolitionist at heart.[15] The *Daily American,* the only newspaper that warmly endorsed the meeting, gave the fullest accounts of the proceedings.[16]

The second session formally opened on Monday, 11 November, with ninety-five persons, including the spectators, in attendance.[17] On a motion by Gideon Pillow of Tennessee, who called the meeting to order, the convention called Vice President McDonald to the chair.[18] Following the custom of the previous session, a clergyman delivered an invocation, and then McDonald delivered a short speech. The June session, he said, was entitled to a decent consideration by Congress, but the lawmakers had treated it with contempt and scorn. They had not only admitted California as a free state, but they had disregarded the principle of equal rights to the public territories. Changing the Constitution was a far greater wrong; everything depended on its preservation, unchanged and unbroken. His eloquent pro-southern speech concluded, "If the Constitution be doomed to perish, we must nerve our arms to secure the rights it was intended to guarantee, relying on the guidance and aid of the Omnipotent in so just a cause." Clay of Alabama moved that the convention authorize the president to fill vacancies on the credentials committee, and he then proposed adjournment until 12 o'clock the next day, as the Mississippi delegates and some from Alabama, Georgia, and South Carolina had not arrived.[19] On Tuesday, Clay nominated

McDonald as president, and Barnwell nominated Reuben Chapman of Alabama as vice president. Both were elected by acclamation. E. G. Eastman, now *American* editor, W. F. Cooper, and Thomas Boyers served as secretaries. The chairman then requested the delegations to fill vacancies on the resolutions committee. Since many of the delegates had been so slow in reaching Nashville, little was accomplished the first two days.

Pillow, chairman of the credentials committee, reported the new delegates on Wednesday. Clay offered a preamble that delineated the grievances of the South, which stood on the defensive invoking the spirit of the Constitution and claiming its guaranties. If the North disregarded its provisions and endangered southern peace and existence by united and deliberate action, the states had a right to secede. Clay also delivered resolutions that explained the constitutional principles endorsing the right of secession, affirmed any state's right to secede, and recommended that the southern states pledge themselves to support with all their resources any state that might secede from the Union upon coercion by the general government. Furthermore, Clay recommended that a southern congress meet at Montgomery, with delegates fully authorized to represent their states in determining a course for maintaining their rights and institutions. He also recommended a second objective: southerners should abstain from all intercourse with northerners, including shipping and product consumption. The *Republican Banner* claimed that Clay's resolutions told the whole story of the dream of some delegates—a Southern Confederacy. Charles H. DuPont of Florida presented a series of resolutions that stated the unanimous sentiment of his state delegation on the Compromise and also recommended a general convention, whose only object was to promote harmony and unity of action, for each state had the right to determine her relations to the Federal government. The last of DuPont's resolutions stated clearly that secession was "one amongst the unalienable rights, *reserved* by the States," and any force on the part of the Federal Government should be "unanimously resisted" by the other states.[20]

Thursday, the busiest day of the entire session, was

crowded with resolutions, one long speech, and two other incidents worth noting. The president presented a letter from Dr. W. P. Rowles of Lawrenceburg, who had served as a Tennessee delegate in June, expressing regret for his inability to attend. He did not consider the question settled but merely postponed; apparently he was dissatisfied with the congressional adjustment. The delegates also invited the most "ultra" southern spokesman in Tennessee, Senator Hopkins L. Turney, who was in the galleries, to take an honorary seat in the convention. Jones of Georgia offered two resolutions, dealing primarily with nonintercourse and prefaced by a short preamble: "Equality of rights . . . that has been grossly, fraudulently, and oppressively violated by the acts of Congress. . . . We cannot now shut our eyes to the fact that in the public mind of the North of every sect and party, there is a settled purpose to deprive us of our slave property." Hunter of Georgia introduced six resolutions, one stating plainly that the slave states had a duty to resist the late congressional legislation; if resistance failed, each state might decide for itself. These and all other resolutions were referred to the resolutions committee without debate.[20] J. J. Davenport of Mississippi offered resolutions similar to Clay's in tone and spirit: the original object of the convention was to preserve the Constitutional Union of the states, but the Union was one of equal and independent sovereignties, each of which could resume the powers delegated to the Federal government whenever necessary. The failure to extend the Missouri Compromise line to the Pacific and the late congressional acts had confirmed all of the anticipated evils. Davenport recommended a general congress with full authority of deliberation and action to restore the constitutional rights of the South if possible, or if not, to provide for safety and independence of the South in the last resort. He urged southerners to adopt measures for nonintercourse, to promote southern institutions, and to boycott national presidential nominating conventions until their constitutional rights were secured.[21]

Pillow, speaking on behalf of most of the Tennessee delegation, introduced resolutions that contrasted strongly with the others. They accepted the Compromise measures on condition that the North faithfully carry out its part, and they interpreted the Compromise as the North's final action regarding slavery. The resolutions set forth certain contingencies, however, which would bring about an immediate convention of states and the institution of a rigid system of nonintercourse, should they materialize. The theme of the Tennessee resolutions was, therefore, acquiescence, but acquiescence determined to resist further aggression.[22] "The Tennessee resolutions are for the perpetuity of the Union," wrote the editor of the Nashville *Union*; "the resolutions of the other states look to secession and the ultimate dissolution of the Union." A. J. Donelson thought some of his delegation's resolutions were too strong and presented some of his own, advising acquiescence in the Compromise and open resistance only when the Federal government became an instrument of "intolerable tyranny." But Thomas Claiborne objected to these resolutions, causing the *Mercury* reporter to declare that extraordinary unanimity prevailed in all delegations except Tennessee's.[23]

For South Carolina, Langdon Cheves rose and offered a single resolution: secession was the only remedy. Before traveling to Nashville he had written his daughter that he expected his attendance to be the last public act of his life. He evidently had this in mind when he prepared the lengthy speech that he now read. Beginning with the admission of California—"fraudulent, insulting, tyrannical"—he catalogued the wrongs the South had endured at northern hands. "There is no doubt that they have abolished the Constitution. The carcass may remain, but the spirit has left. . . . It stinks in our nostrils." The only remedy lay in united secession of the slaveholding states. "Nothing else will be wise—nothing else will be practicable. The Rubicon is passed—the Union is already dissolved." If four or five adjoining states would unite, the enemy would not venture an attack; the Constitution protected the South from any war. Cheves concluded eloquently, "O! great God, unite us, and a tale of submission shall never be told." The *Mercury* described the speech as "elaborate, profound, eloquent, sometimes brilliant and all together unanswerable." The reporter added that the courageous old man whose "voice sometimes filled the hall like a bugle," had thrown down the gauntlet to submissionists in Tennessee's capital, where loud applause of the illustrious Union was "the surest passport to popular favor," and poured forth his indignant scorn on all who would shrink from the defense of southern rights. If the convention accomplished nothing else, the value of this speech to the South would be inestimable: it would compensate the delegates for all their trouble and expense.[24]

On Friday the resolutions committee met, and the main body listened to the addresses of anyone who desired to speak. The most outstanding was an hour-long oration by McWhertor of Georgia supporting his resolution urging the convention to retain its emphasis on southern rights but also to restrain those who would be hasty. He professed a love for the Union of his fathers but denounced the Fugitive Slave Law as a "*quid pro quo* of a false character" and declared that Union and slavery could not long exist together. W. F. Cooper found McWhertor's speech "handsome . . . well delivered, full of fine passages," but he was not sure whether it put forth more union or disunion sentiments. "Sheer hypocrisy," observed John L. Marling, editor of the Nashville *Gazette,* whose outspoken criticism had caused the delegates to consider ousting him the day before. Claiborne delivered a brief address similar to that of McWhertor, but he spoke for himself rather than for his state, as he was in the minority.[25] The report of the resolutions committee, given by Chairman Gordon on Saturday, offered a series of resolutions that substantially duplicated those of Clay. The Tennessee delegation did not concur, and Aaron V. Brown submitted a minority report. In the discussion Clay and Pillow were the principal speakers, McWhertor suggested amendments, and Gordon moved for adoption.

The Mississippi members would not support Clay's resolutions, however, and on Monday Gordon requested that the resolutions be resubmitted to the committee. A brief conference of the committee resulted in the adoption of the Alabama preamble with the substitution of a new set of resolutions, essentially those of Mississippi. The committee had, therefore, bypassed South Carolina's resolution advocating united secession, but it had approved measures affirming the right of secession, denouncing the Compromise, and recommending a southern congress. A. O. P. Nicholson and Brown dissented from the report but rejected debate, saying they would present their views to the public in some other way.[26] After Gordon presented the preamble and resolutions, Donelson rose, evidently to address the galleries, but the chairman called him to order; Donelson denounced the admonition as "unworthy of the convention." Upon the roll call of states, only Tennessee voted "no," whereupon Donelson requested a reconsideration of the vote. Since Donelson's state had voted in the negative, McDonald ruled that the motion was out of order. Yet Donelson demanded the floor. He castigated the purposes of the convention as "unhallowed," bringing forth vociferous applause from the audience and creating a good deal of confusion. While he was still speaking, the convention adjourned in "undignified haste." According to the *American,* some of Nashville's most prominent citizens participated in the disorder, but the behavior of the out-of-state delegates and most of the other Tennesseans was orderly and dignified. In fact, the incident deeply mortified all of the Tennessee delegation except Donelson. Secretary Eastman, however, explained that no disgrace existed: everyone understood that the convention had to adjourn Monday morning because the congregation needed to use the church for a funeral.[27] Thus the second session ended in hasty confusion, in sharp contrast to the formal valedictories that had characterized the first.

Again contemporaries provide the most telling commentaries on the meeting. Marling, the most extreme critic of the convention, accused the delegates of turning the house of God "into a court of Radamanthus"[28] and polluting it with "sentiments worthy only of Lucifer." He had watched the proceedings with "chagrin and mortification" and was convinced that all of the delegates except the Tennesseans cherished feelings of hostility against the Union, but the real moving power was South Carolina. "Her supple and cunning statesmen" had found in Clay "a cat's paw" to accomplish their object.[29]

Hammond now believed that his forebodings had come

true. He had thought that those who acquiesced would either send recruits in order "to throw cold water on the Georgia movement," or if they remained at home would regard the action as that of a group of ultras which would "drive off Tennessee." The latter had happened. Well satisfied that he had not returned, Hammond declared the Nashville Convention had proved a "total failure" and a "mere abortion" from the beginning. The moderation of the first session and Cheves' speech in the second were all that had saved the convention "from being the laughing stock of the parties," and the sooner it faded into "utter oblivion the better." Since so many June delegates had failed to return, he believed many of them shared his opinion.[30]

In contrast to Hammond's pessimism, however, the city of Jackson saluted the gathering on the day of adjournment with three cheers in the name of Mississippi. The special session of the legislature had convened, Governor Quitman's message was "all right," and the Southern Rights party was in "high spirits." In his message to the legislature, Quitman had reviewed the entire controversy and recommended authorizing a state convention, either with the other states or separately, to adopt "such measures as may best comport with dignity and safety of the state and effectually correct the evils complained of." The legislature issued a call for the election of delegates in September 1851 for a state convention to meet that November to consider the future relationship between the state and Federal government. The extremists regarded this as a triumph, in light of the strong opposition minority and unsettled public opinion in some counties. The editor of the Vicksburg *Whig*, however, asserted that the legislature had usurped authority by refusing to let the people decide whether they needed a convention. The legislature also censured Foote and endorsed the position of Jefferson Davis and the state's representatives.[31]

At the same time, some fifteen hundred Unionists were gathering in a bipartisan convention in the city hall to rebuke the "treasonable action" of the legislature and "to censure the censurers." Their president was William L. Sharkey. Senator

Foote, who had returned to Jackson in October, addressed the meeting. The participants approved his position on the Compromise, voted to support it unless egregious violations occured, and formed the Union party, composed of both Whigs and Democrats.[32]

The Georgia campaign for election of delegates to the state convention that Governor Towns had called probably aroused the greatest interest, however, as Georgia's decision would largely determine the success of southern cooperative action and probably the fate of the whole resistance movement. During the summer and fall of 1850 the masses continued to oppose or ignore the sectional appeal. Toombs, Stephens, and Howell Cobb led the Union campaign for acceptance of the Compromise; Stephens traveled some three thousand miles explaining the Compromise measures and advising the people to accept them. Colquitt and Benning were the most prominent extremists, openly advocating secession. Their avowed opinions brought forth charges of disunion against the southern rights men who urged the election of delegates opposed to the Compromise measures. This affected the campaign considerably, and by late October all except one or two of the radical papers had noticeably moderated their sentiments. Southern rights leaders ceased to counsel secession and began to speak only of "resistance to oppression." Some papers that had advocated secession in September stopped at the halfway point of nonintercourse or another southern convention, and many even recommended accepting the Compromise. Richard Shryock finds this "swing to the right" the most noticeable and significant feature of the entire campaign. Senator Berrien led a third very small group that advocated economic resistance to the North. They urged resistance *within* the Union and the Constitution; secession would be impractical, but nonintercourse would encourage the economic life of the South and bring pressure upon northern conservative business interests.[33]

The election result on 25 November was largely a repetition of the April fiasco, as the Union claimed a majority greater than any party had ever polled in the state—46,000 for Union candidates and only 24,000 for southern rights. Of the ninety-three counties only ten chose southern rights delegates. The editor of the Savannah *Morning News* warned, however, that the North must not regard the results as indicative of any lack of resolute determination on the part of Georgia's citizens to resist all further aggression on their constitutional rights. In spite of all the expressed devotion to the Union, he believed a unanimity of sentiment existed among all Georgia parties on the question of southern rights.[34]

The Georgia State Convention, composed of 264 men, most of whom were Unionists, met at Milledgeville from 10 to 14 December 1850. A remarkably large number were able and influential citizens of a conservative vent; more than half of them held slaves. Thomas Spalding of Sapelo Island, a Union Democrat and the last living signer of the state constitution, was elected president. He then chose a committee of thirty-three (three from each state judicial district) to whom all resolutions were referred. The result was the adoption of the "Georgia Platform," a set of five resolutions probably written by Charles J. Jenkins, the chairman of the committee, although Alexander Stephens later claimed authorship. Basically, the resolutions and preamble rejected disunion while warning the North that Georgia did not wholly approve the late Compromise but would abide by it as an adjustment of the controversy; if the Compromise were violated, however, Georgia would secede. The fourth and fifth resolutions listed a series of encroachments on southern rights that would justify secession: abolition of slavery in the District of Columbia, congressional suppression of the internal slave trade, prohibition of the introduction of slaves into Utah or New Mexico territories, refusal to admit a slave state into the Union, and most important, failure to execute the fugitive slave law.[35] Significantly, the "Georgia Platform" strikingly resembled the Tennessee Resolutions that Pillow had introduced at Nashville. The theme of both was an acceptance of the Compromise with a determination to resist any further aggression against southern rights.

In the election of October 1851, Georgia Unionists repeated the victory of the preceding year, when Howell Cobb defeated C. J. McDonald, the fire-eating president of the second session of the Nashville Convention, for governor. Cobb carried all except twenty-one of the ninety-five counties and received a majority of about 18,000 votes. The Unionists also secured an unprecedented majority in the legislature, electing six out of eight congressmen. Thus the election confirmed the Unionist victory of 1850. The majority of the people were willing to give the Union another trial.[36]

The states of the upper South had accepted the Compromise with little fanfare,[37] and the Florida legislature virtually ignored the convention's proposals for a southern congress. Governor Brown told the lawmakers that only willing submission by all sections would preserve the Union. In fact the legislative session of 1850-51 took no action regarding the slavery controversy, but it was responsible for the election of Stephen R. Mallory, a moderate Democrat, as United States Senator to replace fire-eater David L. Yulee. Mallory's election, however, was not a manifestation of Florida's approval of the Compromise, as Mallory was a states' rightist himself, who had favored the Nashville Convention and had been elected as an alternate to it. Yet he had attempted to hold back the disunionists. Florida Democrats finally accepted the Compromise toward the end of 1851, while the Whigs continued to discuss a Constitutional Union party.[38]

In the Alabama elections of August 1851, the Unionists, led by Congressman Hilliard, elected a majority of the legislature and the congressional delegation by 6,000 votes, thus defeating W. L. Yancey's states' rights party. But Yancey's group aided in the reelection of Governor Collier, candidate of the Southern Rights Unionists, over his opponent B. G. Shields, an ultra Unionist. In the 1851-52 session, the Unionists in the legislature finally succeeded in securing acceptance of the Compromise resolutions as the final settlement. Alabama Whigs were also interested in the continuance of a Constitutional Union party, as they found themselves experiencing increasing difficulty with northern Whigs, as were their counterparts elsewhere in the South.[39]

Since the Unionists were apparently sweeping the South,

the hope of those who opposed acceptance of the Compromise lay with Mississippi and South Carolina, the originators of the Nashville Convention. There only did the fire-eaters remain powerful. The struggle in Mississippi centered around two elections—for state convention delegates in September 1851 and for governor in November—that involved personalities as well as the Compromise issue. The Union party convention nominated Henry Foote for governor, while the Democratic States Rights convention nominated former Governor Quitman, who had resigned upon federal indictment for his support of General Narciso López, and his abortive filibustering expedition to Cuba. The government later dropped the charge. Foote considered the acceptance of the Compromise to be the main issue, yet his opponents denied this and attacked Foote personally. "Mississippi was in a blaze from east to west, and from north to south," Reuben Davis, a leading politician, later recalled; "both parties were pervaded by a spirit of intolerance, and the presence of ten men at any one point involved the possibility of serious trouble." The Unionists won the convention election on 1 and 2 September by a vote of 28,402 to 21,241, or 57 percent. Francis Lieber's son, who was assistant professor of geology at the University of Mississippi, reported to his father that the Unionists had "so completely routed" the secessionists that many secessionists thought Foote might even be elected governor. Foote was, however, very unpopular even with many of the Union party, and Quitman, except for his Cuban affair, was well liked, even outside his own party.[40]

Quitman interpreted the Union victory as a condemnation of his position and withdrew four days later. Jefferson Davis, a more effective campaigner, replaced him as the gubernatorial candidate of the States Rights Democrats, who now faced the difficult problem of removing the disunion label pinned on them by the Union party before the September election. The States Rights Democrats concentrated their attack on the alliance between Foote and the Whigs in the Union party, Foote's delayed Senate resignation, and the vacant Senate seat of Davis if Foote should be elected governor.[41] While Foote and his supporters continued to campaign on the defense of the

Constitution and the Union, Davis lay ill with malaria and an eye inflammation, contracted shortly after his nomination, until less than three weeks before the election. Foote won the governorship on 3 and 4 November, by the slim margin of 999 votes; he carried thirty-one counties and Davis twenty-eight. The Union party also elected sixty-three out of ninety-eight members of the lower house of the legislature and seven of sixteen members of the Senate chosen that year. Three Union candidates won seats in Congress, but Albert Gallatin Brown, who violently opposed the Compromise, was reelected. The Union party, though, had lost ground between September and November, partially because weariness and self-satisfaction with their September success had caused apathy within the party. Some Davis supporters rationalized that their candidate, who was personally popular, would have won had the campaign lasted a few weeks longer.[42] Almost two years later, Davis wrote that he resigned as senator to run for governor in order to serve his party where he was needed. Moreover, he never considered the result of the election as a decision against states' rights or a condemnation of his course in the Senate, which he believed was right.[43]

Before leaving the state for Washington, Senator (now governor-elect) Foote addressed the state convention originally instigated by Quitman to consider secession. By a vote of 72 to 17 the meeting adopted resolutions stating that the majority of the people of Mississippi had accepted the Compromise, so long as it was "faithfully adhered to and enforced." Thus, even the state that had originally called the Nashville Convention had acquiesced in the settlement.[44] South Carolina stood alone.

Meanwhile, in the Palmetto State, the demarcation between those who wanted united action by the South and those who preferred independent state action was increasing. Both groups and almost all South Carolinians desired secession; the issue was secession alone or in concert. The R. B. Rhett faction of single-state secessionists, which included such leaders as R. F. W. Allston and Maxcy Gregg, at first was willing to wait upon a southern congress as recommended by the Nashville

Convention, but they wanted the state to declare for secession in advance and then act alone if necessary. The cooperationists opposed the secessionists, advocating secession only if the states of the lower South would join together. The few Unionists in the state supported this group. Only five leading men publicly opposed secession in the fall of 1850—W. J. Grayson, Joel Poinsett, former Governor James Hamilton, Waddy Thompson, and Benjamin F. Perry. Since every newspaper in the state either advocated secession or was silent, Perry, Thompson, and a group of Greenville men established a new paper, the Greenville *Southern Patriot,* to oppose separate state action and immediate disunion, and to advocate the union of the South in a congress for the defense of southern rights and the preservation of the Union. Senator Andrew P. Butler, Langdon Cheves, and Robert Barnwell were the leaders of the cooperationists, but this group also included such prominent men as W. C. Preston, president of South Carolina College; James Chesnut; Representatives James L. Orr and Armistead Burt; and James H. Hammond.[45]

On 30 November Hammond confided to his diary that he had favored disunion and considered it inevitable for almost twenty years and would favor immediate secession if he thought it was "judicious." No state except South Carolina was, however, ready to act, and since South Carolina would stand alone, he believed secession was "impolitic" at this time. He wrote W. H. Gist of his opposition to a state convention or any steps against the Federal government now, but he believed that South Carolina would ultimately have to take the lead in seceding—perhaps to secede alone. Such action now, however, would inevitably divide the South.[46]

Two absorbing questions confronted the newly elected South Carolina legislature when it convened late in November 1850: Should the state proceed immediately to secession? Should it fill Calhoun's seat in the United States Senate? Governor Seabrook's message, which dealt almost exclusively with federal relations, concluded with the admonition that "while adhering faithfully to the remedy of joint state action for redress of common grievances, I beseech you to remember, that no conjunction of events ought to induce us to abandon the right of deciding ultimately our own destiny."[47] Perry, who bore the brunt of the battle against the radicals, said that the legislature contained no more than four or five men opposed to disunion, while Seabrook informed Quitman that only one man favored ultimate submission. Nevertheless, a very stormy session ensued; the members voted again and again on the same thing, as the disunionists could not agree on what course to follow. The majority, who favored immediate secession, attempted to push through a state convention bill but lacked the necessary two-thirds vote. Determined not to alienate South Carolina from her sister states, the minority insisted on electing delegates to the southern congress recommended by the Nashville Convention.[48] Harry Hammond reported from South Carolina College that he had attended the legislative debates and believed his father agreed with C. G. Memminger, who had made a three-hour speech calling immediate secession "madness." Memminger opposed a state convention except for "striking the final blow," advocated a southern congress preliminary to a dissolution, thought South Carolina should remain in the Union with a full congressional delegation as long as possible, and advised appropriation of $400,000 for arming the state. The legislative conflict raged for days, but finally the legislators passed an omnibus bill for the call and election of delegates to a southern congress and a state convention. Eighteen delegates would be chosen for the congress on 13 and 14 October 1851; the bill suggested that the congress assemble at Montgomery, Alabama, on 2 January 1852. On the second Monday in February 1851, delegates would be elected to a state convention to meet on an unspecified date after the projected congress to accept or reject any measures it had adopted. The legislature also elected Rhett to the United States Senate, but the choice between him and Hammond required four ballots. One of Hammond's friends wrote him, "Your not going to Nashville defeated your election. You should have gone and I told you so last summer."[49]

As the critical year of 1850 ended on a note of comparative quiet, George W. Harris, a resident of Yorkville, South Carolina, described for a Florida relative the determination of the people of his state and noted, "Would to God that this was the case throughout the South it would soon silence the clamor of northern fanaticism . . . and stay the tide of aggression which is bearing against us with such fearful force." South Carolina would never recede from her position based on the Constitution, and if necessary she would fight her battle alone in defense of her rights.[50]

During the first five months of the following year, the advocates of immediate secession conducted an intense propaganda campaign. But few voters participated in the election of state convention delegates in February, as the campaign was almost wholly devoid of interest. A large majority of those elected, however, favored immediate secession.[51] Rhett redefined the issue for the Charleston Southern Rights Association on 7 April by declaring his opposition to a general southern convention. "Southern cooperation is at an end. . . . A Southern Congress now would be our ruin. . . . It would counsel submission or secession by South Carolina alone." He presented three main arguments for the latter course: the temperamental one—a state must defend her rights, regardless of cost; the diplomatic—self-preservation would force other southern states to take sides with the seceder whether they wanted to or not; the commercial—South Carolina might deflect all southern trade from the North by charging a much lower duty than the Federal government.[52]

The secession agitation reached its peak in May, when the local Southern Rights Associations held a convention in Charleston. Senator Butler presented the arguments of the cooperationists very forcefully. He charged that the policy of his opponents was virtually a coercion of the other southern states through their economic and emotional interests. No South Carolinian, foreseeing the economic consequences of secession, would place his state in this position if he did not believe circumstances would force other southern states to come to her aid. To force a sovereign state to take a position against its consent, however, was to create a reluctant associate. Both interest and honor required that the southern states take counsel together. Representative Orr added that secession alone would cause two-thirds of Charleston's commerce to disappear and bring about economic decay in the interior of the state. An attempt to force other southern states might defeat the establishment of a Southern Confederacy by an "inconsiderate zeal to thrash off blushing fruit" before it was ready. Although the convention adopted resolutions that support of the other southern states was desirable but not indispensable, this meeting marks the ultimate downfall of the single-state secessionists.[53]

With the arguments of the two opposing sides well defined, a battle of words in newspapers, speeches, and pamphlets took place between May and October, the date for the election of delegates to a southern congress. Starting in Charleston, "the soul of resistance to immediate secession," and Greenville in the up-country, the cooperation leaders gradually organized support and gained converts throughout the state. These leaders spoke for a nationalized South—a South of related interests and institutions with a common destiny—as opposed to an older viewpoint of states' rights in 1830. Their ultimate goal was the formation of a Southern Confederacy, and therefore separate secession was not only foolhardy but unpatriotic. Surely John C. Calhoun, whose great dream was the unity of the South, would have been a leader on the cooperation side. Christopher W. Dubley pointed out that the other southern states had met with South Carolina at Nashville with the assurance that she would not take the lead in secession. Would not South Carolina's taking a different course from that agreed upon in common counsel be a breach of faith with the other southern states?[54]

At a public rally, on the stormy night of 29 July in Charleston, called by the cooperationist majority of St. Philip and St. Michael Southern Rights Association, Barnwell and Butler spoke in opposition to separate state secession. A participant read a letter from Cheves which stated that separate secession was an "undoubted legal and public right" but "scarcely a moral and social one on the part of one southern state in reference to her sister states in the South." Both this meeting and the May convention of Southern Rights Associations indicate the importance of Charleston, where businessmen had begun to voice fears of economic disaster. What would happen if the Federal government blockaded the coast of the state, and Charleston's trade was diverted to Savannah or Wilmington?[55]

The last round in the struggle over secession occurred in the two months between the July meeting and the election. Barnwell wrote Orr on 25 August that he had told the secessionists that the contest would lose its bitterness if they would agree not to secede until two-thirds of the people desired such action. If the secessionists, however, insisted on using their majority in the state convention to plunge South Carolina into "the gulf of ruin," the cooperationists must oppose them "tooth and nail." Although the other southern states had not answered the call for a southern congress and no one expected it to meet, both the secessionists and cooperationists were willing to hold the election as a test of opinion to decide whether the people wanted to secede or remain in the Union.[56]

The cooperationists carried six of the seven congressional districts and received almost twice as many votes as the secessionists did in an outstanding victory on 13 and 14 October. The distribution of the vote for and against secession is significant. The secessionists were victorious only in the seventh congressional district in the southwest corner of the state, Rhett's former congressional district. In Charleston they received only 1,018 votes compared to 2,454 for the cooperationists, yet they carried all except three of the low-country parishes. The cooperationists received more votes in the up-country and in the districts with a higher percentage of whites. The election was, therefore, a clear victory for southern nationalism and a repudiation of the proposed course of the secessionists. Although the right of secession was "fundamental and indisputable," the exercise of it by a single state without the concurrence and support of the other states was not a proper remedy. Governor John H. Means lamented, "The noble attitude of resistance which I supposed the State about to assume . . . seems to have been delayed or abandoned."[57]

Although the original purpose of the state convention was

now void, the legislature of 1851, in which the secessionists had a majority, set the meeting for 26 April 1852. Both single-state secession and cooperation were dead for the present; therefore the preservation of the doctrine of secession was all that could possibly be accomplished. The convention adopted two resolutions to the effect that South Carolina had ample justification to secede, but her decision to remain in the Union was for reasons of expediency; secession remained a legal right of the states. South Carolina had thus yielded. Most of the state's leaders regarded the convention as a humiliation and an embarrassment; Hammond described the results as "too pitiful for comment." Since the action of the convention had imposed submission on South Carolina, Rhett considered himself no proper representative and promptly resigned his seat in the United States Senate.[58]

Thus the movement for southern unity had collapsed. The crisis had passed, the South had acquiesced on condition, and the Union was saved. Ironically, the Georgia Platform united the South more successfully than the Nashville Platform. Why? Because the Georgia Platform was an acceptance of the adjustment within the Union—the southern consensus in 1850. It represented the restoration of tranquility in place of agitation, a sincere desire of most southerners. Yet at the same time the Georgia Platform saved southern pride and honor, upheld the legal right of secession, and placed the responsibility for the maintenance of the Union and peace on the North. In contrast, the Nashville Platform was an unrealistic, impractical solution, unacceptable to the North and contrary to the southern position of congressional noninterference of slavery in the territories. If Congress had, however, failed to pass the Compromise measures, the action of the Georgia convention remains a moot question. Certainly there would have been no Georgia Platform such as the one that was adopted, because there would have been no Compromise to accept.

The significant question in this connection is to what extent, if any, the Nashville Convention influenced the passage of the Compromise and in turn the Georgia Platform. Undoubtedly, the convention did influence the passage of the

Compromise, but that is not to say there would have been no Compromise but for the Nashville Convention. The fact that southerners had met and consulted, declared their rights in the territorial controversy, and agreed to meet again is the most important thing to note. During the heated deliberations on the Compromise, Congress never lost sight of this fact. Since moderation had prevailed at Nashville, the convention strengthened the forces of those in Congress who favored the Compromise. Yet there was always the expressed threat of what might happen at the second session if the crisis had not resolved in a manner satisfactory to the South.

Although the Nashville Convention had failed in its most important purpose of uniting the South (realizing Calhoun's dream) against northern aggression, it was not a failure. Paradoxically, the coalition of most Whigs and Union Democrats that opposed the convention was the basis for the nonpartisan Constitutional Union party that united most—but not all—of the South behind the Georgia Platform or conditional acceptance of the Compromise.

Moreover, southerners had weighed the merits of secession and avowed their devotion to the Union. Voices of moderation tempered those of the fire-eaters; careful consideration of the consequences of secession balanced passions inflamed by rhetoric. A confrontation between idealism and pragmatism, the Nashville Convention recorded little concrete accomplishment. Yet as David Potter has pointed out the convention proved an obstacle to secession.

Simultaneously, the Nashville Convention paved the way for a Southern Confederacy in 1861. Southern nationalists had realized the difficulty of securing the cooperation of all the southern states in the defense of southern rights, and southern fire-eaters had learned their lesson well at Nashville. From 1850 on they eschewed cooperation and advocated single state action. Devotion to an ideal of "southern honor" and respect for Calhoun's dream were not enough for the rest of the southern states; henceforth there would be no more conventions.

The nation, however, had also learned something: the South as a whole was a region that demanded only her constitutional rights—no more, no less. She urgently wanted to maintain the Union and would make more than her share of concessions to do so. Secession was a most undesirable last resort, to be used only in the face of intolerable aggression. As in 1832, no other southern state was willing to join South Carolina, who alone undoubtedly would have taken the fatal step in 1850 if assured of southern cooperation. But at the same time, most southerners retained the belief that secession was a legal right of the states. In this respect the South was probably more unified than in any other. By the terms of the Compromise the North was the real gainer; if and when it failed to maintain the bargain, the South stood ready to exercise this right.

# *Appendices*

# *Appendix A*

## *Delegates Chosen to the First Session*[1]

### Alabama

Chosen by the "legislative convention" 6 and 7 February 1850:

*For the State at large*—James Abercrombie†, John A. Campbell†, Nicholas Davis, Benjamin Fitzpatrick†, Thomas J. Judge†, William Mitchell Murphy†, Leroy Pope Walker†, John A. Winston†

*First Congressional District*—T. B. Bethea†, Burwell Boykin†, W. D. Dunn, Robert V. Montague

*Second District*—Jefferson Buford†, George Goldthwaite†, G. W. Gunn†, Reuben C. Shorter†

*Third District*—Andrew B. Moore, W. S. Phillips, Howell Rose, John G. Winer

*Fourth District*—John Erwin, Joshua L. Martin, Joseph W. Taylor, N. L. Whitfield

*Fifth District*—Daniel Coleman, William Cooper, Jesse W. Garth, James H. Weakley

*Sixth District*—George P. Bierne, James M. Gea, James M. Greene, W. O. Winston

*Seventh District*—Charles McLemore, George S. Walden†, Thomas A. Walker†, Alexander White

Substitutes selected at county meetings authorized by the governor:

William Byrd†, Reuben Chapman†, John Starke Hunter†

### Arkansas

Delegates were chosen by county meetings, but most failed to attend. Only two men represented the state in Nashville:

J. H. Powell

Samuel C. Roane

1. Delegates who attended the Nashville meeting in June are indicated with a dagger.

## Florida

Appointed by district conventions:

*Western Judicial District*—E. C. Cabell, James F. McClellan†,
*Middle District*—Charles H. DuPont†, Arthur J. Forman†,
*Eastern District*—Joseph Hernández
*Southern District*—Bird M. Pearson†

## Georgia

Chosen by the legislature 7 February 1850:

*For the State at large*—William Law, Charles Daugherty, M.H. McAllister, Charles J. McDonald†

Elected by the people 2 April 1850:

*First Congressional District*—James M. Cooper, George M. Troup
*Second District*—Henry L. Benning†, Martin J. Crawford†
*Third District*—Obediah Gibson†, James J. Scarborough
*Fourth District*—Edward G. Hill, Obediah Warner†
*Fifth District*—Simpson Fouche†, H. V. M. Miller
*Sixth District*—William Billups, Junius Hillyer

Substitutes appointed by Governor Towns:

Robert Bledsoe†, Walter T. Colquitt†, Andrew H. Dawson†, Jacob G. McWhertor†, James N. Ramsey†

## Mississippi

Appointed by the October Convention:

*For the State at large*—A. M. Clayton†, H. T. Ellett, G. T. Sturges, William L. Sharkey†
*First Congressional District*—Joseph W. Matthews†, T. J. Word†
*Second District*—J. B. Cobb, T. N. Waul
*Third District*—H. C. Chambers, Edward C. Wilkinson†
*Fourth District*—D. H. Cooper, George Winchester

Elected by the legislature 6 March 1850:

*For the State at large*—S. S. Boyd†, A. M. Clayton†, William L. Sharkey†, Cotesworth Pinckney Smith†
*First Congressional District*—Joseph W. Matthews†, T. J. Word†
*Second District*—G. F. Neil†, G. H. Young
*Third District*—John J. Pettus†, W. R. Miles
*Fourth District*—John J. McRae†, T. Jones Stewart†

## South Carolina

Chosen by the legislative caucus 10 December 1849:
*For the State at large*—Robert W. Barnwell†, Langdon Cheves†, Franklin H. Elmore, James H. Hammond†
Elected by district conventions 6 May 1850:
*First Congressional District*—John A. Bradley†, Samuel Otterson†
*Second District*—Joseph N. Whitner†, Henry C. Young†
*Third District*—James Chesnut, Jr.†, Maxcy Gregg†
*Fourth District*—R. F. W. Allston†, William J. Hanna†
*Fifth District*—Drayton Nance†, Francis W. Pickens†
*Sixth District*—William DuBose†, George A. Trenholm†
*Seventh District*—David F. Jamison†, R. Barnwell Rhett†
Substitute appointed by Governor Seabrook:
J. W. Hayne

## Tennessee

Since the delegates were chosen by county meetings and many failed to attend, this list consists only of those who actually attended. Unidentified delegates are indicated by an asterisk.

George W. Allen
Robert Armstrong
H. S. Atkinson
Washington Barrow
William B. Bate
George W. Bond*
F. W. Brents*
Elijah Boddie
Aaron V. Brown
George W. Buchanan
Thomas Buford
Randolph D. Casey
N. Y. Cavett
L. P. Cheatham
Thomas Claiborne
J. P. Clements
George W. Cunningham
John Dargan
Charles J. Dickenson
Samuel Doke
Andrew J. Donelson
Daniel Donelson
John N. Esselman*
Henry R. Estill
James H. Estill
George Everly
Amasa Ezell
Adam Ferguson
G. B. Fowlks
Edward W. Gantt
George H. Gantt
Callaway C. Garner
Boling Gordon
Isaac M. Gower*
Daniel Graham
James F. Green
R. T. Gupton
William Hall
William B. Hall
William G. Harding
E. W. (or H.) Hickman*
Thomas H. Hickman*
Thomas H. Hopkins
Westly H. Humphreys
L. Hunter (probably John Layton)
Andrew Jackson, Jr.
Thomas Jackson*
A. W. Johnson
Len H. Johnson
John R. Jones
T. J. Kennedy
George T. Malone
John Maxey
Frank McGavock
Jacob McGavock
John McIntosh
F. T. McLaurine
S. B. Moore
William Moore
T. D. Moseley
John T. Neil
A. O. P. Nicholson

D. P. F. Norflett
David R. S. Nowlin
Archibald W. Overton
William Overton
William E. Owen
E. L. Paget (possibly Elijah Padgett)
Patillo Patton (probably P. C.)
James Patterson
Robert G. Payne
Gideon J. Pillow
John Poindexter, Jr.
Edwin Polk
William H. Polk
A. J. Porter*
J. M. Quarles
John E. R. Ray
Felix Robertson
William P. Rowles
Basil B. Satterfield
W. A. Sewell
Thomas Shepard
W. B. Shepherd*
J. J. B. Southall
John Stephens (probably Stevens)
V. K. Stevenson
W. J. Strayhorn
Howell Taylor*
W. E. Venable
James Walker
Richard Warner
Frederick H. Watkins
William E. Watkins
Sam H. Whitthorne
W. C. Whitthorne
J. W. Whitfield
William Williams
Willoughby Williams
Richard A. L. Wilkes
George W. Winchester

## Texas

Elected by the people 4 March 1850:

*First Congressional District*—James Davis, J. Pinckney Henderson†, C. C. Mills, John T. Mills

*Second District*—H. P. Bee, Fielding Jones, J. S. Mayfield, H. G. Runnels

## Virginia

Chosen by district conventions:

*First Congressional District*—Tazewell Taylor, Richard Urquhart

*Second District*—Thomas S. Gholson†, William O. Goode†

*Fourth District*—William C. Flourney, James T. Thorne

*Fifth District*—B. Johnson Barbour, William F. Gordon†

*Sixth District*—James Lyons, Robert G. Scott

*Seventh District*—R. H. Claybrook†, Henry A. Wise (Beverley Tucker†, alternate)

*Eighth District*—Willoughby Newton†, William P. Taylor

# APPENDIX B

## ANALYSIS OF FIRST SESSION DELEGATION

Table 1: Alabama Delegation

| Name | Age | Place of Birth | Education | Party | Residence | Occupation | Public Service or Office Holding | Property Holding |
|---|---|---|---|---|---|---|---|---|
| James Abercrombie | 50 | Hancock County Georgia | Common Schools Read Law | Whig | Russell County | Lawyer Planter | State Leg., Both Houses; Congress, 32nd and 33rd | Wealthy 107 slaves $50,000 |
| T. B. Bethea | 40 | Marion District S. Carolina | Plain education Read Law | Democrat | Wilcox Co. | Lawyer Planter | State Sen., 1853; State H.R., 1863-67 | 116 slaves $40,000 |
| Burwell Boykin | 37 | Kershaw District S. Carolina | Graduated Univ. of Alabama | Democrat | Mobile | Lawyer Merchant | State Leg., Dallas Co. twice | 9 slaves No real estate listed |
| Jefferson Buford | 43 | Chester District S. Carolina | Read Law | Whig Democrat | Barbour Co. | Lawyer & prominent political leader Planter | Attempted to settle proslavery advocates in Kansas but failed; Secession Convention last part | 26 slaves $3,500 |

Table 1: Alabama (continued)

| Name | Age | Place of Birth | Education | Party | Residence | Occupation | Public Service or Office Holding | Property Holding |
|---|---|---|---|---|---|---|---|---|
| William M. Byrd | 32 | Perry Co. Mississippi | Miss. College at Clinton & Grad. La-grange Col. 1838 Law | Whig | Marengo Co. Linden | Lawyer | State H.R., Assoc. Jus-tice, State Supreme Ct., 1865 until displaced by Cong. Recon-struction | 15 slaves $11,600 |
| John A. Campbell | 39 | Wilkes Co. Georgia | Grad. Frank-lin Col. 1826, West Point Law | Democrat | Mobile | Lawyer | State Leg.; Assoc. Jus., US Supreme Ct., 1853-61 | 17 slaves $35,000 |
| Reuben Chapman | 56 | Caroline County Virginia | Academy in Virginia Read Law | Democrat | Madison Co. Huntsville | Lawyer Farmer | State Sen.; Congress, 1835-47; Governor, 1847-49; State H.R.; Confederate rep. to France, 1862 | 10 slaves $20,000 |
| Daniel Coleman | 48 | Caroline Co. Virginia | Graduated Transylvania University | Democrat | Athens Limestone Co. | Mercantile Business | State H.R.; Circuit Judge; State Supreme Ct., 1851 | 60 slaves $20,000 |

Table 1: Alabama (continued)

| Name | Age | Place of Birth | Education | Party | Residence | Occupation | Public Service or Office Holding | Property Holding |
|---|---|---|---|---|---|---|---|---|
| William Cooper | 48 | Brunswick County Virginia | Graduated Univ. of Nashville, Read law under Ephriam Foster | Whig | Franklin Co. | Lawyer Planter | Atty. for Chickasaws; Bank commissioner; Sent to Missouri during secession movement | 34 slaves $3,500 |
| Nicholas Davis, Sr. | 69 | Hanover Co. Virginia | Law school | Whig | Limestone County | Planter | 1st State Const. Conv.; State Leg., Both Houses; Mexican War; Secession Convention; Confed. Cong. | 65 slaves $31,840 |
| John L. Erwin | 50 | Pendleton County Virginia | Read Law | Whig Changed to Democrat 1840 | Greene Co. | Lawyer Planter | State Leg., Both Houses; Presided, bolting wing, Charleston Convention | 127 slaves $20,000 |
| Benajmin Fitzpatrick | 47 | Greene Co. Georgia | Read Law | Democrat | Autauga Co. | Lawyer Planter | Solicitor; Governor, 1841-45; U.S. Senator 1848, '53-61; Presided, Ala. Const. Conv, 1865 | 106 slaves $20,000 |

Table 1: Alabama (continued)

| Name | Age | Place of Birth | Education | Party | Residence | Occupation | Public Service or Office Holding | Property Holding |
|---|---|---|---|---|---|---|---|---|
| George Goldthwaite | 41 | Massachusetts | Military School Davis, Lee L. Polk and J. E. Johnson Read Law | Democrat | Montgomery County | Lawyer (Jurist) Planter | Judge State Supreme Ct.; Adj. Gen. Ala. during Civil War; U.S. Senator 1870-77 | 119 slaves $34,000 |
| G. W. Gunn | 40 | Georgia | | Whig | Macon Co. | Lawyer Baptist Minister | State Senate, 1849-51 | 17 slaves $40,000 |
| John Starke Hunter | 51 | Near Camden Kershaw District S. Carolina | Graduated S. Carolina College Law | Democrat Whig (1850) | Dallas Co. Cahaba | Lawyer Planter | Cir. Judge; Presided, First Whig Conv., 1840 | 201 slaves $40,000 |
| Thomas J. Judge | 34 | Richland District S. Carolina | Early schooling meager Read Law | Whig | Lowndes or Montgomery Co. | Lawyer | State Leg., Both Houses; CSA; Judge, Conf. Ala. Mil. Ct.; Judge, Ala. Supreme Ct. | 9 slaves $1,200 |
| William Mitchell Murphy | 44 | N. Carolina Granville County | Univ. of Ala. and Univ. of Virginia | Whig | Greene Co. | Lawyer Planter | State H.R., 1840; State Sen., 1849-51 | 24 slaves $10,000 |

Table 1: Alabama (continued)

| Name | Age | Place of Birth | Education | Party | Residence | Occupation | Public Service or Office Holding | Property Holding |
|---|---|---|---|---|---|---|---|---|
| Reuben C. Shorter | 63 | Culpeper Co. Virginia | Univ. of Pennsylvania | Democrat | Eufaula Barbour Co. | Physician Planter Legislator | State Leg., Both Houses; Major Gen., Ga. Militia | 90 slaves $3,400 |
| George S. Walden | 35 | Georgia | | | Cherokee Co. | Lawyer | None | 4 slaves $800 |
| Leroy Pope Walker | 33 | Madison Co. Alabama | "Thorough"; Univ. of Ala. & Va. Law | Democrat | Lauderdale Co. | Lawyer | State H.R.; Sec. of War, Confederate Cabinet; CSA; Judge, Military Ct. | 4 slaves $10,000 |
| Thomas A. Walker | 39 | Jasper Co. Georgia | Graduated Univ. of Ala. 1833 | | Benton Co. | Lawyer | State Leg.; Both Houses; Cir. Judge; Pres. Selma & Rome RR | 14 slaves $35,000 |
| John A. Winston | 38 | Madison Co. Alabama | Lagrange College & Univ. of Nashville | Democrat | Sumter Co. | Planter | State Leg.; Both Houses; Mexican War; Gov. 1855; Delegate, Charleston Dem. Conv., 1860; CSA | 98 slaves |

Table 2: Arkansas Delegation

| Name | Age | Place of Birth | Education | Party | Residence | Occupation | Public Service or Office Holding | Property Holding |
|---|---|---|---|---|---|---|---|---|
| Samuel C. Roane | 46 | N. Carolina | "Not neglected" | Democrat | Jefferson Co. | Planter Lawyer | U.S. Dist. Atty., AR Terr ; Judge of 1st Terr Ct.; State Const. Conv.; Pres. 1st State Senate | 86 slaves $15,000 Real estate |

Table 3: Florida Delegation

| Name | Age | Place of Birth | Education | Party | Residence | Occupation | Public Service or Office Holding | Property Holding |
|---|---|---|---|---|---|---|---|---|
| Charles H. DuPont | 45 | S. Carolina | | Democrat | Quincy, Gadsden Co. | Attorney | Justice and Chief Just., Supreme Ct. of Florida | 73 slaves $37,000 |
| Arthur J. Forman | 42 | Maryland | | Whig | Quincy, Gadsden Co. | Planter | None | 100 slaves $22,500 |
| James F. McClellan | 26 | Tennessee | | Democrat | Jackson Co. | Lawyer | Made 2nd Digest of FL Laws; Judge, Circuit Ct. | Not on slave census No real estate |

Table 3: Florida Delegation

| Name | Age | Place of Birth | Education | Party | Residence | Occupation | Public Service or Office Holding | Property Holding |
|---|---|---|---|---|---|---|---|---|
| Bird M. Pearson | 43 | S. Carolina | | Democrat | Benton Co. | Lawyer Planter | SC State's Attorney; Just., FL Supreme Ct. | 30 slaves $5,000 |

Table 4: Georgia Delegation

| Name | Age | Place of Birth | Education | Party | Residence | Occupation | Public Service or Office Holding | Property Holding |
|---|---|---|---|---|---|---|---|---|
| Henry L. Benning | 36 | Columbia County, Georgia | Graduated Univ. of GA Adm. to bar 1835 | Democrat | Muskogee County | Lawyer | Sol. Gen.; Gen. Assembly; Assoc. Just.; GA Sup. Ct. 1853-59; Secession Convention; CSArmy | 60 slaves $10,000 |
| Robert Bledsoe | 60 | Virginia | | Whig | Putnam Co. | Farmer | Brig. Gen.; 1st Brigade, 3rd Div., GA Militia, 1833-44 | 57 slaves $2,884 |

Table 4: Georgia (continued)

| Name | Age | Place of Birth | Education | Party | Residence | Occupation | Public Service or Office Holding | Property Holding |
|---|---|---|---|---|---|---|---|---|
| Walter T. Colquitt | 50 | Georgia or Halifax Co., Virginia | Local schools College of New Jersey Read Law Adm. to bar 1820 | Democrat | Columbus, Muskogee Co. | Lawyer | Cir. Judge; State Leg., Both Houses; Congress, 1839-40 & 1842-43 | 34 slaves $10,000 |
| Martin J. Crawford | 30 | Jasper Co., Georgia | Brownwood Institute & Mercer Univ., Macon, GA Read Law Adm. to bar 1839 | Whig | Columbus, Muskogee Co. | Lawyer | State H.R.; Judge Superior Ct.; Congress 1855-61; Confed. Prov. Cong., 1861-62; State Supreme Ct. | 45 slaves No real estate |
| Andrew H. Dawson | 30 | Kentucky | | Democrat | Richmond County | Lawyer | None | Not on slave census No real estate |
| Simpson Fouche | 43 | Georgia | | Democrat | Floyd Co. | Newspaper Editor | Delegate, RR Conv., 1849; Secession Convention | No slaves Real estate? |

Table 4: Georgia (continued)

| Name | Age | Place of Birth | Education | Party | Residence | Occupation | Public Service or Office Holding | Property Holding |
|---|---|---|---|---|---|---|---|---|
| Obediah C. Gibson | 42 | Georgia | | Democrat | Thomaston, Upson Co. | Lawyer Farmer or Planter | State Senator, 1837-38, Upson Co.; State Senator, 1855-56, Pike Co. | 14 slaves $4,500 1,390 acres |
| Charles J. McDonald | 57 | Charleston, S. Carolina | S. Carolina College, Graduated 1816 Adm. to bar 1817 | Democrat | Cobb Co. | Farmer Lawyer | Sol. Gen.; State Leg., Both Houses; Governor, 1839-43; Assoc. Just. GA Sup. Ct. | 18 slaves $38,500 360 acres |
| Jacob G. McWhertor | 61 | S. Carolina | | Democrat | Augusta? Richmond Co. | Doctor? Farmer or Planter | None | 15 slaves $18,000 2,510 acres |
| James N. Ramsey | 29 | Georgia | | Whig | Harris Co. | Lawyer | State H.R., 1845-47; State Sen., 1863-65; Secession Convention | 10 slaves $4,500 |
| Obediah Warner | 39 | | | Democrat | Meriwether County | Lawyer | Judge Superior Ct.; Const. Conv., 1865; State H.R., 1875-76 | Not on slave census Not on census record |

Table 5: Mississippi Delegation

| Name | Age | Place of Birth | Education | Party | Residence | Occupation | Public Service or Office Holding | Property Holding |
|---|---|---|---|---|---|---|---|---|
| S. S. Boyd | 40 | Portland, Maine | Highly Educated | Whig | Natchez, Adams Co. | Judge Lawyer Planter | State Leg., Both Houses | 79 slaves $15,000 |
| Alexander M. Clayton | 49 | Campbell County, Virginia | In Virginia Law | Democrat | Marshall Co. | Lawyer Judge Planter | Judge, MS High Ct. of Errors & Appeals; US Consul, Cuba; Secession Convention; Prov. Conf. Congress | 65 slaves $28,000 |
| Joseph W. Matthews | 43 | TN? or AL? or NC? | Limited | Democrat | Marshall Co. | Planter | State Leg., Both Houses; Governor 1849-50 | 48 slaves $25,000 |
| John J. McRae | 35 | Sansboro, NC(or Sneedsboro) | Frederick School at Pascagoula, MS, Grad. Miami Univ., Ohio; Law | Democrat | Clarke Co. | Lawyer Editor | State H.R.; Congress, Both Houses; Governor, 1853-57; CSArmy | 15 slaves $1,500 |
| G. F. Neil | 39 | Tennessee | | Democrat | Carrollton, Carroll Co. | Farmer | State H.R., 1848, 1850; State Senate, 1858-65; CSArmy | Not on slave census $6,000 |

Table 5: Mississippi (continued)

| Name | Age | Place of Birth | Education | Party | Residence | Occupation | Public Service or Office Holding | Property Holding |
|---|---|---|---|---|---|---|---|---|
| John J. Pettus | 37 | Wilson Co., Tennessee | Read Law | Democrat | Kemper Co. | Farmer Lawyer | State Leg., Both Houses; Governor 5 da., 1854; War governor | 24 slaves $900 |
| William L. Sharkey | 51 | Sumner Co., Tennessee | College at Greeneville, Tennessee; Read Law at Lebanon | Old Line Whig | Hinds Co. | Lawyer Jurist | State H.R.; Chief Just., High Ct. of Errors & Appeals; Reconstruc. Governor June-Oct., 1865 | 18 slaves $25,000 |
| Cotesworth Pinckney Smith | 50 | Natchez District MS or SC | Read Law | Whig Democrat? | Wilkinson County | Lawyer | State Leg., Both Houses; High Ct. Errors & Appeals & Chief Just. 1851-62; CSArmy | 1 slave $1,180 |
| T. Jones Stewart | 51 | Tennessee | | Whig | Wilkinson County | Planter | None | 184 slaves $22,398 |
| Edward C. Wilkinson | 46 | Virginia | Read Law | Probably Whig | Yazoo City, Yazoo Co. | Lawyer | Board of Trustees, U. of MS; Cir. Judge | 55 slaves $15,000 |

Table 5: Mississippi (continued)

| Name | Age | Place of Birth | Education | Party | Residence | Occupation | Public Service or Office Holding | Property Holding |
|---|---|---|---|---|---|---|---|---|
| T. J. Word | 41 | Surrey Co., North Carolina | Educated and admitted to bar in N. Carolina | Whig | Marshall Co. | Lawyer | NC H.R., 1832; Congress, May, 1838–March, 1839 | Not on slave census $16,000 |

Table 6: South Carolina Delegation

| Name | Age | Place of Birth | Education | Party | Residence | Occupation | Public Service or Office Holding | Property Holding |
|---|---|---|---|---|---|---|---|---|
| R. F. W. Allston | 49 | All Saints Parish S. Carolina | Graduated West Point 1821 | Democrat | Georgetown County | Rice Planter | State Leg.; Governor, 1856–58 | 401 slaves $130,000 |
| Robert W. Barnwell | 50 | Beaufort, S. Carolina | Graduated Harvard 1812; Law | Democrat | Beaufort | Lawyer Planter Educator Pres. SC College | State Leg.; Congress, Both Houses | 43 slaves in Beaufort 34 in Colleton $12,500 2,275 acres |
| John A. Bradley | 40 | S. Carolina | | | Chester Co. | Merchant Farmer | Sheriff; State H.R. 1838–40; Com. at Chester to raise RR stock | 6 slaves $5,000 48 acres |

Table 6: South Carolina (continued)

| Name | Age | Place of Birth | Education | Party | Residence | Occupation | Public Service or Office Holding | Property Holding |
|---|---|---|---|---|---|---|---|---|
| James Chesnut, Jr. | 35 | Near Camden, S. Carolina | Graduated Princeton 1835; Law | Democrat | Camden, Kershaw Co. | Lawyer Planter | State Leg., Both Houses; U.S. Senate | 68 slaves $108,000 250 acres |
| Langdon Cheves | 74 | Abbeville District, S. Carolina | Read Law | Democrat | Charleston & Beaufort | Lawyer Planter Financier | State Leg.; Congress; Judge; Pres. U.S. Bank | 284 slaves |
| William DuBose | 63 | St. Stephen Parish, S. Carolina | Graduated Yale 1807; Law | | St. Stephen Parish Pineville, Charleston County | Lawyer Planter | Local Offices; State Leg., Both Houses; Lt. Gov. | 165 slaves $12,000 3,800 acres |
| Maxcy Gregg | 35 | Columbia, S. Carolina | S. Carolina College Law | Democrat | Columbia, Richland Co. | Lawyer | No offices held; Military career | Not on slave census No real estate |
| James H. Hammond | 42 | Newberry District, S. Carolina | Graduated S. Carolina College, 1825 Law | Democrat | Barnwell Co. | Lawyer Planter | Congress, Both Houses; Governor, 1842-44 | 237 slaves $100,000 10,000 acres |
| William J. Hanna | 45 | York District, S. Carolina | Academic Education Law | | Chesterfield County | Lawyer | SC Militia; Local Offices; State Senate; Solicitor | 29 slaves $4,000 |

Table 6: South Carolina (continued)

| Name | Age | Place of Birth | Education | Party | Residence | Occupation | Public Service or Office Holding | Property Holding |
|---|---|---|---|---|---|---|---|---|
| David F. Jamison | 39 | Orangeburg District, S. Carolina | S. Carolina College Law | Democrat | Orangeburg Co. Orange Parish | Planter Lawyer Scholar Writer | State H.R. | 65 slaves $12,000 |
| Drayton Nance | 45 | S. Carolina | Univ. of S. Carolina Graduated 1821 | | Newberry, Newberry Co. | Lawyer RR director Farmer | Commis-sioner's Office in Equity | 19 slaves $13,000 |
| Samuel Otterson | 58 | S. Carolina | | | Spartanburg Co., Limestone Springs | Doctor | State H.R., 1846-48 | 26 slaves $13,000 |
| Francis W. Pickens | 46 | St. Paul's Parish, Colleton County, S. Carolina | Franklin College (Now U. of GA) & S. Carolina College Law | Democrat | Edgefield Co. | Lawyer Planter | State Leg., Both Houses; Congress; Governor 1860-62; Minister to Russia | 299 slaves $90,000 |
| Robert B. Rhett | 49 | Beaufort, S. Carolina | Law | Democrat | St. Barth's Parish, Colleton County | Lawyer Planter | State Leg.; U.S. Senate; State Atty. General | 306 slaves $50,000 |
| George A. Trenholm | 44 | Charleston, S. Carolina | Left school and sought employment early | | Charleston | Merchant Financier Planter | State Leg.; 1852-56; CSA Sec. of Treas., 1864-65 | Not on Charleston or Colleton slave census $60,000 |

Table 6: South Carolina (continued)

| Name | Age | Place of Birth | Education | Party | Residence | Occupation | Public Service or Office Holding | Property Holding |
|---|---|---|---|---|---|---|---|---|
| Joseph Whitner | 51 | Pickens County, S. Carolina | Graduated S. Carolina College, 1818 Law | Democrat | Anderson Co. | Lawyer Solicitor Planter | State Leg. Both Houses; Solicitor W. Jud. Circuit | 78 slaves $20,500 3,000 acres |
| Henry C. Young | 50 | N. Carolina | Limited Read Law | | Laurens Co. | Lawyer | State H.R. 1830-38, State Senator 1842-46 | Not on slave census $10,000 |

Table 7: Tennessee Delegation

| Name | Age | Place of Birth | Education | Party | Residence | Occupation | Public Service or Office Holding | Property Holding |
|---|---|---|---|---|---|---|---|---|
| George W. Allen | 28 | Tennessee | | | Sumner Co. | Lawyer | | No slaves No real estate |
| Robert Armstrong | 57 | Abingdon, Virginia | | Democrat | Davidson Co. | Military (Creek War, New Orleans) Brig. Gen. 2nd Seminole War | Postmaster Nashville; U.S. Consul. to Liverpool; Prop. of Wash. _Union_ | No slaves |

Table 7: Tennessee (continued)

| Name | Age | Place of Birth | Education | Party | Residence | Occupation | Public Service or Office Holding | Property Holding |
|---|---|---|---|---|---|---|---|---|
| H. S. Atkinson | 40 | Tennessee | | | Nashville, Davidson Co. | Carpenter Builder | | 6 slaves $10,000 |
| Washington Barrow | 43 | Davidson Co. Tennessee | | Whig | Edgefield or S. Nash., Davidson Co. | Lawyer President, Gas Co. | 1st Pres. Nashville Gas Co.; Minister to Portugal; Cong. (H.R.), 1847–49; Ed. N. Banner; Gen. Assembly, 1860–61 | No slaves No real estate |
| William B. Bate | 23 | Castalian Springs, Tennessee | | Whig | Sumner Co. | Farmer | Gen. Assem. 1849–51; Dist. Atty. General; Governor; U.S. Sen.; Mexican War; Newspaper Ed.; Maj. Gen., CSArmy | No slaves No real estate |
| Elijah Boddie | 63 | Nash Co., N. Carolina | | Democrat | Gallatin, Sumner Co. | Lawyer Farmer | Gen. Assem. 1827–29, '31–33, '35–37, '43–45; Sumner Co. Court | 16 slaves $18,000 |

Table 7: Tennessee (continued)

| Name | Age | Place of Birth | Education | Party | Residence | Occupation | Public Service or Office Holding | Property Holding |
|---|---|---|---|---|---|---|---|---|
| Aaron V. Brown | 54 | Virginia | U. of NC Read Law | Democrat | Davidson Co. | Planter Lawyer | Both Houses Gen. Assem. 1821-25, '31-33, Cong. (H.R.) 1839-45; Governor; Postmaster General | 20 slaves $30,000 210 acres |
| George W. Buchanan | 29 | Franklin Co., Tennessee | | Democrat | Shelbyville, Bedford Co. | Lawyer | Mexican War, Gen. Assem., 1849-1851; CSArmy | No slaves No real estate |
| Thomas Buford | 36 | Giles Co., Tennessee | | Democrat | Lynnville, Giles Co. | Farmer | Gen. Assem. 1849-51, '53-55; Gen. Assembly of MS; 1st Pres. N & Decatur RR | No slaves $20,000 |
| Randolph D. Casey | 40 | N. Carolina | | | Hardeman Co. | Farmer | | No slaves $2,000 |
| N. Y. Cavett | | | | | Weakley Co. | | | No slaves |
| L. P. Cheatham | 58 | Virginia | | | Nashville, Davidson Co. | Deputy of Co. Court Clerk | | 5 slaves No real estate |

Table 7: Tennessee (continued)

| Name | Age | Place of Birth | Education | Party | Residence | Occupation | Public Service or Office Holding | Property Holding |
|---|---|---|---|---|---|---|---|---|
| Thomas Claiborne | 70 | Brunswick Co., VA | "Common schools," VA; Read Law, Nashville | Democrat | Davidson Co. | Lawyer | War of 1812; Gen. Assem. 1811-15, '31- 33; Mayor of Nashville; Cong. (H.R.) 1817-19 | No slaves $8,000 |
| J. B. Clements | 50 | S. Carolina | | | Edgefield, Davidson Co. | Surveyor City & Supt. of City Cemetery | | 6 slaves $175 Livestock |
| George W. Cunningham | 48 | N. Carolina | | | Bedford Co. | Farmer | | 4 slaves $10,000 |
| John Dargan | 59 | N. Carolina | | | Henry Co. | Farmer | | No slaves $1,500 |
| Charles J. Dickerson | 29 | Illinois | | | Columbia, Maury Co. | Newspaper Editor, Lawyer | Delegate to Memphis RR Conv. 1849 | No real estate |
| Samuel Doke | 48 | Kentucky | | | Bedford Co. | Planter | | 24 slaves $10,000 |

Table 7: Tennessee (continued)

| Name | Age | Place of Birth | Education | Party | Residence | Occupation | Public Service or Office Holding | Property Holding |
|---|---|---|---|---|---|---|---|---|
| Andrew J. Donelson | 50 | Sumner Co., Tennessee | Cumberland College, West Point, Law at Transylvania Univ. | Democrat | Davidson Co. | Lawyer Planter | FL (Mil.) Campaign; Secy., Pres. Jackson; Know Nothing Candidate for Vice Pres.; Minister to Prussia; Ed. Wash. Union | 66 slaves $47,000 1,200 acres |
| Daniel Donelson | 48 | Sumner Co., Tennessee | West Point | Democrat | Sumner Co. | Farmer Military | Gen. Assem., 1842-43, 1855-59; Speaker of House, 1857-59; Deleg. Dem. Nat. Conv., Baltimore, 1860; Brig. Gen. CSArmy | No slaves |
| John N. Esselman | | | | | Davidson Co. | Physician | | No slaves |
| Henry R. Estill | 28 | Tennessee | | | Franklin Co. | Physician | | 1 slave $600 |
| James H. Estill | 52 | Virginia | | | Franklin Co. | Farmer | | 6 slaves $10,000 104 acres |

Table 7: Tennessee (continued)

| Name | Age | Place of Birth | Education | Party | Residence | Occupation | Public Service or Office Holding | Property Holding |
|---|---|---|---|---|---|---|---|---|
| George Everly | 57 | Virginia | | | Giles Co. | Farmer | | No slaves<br>$7,250 |
| Amasa Ezell | 42 | S. Carolina | | Democrat | Giles Co. | Farmer | | 16 slaves<br>$4,000 |
| Adam Ferguson | 51 | N. Carolina | | | Smith Co. | Planter | | 24 slaves<br>$6,000 |
| G. B. Fowlks | 36 | Tennessee | | | Hickman Co. | Carpenter | | 6 slaves<br>$1,500 |
| Edward W. Gantt | 22 | Tennessee | | | Maury Co. | Lawyer | | No real estate |
| George Gantt | 24 | Tennessee | | | Maury Co. | Lawyer | Gen. Assem. 1849-51, '59-61; Pres. elector 1860; Lt. Col. CSArmy | No real estate |
| Callaway C. Garner | 50 | Rutherford County, N. Carolina | | | Franklin Co. | Farmer | | 18 slaves<br>$3,500<br>155 acres |
| Boling Gordon | 49 | Nashville, Tennessee | Excellent educ. in Nashville | Democrat | Hickman Co. | Planter | Both Houses Gen. Assem., 1829-37, '43-45; State Constitu. Convention 1834, 1870 | 48 slaves<br>$8,000<br>Plantation "Cottage Hill" |

Table 7: Tennessee (continued)

| Name | Age | Place of Birth | Education | Party | Residence | Occupation | Public Service or Office Holding | Property Holding |
|---|---|---|---|---|---|---|---|---|
| Daniel Graham | 61 | N. Carolina | Univ. of N. Carolina Read Law | Democrat | Davidson Co. | Planter | Sec. of State, TN, 1818-30; Register of U.S. Treas., 1847-48 | 44 slaves 921 acres |
| James F. Green | 54 | Virginia | | | Franklin Co. | Planter | | 34 slaves $4,500 865 acres |
| R. T. Gupton | 38 | Tennessee | | | Montgomery Co. | Farmer | | No slaves No real estate. |
| William Hall | 75 | N. Carolina | | | Sumner Co. | Planter | Gen. Assem., 1797-1805, 1821-29; Governor, 16 Apr 1829-1 Oct 1829, Cong., 1831 | 49 slaves $17,500 700 acres |
| William B. Hall | 52 | N. Carolina | | Democrat | Lawrence Co. | Planter | | 91 slaves $6,000 |
| William G. Harding | 41 | Tennessee near Nashville | Grad. of Amer. Lit. & Science Academy, Middletown, Conn. | Democrat | Davidson Co. | Planter | | 93 slaves $170,000 4,000 acres Plantation "Belle Meade" |

Table 7: Tennessee (continued)

| Name | Age | Place of Birth | Education | Party | Residence | Occupation | Public Service or Office Holding | Property Holding |
|---|---|---|---|---|---|---|---|---|
| Thomas H. Hopkins | 44 | Kentucky | Read Law | Democrat? | Marion Co. | Lawyer | Gen. Assem.; 1841–43 | No slaves |
| Westly H. Humphreys | 43 | Williamson County, Tennessee | Read Law | | Fayette or Davidson Co. | Lawyer Jurist Writer | Gen. Assem. 1835-37; Constitu. Conv., 1834; Atty. Gen., TN; U.S. Dist. Judge; Judge CSA | No slaves Real estate? |
| L. Hunter (poss. John Layton Hunter) | 52 | Tennessee | | | Davidson Co. | Farmer | | Poss. 1 slave $2,000 |
| Andrew Jackson, Jr. | 40 | Tennessee near Hermitage, Adopted son of President Jackson | Graduated Univ. of Nashville | Democrat | The Hermitage, Davidson Co. | Planter Lawyer | | 137 slaves $50,000 1,000 acres |
| A. W. Johnson | 53 | New Hampshire | "Common Schools," Cumberland College | Democrat? | Edgefield, Davidson Co. | Merchant (wholesale commission business) Farmer | TN Militia, 1829; bank director; Gen. Assem., 1855–57 | 15 slaves $60,000 250 acres |

Table 7: Tennessee (continued)

| Name | Age | Place of Birth | Education | Party | Residence | Occupation | Public Service or Office Holding | Property Holding |
|---|---|---|---|---|---|---|---|---|
| L. H. (prob. Len H.) Johnson | 33 | Virginia | | | Montgomery Co. | Farmer | | No slaves $2,650 |
| John R. Jones | 52 | N. Carolina | | | Marshall Co. | Planter | | 41 slaves $8,000 |
| T. J. Kennedy | 50 | Botetourt County, Virginia | Studied Medicine | Democrat | Giles Co. | Physician | General Assembly, 1859-61 | 18 slaves $4,000 |
| George T. Malone | 45 | Virginia | | Democrat | Giles Co. | Farmer | Delegate Dem. State Conv., 1847 | No slaves $9,200 |
| John Maxey | 62 | Virginia | | | Davidson Co. | Physician | | 6 slaves $5,000 $225 livestock |
| Frank McGavock | 56 | Wythe Co., Virginia | Univ. of Nashville | | Davidson Co. | Planter | None | 22 slaves $80,000 800 acres |
| Jacob McGavock | 59 | Virginia | | | Cherry St. Nashville, Davidson Co. | Planter | Clerk, U.S. Cir. & Dist. Courts for Nashville District; Creek War | 24 slaves $25,000 |

Table 7: Tennessee (continued)

| Name | Age | Place of Birth | Education | Party | Residence | Occupation | Public Service or Office Holding | Property Holding |
|---|---|---|---|---|---|---|---|---|
| John McIntosh | 54 | Fayette County, Kentucky | Wife taught him to read | Democrat | Nashville, Davidson Co. | Railroad Contractor; In charge State prison more than 30 years | None Military, Battle of Thames | 14 slaves Considerable Plantation in LA (place of deatn) No real estate Tennessee |
| F. T. McLaurine | 39 | Tennessee | | Democrat | Giles Co. | Merchant | Delegate, Dem. State Conv. 1847 | No slaves $6,000 |
| S. B. Moore | 41 | Smith County, Tennessee | Studied Medicine | Democrat | Centerville, Hickman Co. | Physician, Manuf. of Iron | Both Houses, Gen. Assem., 1847-51, '53-55 | 10 slaves Real estate not determined |
| William Moore | 52 | Kentucky | | Democrat | Lincoln Co. | Soldier Politician Farmer | Both Houses, Gen. Assem. 1825-29, 1833-37; President Fayette-ville, Lynchburg & Mulberry Turnpike | 17 slaves No real estate |
| T. D. Moseley | 44 | Tennessee | | | Nashville, Davidson Co. | Lawyer Office Ct. House | | 3 slaves $500 12 acres $175 livestock |

Table 7: Tennessee (continued)

| Name | Age | Place of Birth | Education | Party | Residence | Occupation | Public Service or Office Holding | Property Holding |
|---|---|---|---|---|---|---|---|---|
| John T. Neil | 47 | Georgia | | | Bedford Co. | Clerk Circuit Court | | 11 slaves $13,000 |
| A. O. P. Nicholson | 47 | Tennessee | Studied Medicine 1 year, then law | Democrat | Nashville, Davidson Co. | Lawyer, Newspaper editor | U.S. Senate 1857-61; Chanc. Maury Co. Div.; Pres. State Bank; Chief Just. TN Supreme Court, 1870 | 7 slaves $5,000 |
| D. P. F. Norflett | 47 | Tennessee | | | Montgomery Co. | Physician | | No slaves None |
| David R. S. Nowlin | 28 | Virginia | | | Henry Co. | Physician | | 18 slaves None |
| Archibald W. Overton | 66 | Louisa Co., Virginia | "Common Schools," Kentucky, Graduated Transylvania University, Law under Clay & John Overton | | Smith Co. | Planter Lawyer | Clerk, Sup. Court of Errors & Appeals; Both Houses, Gen. Assem., 1823-25, 1829-31 | 79 slaves $73,000 |

Table 7: Tennessee (continued)

| Name | Age | Place of Birth | Education | Party | Residence | Occupation | Public Service or Office Holding | Property Holding |
|---|---|---|---|---|---|---|---|---|
| William Overton | Bet. 40 & 50 | Montgomery County, Tennessee | Read Law | Democrat | Montgomery Co. | Lawyer Journalist | Editor of Clarksville *Chronicle*; Gen. Assem., 1835-37 | No slaves Real Estate? |
| William E. Owen | 60 | Virginia | | | Davidson Co. | Planter | | 20 slaves $10,220 334 acres |
| E. L. Paget (prob. Elijah Padgett) | 39 | Kentucky | | | Sumner Co. | Farmer | | $300 |
| Patillo Patton | 40 | Tennessee | | | Maury Co. | Planter | Delegate, RR Conv. Memphis, 1849 | 42 slaves $20,000 1,200 acres |
| James Patterson | 66 | Virginia | | | Giles Co. | Planter | Fought Creeks 1813, helped promote schools and public enterprises | 20 slaves $22,000 |
| Robert G. Payne | 37 | Virginia | | Democrat | Columbia, Maury Co. | Lawyer | Delegate, Dem. Conv. & RR Conv., Memphis, 1849 | No slaves None |

Table 7: Tennessee (continued)

| Name | Age | Place of Birth | Education | Party | Residence | Occupation | Public Service or Office Holding | Property Holding |
|---|---|---|---|---|---|---|---|---|
| Gideon J. Pillow | 47 | Williamson County, Tennessee | Graduated Univ. of Nashville | Democrat | Maury Co. | Planter Lawyer | No civil office; Law partner of J. K. Polk & I. G. Harris; Mexican War; Brig. Gen. CSArmy | 75 slaves $133,370 2,007 acres |
| John Poindexter, Jr. | 32 | Virginia | | | Montgomery Co. | Lawyer | | 3 slaves None |
| Edwin Polk | 32 | Tennessee | | Democrat | Hardeman Co. | Planter Lawyer | Both Houses, Gen. Assem., 1847-55; Speaker of Senate, 1853 | 34 slaves $15,000 |
| William H. Polk | 34 | Maury Co. Tennessee, Brother of J. K. Polk | Attended Univ. of NC, Grad. U.T. | Democrat | Columbia Maury Co. | Lawyer | Gen. Assem. 1842-46; Minister to Naples; Mexican War; Cong. (H.R.) 1851-53 | 12 slaves $7,000 |

Table 7: Tennessee (continued)

| Name | Age | Place of Birth | Education | Party | Residence | Occupation | Public Service or Office Holding | Property Holding |
|---|---|---|---|---|---|---|---|---|
| J. M. Quarles | 27 | Louisa Co., Virginia | "Common Schools" Read Law | Prob. Whig | Montgomery Co. | Lawyer | Atty. Gen., TN; Cong. (H.R.), 1859-61; CSArmy, Author of "Quarles' Criminal Digest" | No slaves None |
| John E. R. Ray | | | | Democrat | Weakley Co. | | Sec. of State TN 1859-1862; Gen. Assem. 1849-1853 | ? |
| Felix Robertson | 69 | 1st white male born at Nashville TN (son of James Robertson) | M.D. Degree Univ. of PA | | Davidson Co. | Physician (Introduced use of quinine 1829) | Physician State Peniten.; Chm. Medical Dept. Univ. of Nashville | No slaves $6,000 |
| William P. Rowles | 50 | Maryland | | Democrat | Lawrence Co. | Lawyer Physician Editor Writer | Gen. Assem. 1847-49; Editor; Author, biog. Wm. B. Allen | 3 slaves $1,100 |
| Basil B. Satterfield | 47 | S. Carolina | | | Hickman Co. | Carpenter | | 8 slaves $450 |

Table 7: Tennessee (continued)

| Name | Age | Place of Birth | Education | Party | Residence | Occupation | Public Service or Office Holding | Property Holding |
|---|---|---|---|---|---|---|---|---|
| W. A. Sewell | 23 | Alabama | | | Marshall Co. | Merchant | | 1 slave $150 |
| Thomas Shepard | 50 | New York | | | 50 Cedar St., Nashville, Davidson Co. | Coach Maker | | No slaves No real estate |
| W. B. Shepherd | 30 | Tennessee | | | Davidson Co. | Clerk | | No real estate |
| J. J. B. Southall | 37 | N. Carolina | | | Davidson Co. | Lawyer | | 24 slaves $28,000 150 acres |
| John Stephens | 55 | Virginia | | | Smith Co. | Saddler | | 8 slaves $2,010 |
| V. K. Stevenson | 38 | Kentucky | | | Nashville Davidson Co. | Merchant Pres. of Nash. & Chatt. RR system 1848-65 | Called father of RR system in Nashville; Quarter-Master Gen., CSArmy | 11 slaves $50,000 |
| W. J. Strayhorn | 41 | Orange Co., N. Carolina | | Democrat | Columbia, Maury Co. | Farmer | Gen. Assem. 1849-51 | 25 slaves $4,500 350 acres |

Table 7: Tennessee (continued)

| Name | Age | Place of Birth | Education | Party | Residence | Occupation | Public Service or Office Holding | Property Holding |
|---|---|---|---|---|---|---|---|---|
| W. E. Venable | 46 | Prince Edward Co., Virginia | Read Law | Democrat | Franklin Co. | Lawyer Teacher Diplomat | An organizer of Mary Sharp College, Winchester; Gen. Assem. 1847-49 | 5 slaves $1,500 |
| James Walker | 55 | Kentucky (brother-in-law of J. K. Polk) | | Democrat | Columbia, Maury Co. | Newspaper editor; Manufacturer | Started 1st newspaper in Columbia, 1810; 1810; Leading churchman (Episcopal) | 12 slaves $100,000 |
| Richard Warner | 54 | N. Carolina | | Democrat | Marshall Co. | Farmer | War of 1812; Both Houses, Gen. Assem. 1833-35, '37-43, '45-47 | No slaves $9,684 |
| Frederick H. Watkins | 34 | Lunenburg County, Virginia | | | Maury Co. | Planter | | 94 slaves $16,250 650 acres |
| William E. Watkins | 62 | Penn. | | | Davidson Co. | Planter | | 42 slaves $12,000 |
| Sam H. Whitthorne | 22 | Tennessee | | | Bedford Co. | Lawyer | | No slaves None |

Table 7: Tennessee (continued)

| Name | Age | Place of Birth | Education | Party | Residence | Occupation | Public Service or Office Holding | Property Holding |
|---|---|---|---|---|---|---|---|---|
| W. C. Whitthorne | 25 | Marshall Co., Tennessee | Arrington Acad. in Williamson County; Campbell Acad. Lebanon | Democrat | Columbia, Maury Co. | Lawyer | Both Houses, Gen. Assem. 1855-61 Congress (H.R.) 1871-83, 1887-1901; U.S. Senate 1886-87; CSArmy | 6 slaves $2,500 |
| J. W. Whitfield | 31 | Williamson County, Tennessee | Elementary & Secondary schools Franklin | Democrat | Hickman Co. | Public Servant | Gen. Assem. 1849-53; Rep. Kansas in Congress 1854-57; Mexican War; CSArmy; TX House of Rep. | No slaves None |
| William Williams | 74 | Halifax Co., N. Carolina | Graduate of Harvard 1799 | | Edgefield, Davidson Co. (came in 1804) | Farmer (breeder of thoroughbred horses) | Circuit Court Judge; Trustee Univ. of Nashville & other schools; Gen. Assem. 1819-1821 | 41 slaves $19,000 640 acres |

Table 7: Tennessee (continued)

| Name | Age | Place of Birth | Education | Party | Residence | Occupation | Public Service or Office Holding | Property Holding |
| --- | --- | --- | --- | --- | --- | --- | --- | --- |
| Willoughby Williams | 51 | N. Carolina | | | Davidson Co. | Planter | | 111 slaves<br>$110,000<br>1,300 acres |
| Richard A. L. Wilkes | 50 | Virginia | | | Near Culleoka, Maury Co. | Planter | Both Houses, Gen. Assem. 1847-51; Active patron of education & church work; | 54 slaves<br>$12,000<br>827 acres |
| George W. Winchester | 28 | Sumner Co., Tennessee | Graduated Univ. of Nashville<br>Read Law | Democrat | Cragfont, Sumner Co. | Lawyer, Editor of the *Tenth Legion* | Gen. Assem. 1853-55; CSArmy | No slaves<br>None |

Table 8: Texas Delegation

| Name | Age | Place of Birth | Education | Party | Residence | Occupation | Public Service or Office Holding | Property Holding |
| --- | --- | --- | --- | --- | --- | --- | --- | --- |
| J. Pinckney Henderson | 42 | N. Carolina | Lincoln Academy, Univ. of NC<br>Read Law | Democrat | San Augustine County | Public Service | Atty. Gen., Sec. of State & Diplomat for TX Republic; Const. Conv. & 1st Gov., TX; Mex. War; US Sen., 1857-59 | 9 slaves<br>$30,000<br>Real Estate |

Table 9: Virginia Delegation

| Name | Age | Place of Birth | Education | Party | Residence | Occupation | Public Service or Office Holding | Property Holding |
|---|---|---|---|---|---|---|---|---|
| R. H. Claybrook | 33 | Virginia | | Whig | North-umberland Co. Tidewater Area | Planter | None | 33 slaves $10,000 |
| Thomas S. Gholson | 41 | Gholsonville, Brunswick County, VA | Graduated Univ. of VA 1827 Law | Whig | Petersburg, Brunswick County | Capitalist Lawyer Judge | Judge, 5th Judicial Circuit in VA,1859-63 | Not on slave census |
| William O. Goode | 52 | Mecklenburg County, VA | Graduated William & Mary, 1819 Law | Democrat | Boydton, Mecklenburg County | Planter Lawyer | State Leg.; Congress, 1853-59 | 40 slaves $52,285 |
| William F. Gordon | 63 | Germana, Orange County, VA | Spring Academy No college Law | Democrat Whig Democrat | Charlot-tesville, Albemarle County, | Planter Lawyer | State Leg.; State Const. Convention, 1829-30; Congress, 1830-35 | 54 slaves $21,500 |
| Willoughby Newton | 48 | Westmoreland County, VA | Limited | Whig | Westmoreland County | Planter | Congress, 1843-45 | 86 slaves $30,000 |
| Beverley Tucker | 66 | "Matoax" Chesterfield County, VA | Graduated William & Mary, 1801 Law | Democrat | Williamsburg, James City County | Lawyer Writer Professor Judge | Judge, MO Territory and State | Not on slave census |

# *Appendix C*

## *Committees on Resolutions and Business*

### First Session[1]

*Alabama*—J. A. Campbell, W. M. Murphy
*Arkansas*—J. H. Powell, S. C. Roane
*Florida*—B. M. Pearson, A. J. Forman
*Georgia*—C. J. McDonald, H. L. Benning
*Mississippi*—A. M. Clayton, S. S. Boyd
*South Carolina*—R. W. Barnwell, J. H. Hammond
*Tennessee*—A. V. Brown, A. O. P. Nicholson
*Texas*—J. P. Henderson
*Virginia*—Willoughby Newton, W. F. Gordon

### Second Session[2]

*Alabama*—Jefferson Buford, C. C. Clay
*Florida*—J. C. McGehee, C. H. DuPont
*Georgia*—C. J. McDonald, W. C. Daniel
*Mississippi*—J. C. Thompson
*South Carolina*—R. W. Barnwell, F. W. Pickens
*Tennessee*—A. V. Brown, A. O. P. Nicholson
*Virginia*—W. F. Gordon

---

1. *Resolutions, Address, and Journal of Proceedings of the Southern Convention, Held at Nashville, Tennessee, June 3d to 12th, Inclusive in the Year 1850* (Nashville, 1850), 29.
2. Nashville *Daily American,* 14 November 1850.

# *Appendix D*

## *Delegates to the Second Session*[1]

**Alabama**

Jefferson Buford†
James M. Calhoun
Reuben Chapman†
Clement C. Clay, Sr.
George W. Williams

**Florida**

Charles H. DuPont†
John C. McGehee
J. H. Verdier
P. Woodson White

**Georgia**

Henry L. Benning†
James N. Bethune
Robert Bledsoe†
William C. Daniel
George R. Hunter
John A. Jones
Charles J. McDonald†
Jacob G. McWhertor†
William B. Parker
John C. Sneed
John P. Snell (or Stell)

**Mississippi**

Joel M. Acker
James J. Davenport
Austin Hutchinson
William H. Kilpatrick
Charles McClaran
Pearson Smith
John C. Thompson
Thomas J. Wharton

1. Delegates to the first session who returned for the second session are indicated with a dagger.

**South Carolina**

R. W. Barnwell†
James Bradley
James Chesnut, Jr.†
Langdon Cheves†
William DuBose†
Maxcy Gregg†
W. J. Hanna†
D. F. Jamison†
Drayton Nance†
Samuel Otterson†
F. W. Pickens†
R. B. Rhett†
G. A. Trenholm†
J. N. Whitner†
John S. Wilson
H. C. Young†

**Tennessee**

Aaron V. Brown†
L. P. Cheatham†
Thomas Claiborne†
J. B. Clements
A. J. Donelson†
J. N. Esselman†
W. G. Harding†
Thomas Martin
F. McClaran
Frank McGavock†
T. D. Moseley†
A. O. P. Nicholson†
Gideon J. Pillow†
William H. Polk†

**Virginia**

William F. Gordon†

*Notes*

*Bibliographical Essay*

*Index*

# *List of Repository Abbreviations*

AAH—Alabama Department of Archives and History
DUL—Duke University Library
GAH—Georgia Department of Archives and History
HSP—Historical Society of Pennsylvania
LC—Library of Congress
MAH—Mississippi Department of Archives and History
NCAH—North Carolina Department of Archives and History
SHC—Southern Historical Collection, University of North Carolina at Chapel Hill
SCHS—South Carolina Historical Society
SCL—South Caroliniana Library, University of South Carolina
SCAH—South Carolina Department of Archives and History
TSL—Tennessee State Library and Archives
UAL—University of Alabama Library
UFL—University of Florida Library
UGL—University of Georgia Library
UTL—University of Tennessee Library
UTxL—University of Texas Library
UVL—University of Virginia Library
VHS—Virginia Historical Society

# Notes

## Chapter 1

1. Hammond to William Gilmore Simms, 16 June 1850, in Hammond Papers, LC; Sharkey to the editor of *The Southron* (Jackson), 21 June 1850; Mobile *Daily Register,* 4 March 1850.

2. See the Bibliographical Essay for a discussion of interpretation.

3. Milo M. Quaife (ed.), *The Diary of James K. Polk During His Presidency, 1845-49,* 4 vols. (Chicago, 1910), 4:249-52, 284-88; John C. Calhoun to Mrs. Thomas G. Clemson, 24 January 1849, in J. Franklin Jameson (ed.), *Correspondence of John C. Calhoun,* American Historical Association, *Annual Report, 1899,* pt. 2 (Washington, 1900): 710.

4. J. D. B. DeBow, *Statistical View of the United States . . . Being a Compendium of the Seventh Census* (Washington, 1853), xlvi, lxxxvii.

5. Charles L. Wiltse, *John C. Calhoun,* 3 vols. (Indianapolis, 1944-54), 3:293; *Cong. Globe,* 29 Cong., 2 Sess., 425, 453-55; David M. Potter, *The Impending Crisis, 1848-1861* (New York, 1976), 61. Potter states that historians have not sufficiently noted that in stating the southern position, Calhoun gained one of his few "clear-cut successes."

6. Calhoun to Andrew P. Calhoun, 23 February 1848, in Jameson, *Calhoun Correspondence,* 744; Calhoun to John H. Means, 13 April 1849, in ibid., 764-66.

7. Wiltse, *Calhoun,* 3:378-88. See also Quaife, *Polk's Diary* 4:249-52, 284-88.

8. Richard K. Crallé (ed.), *The Works of John C. Calhoun,* 6 vols. (New York, 1854-57), 6:285-313 includes a few letters related to the address and a list of the signers, as well as the address itself.

9. William W. Freehling, *Prelude to Civil War: The Nullification Controversy in South Carolina, 1816-1836* (New York, 1965), 201-207, 237-39, 323-27. Dr. Thomas Cooper, influential president of South Carolina College for several years, especially promoted the idea of a southern convention in the immediate postnullification period. See Dumas Malone, *The Public Life of Thomas Cooper, 1783-1839* (Columbia, 1961), chapters 9, 10, and 11. Herbert Wender, *Southern Commerical Conventions, 1837-1859* (Baltimore, 1930); Weymouth T. Jordan, *Rebels in the Making: Planters Conventions*

*and Southern Propaganda* (Tuscaloosa, 1958); Chauncey S. Boucher, "The Annexation of Texas and the Bluffton Movement in South Carolina," *Mississippi Valley Historical Review* 6 (June 1919):3-33.

10. *South Carolina Tri-weekly,* 25 May 1850, as cited in Herman V. Ames, "John C. Calhoun and the Secession Movement of 1850," University of Pennsylvania *Lectures* 5 (Philadelphia, 1918): 125.

11. Virginia Mason, *The Public Life and Diplomatic Correspondence of James M. Mason with Some Personal History* (New York, 1906), 72-73.

12. *Journal of the House of Representatives of the State of Mississippi* (Jackson, 1850), pp. 288-89.

13. George W. Gordon and James W. Paige (eds.), *The Works of Daniel Webster,* 6 vols. (Boston, 1851), 5:429.

14. Avery Craven, *The Growth of Southern Nationalism* (Baton Rouge, 1953), 112.

15. Allan Nevins, *Ordeal of the Union,* 2 vols. (New York, 1947), 1:356.

16. Potter, *The Impending Crisis,* 90-120. Potter questions whether the settlement was really a compromise and chooses to refer to it as the "armistice."

17. David M. Potter, *The South and the Sectional Conflict* (Baton Rouge, 1968), 30-31.

18. Hammond's Diary, 30 November 1850, in Hammond Papers, SCL.

19. Ames, "Calhoun and the Secession Movement," 129.

20. The circumstances of both Taylor's nomination and election in 1848, as well as his pro-northern policies, contributed greatly to the Whig party's downfall. See Chapter 2.

21. For an excellent discussion of "the political parties in metamorphosis" during the decade of the Fifties see Potter, *Impending Crisis,* 225-65.

22. Hammond's Diary, 30 November 1850, in Hammond Papers, SCL.

## *Chapter 2*

1. Herman V. Ames, *State Documents on Federal Relations* (Philadelphia, 1906), 244-47; Henry T. Shanks, *The Secession Movement in Virginia, 1847-1861* (Richmond, 1935), 22-23.

2. Charleston *Mercury,* 10 March 1847; see also 18 March for a similar meeting at Columbia on 15 March to welcome Senator A. P. Butler. Calhoun to Duff Green, 9 March 1847, in Jameson, *Correspondence of Calhoun,* 718-20. Calhoun reported that he found "perfect unanimity . . . including Whigs and Democrats" in Charleston. Calhoun's speech in Crallé, *Calhoun's Works,* 4:382-96.

3. Clarence P. Denman, *The Secession Movement in Alabama* (Montgomery, 1933), 7-9; *Niles' Register,* 22 May 1847; Richard H. Shryock, *Georgia and the Union in 1850* (Durham, 1926), 139-41; Ames, *State Documents on Federal Relations,* 245; Phillip M. Hamer, *The Secession Movement in South Carolina, 1847-52* (Allentown, Penn., 1918), 16-17.

4. Hamer, *Secession Movement in South Carolina,* 23; Ames, "Calhoun and the Secession Movement," 109; Charleston *Mercury,* 12, 25, 29 September 1848.

5. R. F. W. Allston to Adele Petigru Allston, 8 December 1848, in R. F. W. Allston Papers, SCL; Ames, "Calhoun and the Secession Movement," 109, quote; Whitemarsh B. Seabrook to Calhoun, 13 January 1849, in John C. Calhoun Papers, SCL.

6. Arthur C. Cole, *The Whig Party in the South* (1914, rpt. Gloucester, MA, 1962), 133-34; Wiltse, *Calhoun,* 3:369-72.

7. Robert Toombs to John J. Crittenden, 3 and 22 January 1849, in John J. Crittenden Papers, LC.

8. Calhoun to Mrs. T. G. Clemson, 24 January 1849, in Jameson, *Correspondence of Calhoun,* 761-62.

9. Conner to Calhoun, 12 January 1849, in ibid., 1188-90. Governor Moseley of Florida also deplored "the apathy of a large part of the Southern public." See Moseley to Seabrook, 18 May 1849, in Whitemarsh B. Seabrook Papers, LC.

10. William Gilmore Simms to Calhoun, 19 February 1849, in Chauncey S. Boucher and Robert P. Brooks (eds.), "Correspondence Addressed to John C. Calhoun, 1837-1849," American Historical Association *Annual Report, 1929* (Washington, 1930), 498-99; V. D. V. Jamison to Calhoun, 29 January 1849, in Calhoun Papers, SCL; Hammond to Calhoun, 19 February 1849, in Jameson, *Correspondence of Calhoun,* 1192-94.

11. Cleo Hearon, "Mississippi and the Compromise of 1850," Mississippi Historical Society *Publications* 5 (1905): 42-44.

12. Shanks, *Secession Movement in Virginia,* 24-26, quote, 25; Richmond *Whig and Public Advertiser,* 2, 12, 15, 16, 19 and 22 January 1849; Crallé to Calhoun, 25 July 1849, in Jameson, *Correspondence of Calhoun,* 1199-1202.

13. *The Weekly Raleigh Register and North Carolina Gazette,* 24 January, 21 February 1849; J. Carlyle Sitterson, *The Secession*

*Movement in North Carolina* (Chapel Hill, 1939), 44-48; Badger to Crittenden, 13 January 1849, in Crittenden Papers, LC.

14. Wilmington *Journal,* 2 February 1849; Haywood to Martin Van Buren, 11 March and 30 May 1849, in Martin Van Buren Papers, typescript copy, NCAH, orig., LC; *The Weekly Raleigh Register and North Carolina Gazette,* 11 July 1849. See also 1 August and 24 October 1849.

15. Edwin L. Williams, Jr., "Florida in the Union, 1845-1861" (Ph.D. dissertation, University of North Carolina, Chapel Hill, 1951), 494-504; *Niles' Register,* 7 February 1849.

16. Herbert J. Doherty, Jr., "The Florida Whigs" (MA thesis, University of Florida, 1949), 124-25; *Florida Sentinel* (Tallahassee), 20 February 1849.

17. Moseley to Seabrook, 18 May 1849, in Seabrook Papers, LC; D. S. Walker to Crittenden, 19 January 1849, in Crittenden Papers, LC.

18. Yulee to Calhoun, 10 July 1849, in David L. Yulee Papers, UFL.

19. Denman, *Secession Movement in Alabama,* 22; Hilliard M. Judge to Calhoun, 29 April 1849, in Jameson, *Correspondence of Calhoun,* 1195-97.

20. Ruth H. Nuermberger, *The Clays of Alabama: A Planter-Lawyer-Politician Family* (Lexington, 1958), 109; Greensboro *Beacon,* 24 February 1849; Austin L. Venable, "Alabama's 'War of the Roses'," *Alabama Review* 8 (October 1955): 250.

21. Lewy Dorman, *Party Politics in Alabama from 1850 through 1860* (Wetumpka, 1935), 31-32; Venable, "Alabama's 'War of the Roses'," 250-59; King to John W. Womack, 10 March 1849, in William R. King Papers, SHC.

22. Houston to Cobb, 22 March 1849, in Ulrich B. Phillips (ed.), *The Correspondence of Robert Toombs, Alexander H. Stephens, and Howell Cobb,* American Historical Association, *Annual Report, 1911,* pt. 2 (Washington, 1913): 158-59; Judge to Calhoun, 29 April 1849, in Jameson, *Correspondence of Calhoun,* 1195-97.

23. "To Our Constituents" signed Howell Cobb, Linn Boyd, Beverley Clarke, and John H. Lumpkin, 26 February 1849, in the De Renne Special Collections, University of Georgia, Athens. This is often referred to as the minority address; Cobb to Buchanan, 17 June 1849, in Phillips, *Correspondence,* 163-64.

24. Letters to Cobb include Thomas W. Thomas, 16 February 1849; Holsey, 24 February 1849; and Lumpkin, 6 June 1849, in Phillips, *Correspondence,* 149-52, 154-55, 160-61.

25. See *The Southern Museum* (Macon) and *The Federal Union* (Milledgeville), both Democratic papers, January-March 1849.

26. Benning to Cobb, 1 July 1849, in Phillips, *Correspondence,* 168-72; Lumpkin to Calhoun, 3 January 1849, in Boucher and Brooks, "Correspondence Addressed to Calhoun," 492-93; Johnson to Calhoun, 28 June and 20 July 1849, in Herschel V. Johnson Papers, DUL.

27. Shryock, *Georgia and the Union,* 197-98.

28. *Georgia Journal and Messenger,* 24 January 1849. See also 7 February 1849.

29. Shryock, *Georgia and the Union,* 191-95. For the Whig opinion see *Georgia Journal and Messenger* (Macon) and *The Southern Recorder* (Milledgeville) both Whig papers, January-March 1849.

30. Chauncey S. Boucher, "The Secession and Cooperation Movements in South Carolina, 1849-52," Washington University *Studies* 5, Humanistic Series, pt. 2, no. 2 (St. Louis, 1918), 78-79; See Charleston *Mercury,* February-March 1849, for accounts of various meetings.

31. Calhoun to John H. Means, 13 April 1849, in Jameson, *Correspondence of Calhoun,* 764-66. For the proceedings of the convention see Charleston *Mercury,* 15, 16 May 1849.

32. Elmore to Seabrook, 30 May 1849, in Seabrook Papers, LC.

33. *Mississippi Free Trader* (Natchez), 10 February 1849; Hearon, "Mississippi and the Compromise of 1850," 39, 45-46; C. R. Clifton to Calhoun, 30 January 1849, in Boucher and Brooks, "Correspondence Addressed to Calhoun," 496.

34. Dunbar Rowland, *History of Mississippi: The Heart of the South,* 2 vols. (Chicago-Jackson, 1925), 1:709; Vicksburg *Whig,* 10 May 1849; C. S. Tarpley to Calhoun, 9 May 1849, in Calhoun Papers, SCL. The official account of the May convention is in the *Journal of the House of Representatives of Mississippi,* 269-76. Sharkey later served as president of the Nashville Convention.

35. *Republican Banner* (Nashville), 19, 21 February, 23 March 1849. Nashville *Union,* 3, 14 February, 24 March 1849; Joseph Parks, *John Bell of Tennessee* (Baton Rouge, 1950), 229-39, 208-209; Mary Emily Robertson Campbell, *The Attitude of Tennesseans Toward the Union, 1847-1861* (New York, 1961), 34-38.

36. Paul H. Bergeron, "Tennessee's Response to the Nullification Crisis," *Journal of Southern History* 39 (February 1973): 23-44; St. George L. Sioussat, "Tennessee and National Political Parties, 1850-1860," American Historical Association *Annual Report, 1914,* pt. 1 (Washington, D.C., 1916): 250; Nashville *Union,* 26 April 1849.

37. *Republican Banner,* 21, 30 April 1849; J. T. Trezevant to Calhoun, 7 June 1849, in Boucher and Brooks, "Correspondence Addressed to Calhoun," 508-10.

38. Elsie Mae Lewis, "From Nationalism to Disunion: A Study of

the Secession Movement in Arkansas: 1850-1861" (Ph.D. dissertation, University of Chicago, 1946), 110-14; *Arkansas State Democrat* (Little Rock), 12 January 1849.

39. Contrast the *Arkansas State Democrat* with the *Arkansas State Gazette* (Little Rock), January-April 1849.

40. Roger W. Shugg, *Origins of Class Struggle in Louisiana: A Social History of White Farmers and Laborers During Slavery and After, 1840-1875* (Baton Rouge, 1939), 157-58. See New Orleans *Daily Picayune,* 1847-49, editorial, 14 January 1848; governor's message, 19 January 1848. (Anonymous), "Slavery in the New Territories," *DeBow's Review* 7(1849): 62-73.

41. James K. Greer, "Louisiana Politics, 1845-1861," *Louisiana Historical Quarterly* 12 (1929): 557-67; New Orleans *Daily Picayune,* 30 December 1848, 20, 25, 27, 30 January, 1, 7, 11 February 1849; New Orleans *Bee,* 26 January 1849.

42. Anna Irene Sandbo, "Beginnings of the Secession Movement in Texas," *Southwestern Historical Quarterly* 18 (July 1914): 43-48; Alvy L. King, *Louis T. Wigfall: Southern Fire-eater* (Baton Rouge, 1970), 51-56; Wigfall to Calhoun, 4 January 1849, in Brooks and Boucher, "Correspondence Addressed to Calhoun," 493-95; Randolph Campbell, "Texas and the Nashville Convention of 1850," *Southwestern Historical Quarterly* 76 (July 1972): 1-14. Campbell's thesis is that Texas had more interest in the southern movement and the Nashville Convention than historians have formerly noted.

43. Rusk to Unknown, 30 January 1849, in Rusk Papers, UTxL; Wiltse, *Calhoun,* 3:388.

44. Houston to Henderson Yoakum, 31 January 1849, in Amelia W. Williams and Eugene C. Barker (eds.), *The Writings of Sam Houston, 1813-1863,* 8 vols. (Austin, 1938-43), 5:70-72, address to constituents, 78-88; *Cong. Globe,* 31 Cong. 1 Sess., Appendix, 97-102.

45. Thomas D. Raymond, "A Study in Missouri Politics, 1840-1870," *Missouri Historical Review* 21 (1927): 171-80; *Cong. Globe,* 31 Cong., 1 Sess., 97-98; Benjamin C. Merkel, "The Slavery Issue and the Political Decline of Thomas Hart Benton, 1846-1856," *Missouri Historical Review* 38 (1944): 393. See Wiltse *Calhoun* 3:401-404 for Calhoun's reply to Benton.

46. James B. Bowlin to Cobb, 6 June 1849, in Phillips, *Correspondence,* 159-60; Treat to Calhoun, 17 June 1849, in Boucher and Brooks, "Correspondence Addressed to Calhoun," 515; William E. Parrish, *David Rice Atchison of Missouri: Border Politician* (Columbia, MO, 1961), 89-93; William N. Chambers, *Old Bullion Benton: Senator from the New West* (Boston, 1956), 340-42.

47. *Republican Banner,* 26 February, 9, 26 March, 1 May 1849; Mrs. Chapman Coleman, *The Life of John J. Crittenden with Selec-*

*tions from His Correspondence and Speeches,* 2 vols. (Philadelphia, 1871), 1:330-35; Crittenden to Clayton, 7 January 1849, in John M. Clayton Papers, LC.

48. H. Jenkins to Clayton, 15 January 1849, in Clayton Papers, LC.

49. Weems to Calhoun, 19 February 1849, in Boucher and Brooks, "Correspondence Addressed to Calhoun," 49; Baltimore *Sun,* 29 December 1848, 22, 30 January, 3 February 1849.

50. Letters to John J. Crittenden from George E. Badger, 13 January 1849; Garrett Duncan, 22 January 1849; and Alexander H. Stephens, 6 February 1849, in Crittenden Papers, LC; Holman Hamilton, *Zachary Taylor: Soldier in the White House,* 2 vols. (Indianapolis, 1951), 2:162-83; Crittenden to Clayton, 7 January 1849, in Clayton Papers, LC. See also Clayton to Crittenden, 18 April 1849, in Crittenden Papers, LC.

51. Hamilton, *Zachary Taylor,* 2:224-25; King to Clayton, 22 July 1849, in Clayton Papers, LC; Craven, *Growth of Southern Nationalism,* 58-61.

52. Johnson to Sampson W. Harris, 22 July 1849, in Johnson Papers, DUL; Calhoun to Thomas G. Clemson, 24 August 1849, in Jameson, *Correspondence of Calhoun,* 771-72; Claiborne to his son, 20 August 1849, in Thomas Claiborne Papers, SHC; Toombs to Mrs. Chapman Coleman, 22 June 1849, in Crittenden Papers, LC.

53. Johnson to Calhoun, 25 August, 1849, in Johnson Papers, DUL.

54. *Journal of the House of Representatives of Mississippi,* 277-310, gives the official account of the October Convention, including the resolutions and the address to the southern states.

55. Wallace was a special agent of Governor Seabrook. Wallace to Seabrook, 8 June, 20 October, 7 November 1849, in Seabrook Papers, LC. Governor Seabrook had also written to a number of southern governors in an attempt to ascertain the degree of cooperation to be expected from their states. See. F. H. Elmore to Seabrook, 30 May 1849, ibid.

56. Hill told Wallace that he felt "constrained" to take no active part in the convention, but according to the official journal Hill was a member of the committee which prepared the address.

57. Tarpley to Calhoun, 9 May 1849, in Calhoun Papers, SCL; Calhoun to Tarpley, 9 July 1849, entire letter quoted in Dallas T. Herndon, "The Nashville Convention of 1850," Alabama Historical Society *Transactions* 5 (1905): 207-208. That Calhoun was thinking of other possible places for the call to be issued is revealed in a letter to Andrew Pickens Calhoun, 24 July 1849, in Jameson, *Correspondence of Calhoun,* 769-70. Calhoun suggested that the southern con-

gressmen might make the call and asked if Alabama could not be induced. He suggested Atlanta as a desirable location for the meeting.

58. Tarpley to the Editors of the *Mississippian,* 16 May 1850, reprinted in the *Black River Watchman* (Sumterville, S.C.), 13 July 1850.

59. Calhoun to Foote, 2 August 1849, in Charleston *Mercury,* 4 June 1851; Anderson Hutchinson to Calhoun, 5 October 1849, in Jameson, *Correspondence of Calhoun,* 1206-1207. Hutchinson states that two of Calhoun's letters to Foote were sent to him for Hutchinson to use at his own discretion, and that he showed the one suggesting a southern convention to Sharkey and Judge C. R. Clifton. The idea of a southern convention had previously occurred in Mississippi, but Calhoun's opinion confirmed those who favored it.

60. Foote to Calhoun, 25 September 1849, in Jameson, *Correspondence of Calhoun,* 1204-1205; *Cong. Globe,* 31 Cong., 1 Sess., Appendix, 97-102.

61. *Cong. Globe,* 32 Cong., 1 Sess., Appendix, 52; and 32 Cong., 1 Sess., 134-35.

62. The editors of the Calhoun papers at the University of South Carolina have not located Calhoun's letter to Hutchinson. See Hutchinson to Calhoun, 5 October 1849, in Jameson, *Correspondence of Calhoun,* 1206-1207. Hutchinson mentioned that he and Sharkey preferred Washington, but the majority thought Nashville was more central. It was the unanimous opinion that February or March was the time for the meeting, but the majority believed that it would require until the first of June for the southern states to act.

# *Chapter 3*

1. Ewing to Adam Ferguson, 20 December 1849, in Adam Ferguson Papers, TSL.

2. Richard M. Johnston and William H. Browne, *The Life of Alexander H. Stephens* (Philadelphia, 1878), 237, 239; James Johnston Pettigrew to William S. Pettigrew, 8 January 1850, in Pettigrew Family Papers, SHC. See also his letter of 9 January 1850 to James C. Johnston, ibid; Calvin H. Wiley to David F. Caldwell, 7 January 1850, in David F. Caldwell Papers, SHC.

3. *Cong. Globe,* 31 Cong., 1 Sess., 1; Horace Montgomery, *Cracker Parties* (Baton Rouge, 1950), 15-16; Toombs to John J. Crittenden,

23 April 1850, in Crittenden Papers, LC; Johnston and Browne, *Life of Stephens,* 237; William Y. Thompson, *Robert Toombs of Georgia* (Baton Rouge, 1966), 56.

4. *Cong. Globe,* 31 Cong., 1 Sess., 28, 29, 66; Johnston and Browne, *Life of Stephens,* 244-47.

5. Calhoun to Mrs. T. G. Clemson, 31 December 1849, in Jameson, *Correspondence of Calhoun,* 778; James Buchanan to Cave Johnson, 1 January 1850, in James Buchanan Papers, HSP.

6. Johnson to Calhoun, 19 January 1850, in Johnson Papers, DUL. See also Johnson to Henry S. Foote, 19 January 1850, ibid. Calhoun to James H. Hammond, 4 January 1850, in Jameson, *Correspondence of Calhoun,* 779-80.

7. *Cong. Globe,* 31 Cong., 1 Sess., 204; King to James Buchanan, 13 Janaury 1850, Buchanan Papers, HSP; *Cong. Globe,* 31 Cong., 1 Sess., 257-61; Alexander H. Stephens to Linton Stephens, 21 January 1850, in Johnston and Browne, *Life of Stephens,* 245; Berrien to Charles J. Jenkins, 7 January 1850, in John M. Berrien Papers, SHC.

8. Ewing to Adam Ferguson, 24 January 1850, in Adam Ferguson Papers, TSL.

9. Buchanan to William R. King, 13 May 1850, in Buchanan Papers, HSP; U. B. Phillips, *The Life of Robert Toombs* (New York, 1913), 54-55; Herschel V. Johnson to Sampson W. Harris, 22 July 1849, and Johnson to Calhoun, 25 August 1849, in Johnson Papers, DUL.

10. Henry Clay to James Harlan, 26 January 1849, in Calvin Colton (ed.), *The Private Correspondence of Henry Clay* (New York, 1855), 583. Clay to James Clay, 2 January 1849, ibid., 582; George Tecknor Curtis, *Life of Daniel Webster,* 2 vols. (New York, 1870), 2:397.

11. *Cong. Globe,* 31 Cong., 1 Sess., 244-52, 115-27; Holman Hamilton, *Prologue to Conflict: The Crisis and Compromise of 1850* (Lexington, 1964), 53-55; David Outlaw to Mrs. Outlaw, 30 January, 2 February 1850, in David Outlaw Papers, SHC.

12. Cole, *Whig Party in the South,* 162-65; Alexander H. Stephens, *A Constitutional View of the Late War Between the States,* 2 vols. (Philadelphia, 1870), 2:200-201.

13. Howell Cobb to Mrs. Cobb, 9 February 1850, in Phillips, *Correspondence,* 183-84; Calhoun to Thomas G. Clemson, 6 February 1850, in Jameson, *Correspondence of Calhoun,* 781.

14. Hamilton, *Zachary Taylor,* 2:287-301. For comments on the breach between Clay and Taylor see Charles S. Morehead to John J. Crittenden, 30 March 1850, and Orlando Brown to Crittenden, 19 April 1850, in Crittenden Papers, LC; Clay to James Harlan, 14 March 1850, in Colton, *Correspondence of Clay,* 603-604.

15. Calhoun to James H. Hammond, 16 February 1850, in Jameson, *Correspondence of Calhoun,* 781-82.

16. *Cong. Globe,* 31 Cong., 1 Sess., 203-206, 149-57.

17. Thompson, *Robert Toombs,* 61; F. H. Hodder, "The Authorship of the Compromise of 1850," *Mississippi Valley Historical Review* 22 (March 1936): 527-28.

18. Hamilton, *Zachary Taylor,* 2:300; Thurlow Weed Barnes (ed.), *Memoirs of Thurlow Weed* (Boston, 1884), 177; Edward Stanly to David F. Caldwell, 1 March 1850, in Caldwell Papers, SHC.

19. Wiltse, *Calhoun,* 3:455-60; New York *Herald,* 8 March 1850.

20. Hamilton, *Prologue to Conflict,* 71-74; *Cong. Globe,* 31 Cong., 1 Sess., 451-55.

21. Calhoun to Thomas G. Clemson, 10 March 1850, in Jameson, *Correspondence of Calhoun,* 784; Outlaw to Mrs. Outlaw, 4 March 1850, in Outlaw Papers, SHC; King to James Buchanan, 11 March 1850, in Buchanan Papers, HSP; John Tyler to Robert Tyler, 12 March 1850, in Lynn G. Tyler (ed.), *The Letters and Times of the Tylers* (Richmond, 1885), 481; Mayo Cabell to Joseph C. Cabell, 13 March 1850, in Joseph C. Cabell Papers; UVL; Marcy to Buchanan, 11 March 1850, in Buchanan Papers, HSP; *Cong. Globe,* 31 Cong., 1 Sess., 461-64.

22. Webster to Peter Harvey, 14, 22 February 1850, in Curtis, *Daniel Webster,* 398-400. *Cong. Globe,* 31 Cong., 1 Sess., Appendix, 269-76.

23. Outlaw to Mrs. Outlaw, 8, 9 March 1850, in Outlaw Papers, SHC; Calhoun to Thomas G. Clemson, 10 March 1850, in Jameson, *Correspondence of Calhoun,* 784. See also Calhoun to H. W. Conner, 18 March 1850, in Calhoun Papers, SCL, in which he seems to have lost hope for any northern support.

24. Hamilton, *Prologue to Conflict,* 81-83; Stephens, *Constitutional View of the War,* 2:211.

25. King to Buchanan, 11 March 1850, in Buchanan Papers, HSP; Toombs to Linton Stephens, 22 March 1850, in Phillips, *Correspondence,* 188; Henry A. Edmundson to Richard B. Gooch, 18 March 1850, in Gooch Family Papers, UVL; William H. Cabell to Joseph C. Cabell, 3 March 1850, in Cabell Papers, UVL; Tyler to Henry S. Foote, 21 May 1850 and Tyler to Alexander Gardiner, 29 May 1850, in Tyler, *Letters and Times of the Tylers,* 484-89.

26. *Cong. Globe,* 31 Cong., 1 Sess., Appendix, 260-69; Potter, *Impending Crisis,* 102.

27. William G. Brownlow to Thomas A. R. Nelson, 2, 19 March 1849, in Thomas A. R. Nelson Papers, McClung Collection, Lawson McGhee Library, Knoxville; *Cong. Globe,* 31 Cong., 1 Sess., 436-39; Joseph H. Parks, "John Bell and the Compromise of 1850," *Journal of Southern History* 9 (August 1943): 340-43.

28. *Republican Banner* 12 March 1850; Stephens, *Constitutional View of the War,* 2:205.

29. Benjamin F. Perry, 19 May, 10 June 1850, MS Journal, SHC; Wiltse, *Calhoun,* 3:476.

30. "Address to the People of the Southern States," Thomas J. Rusk Papers, UTxL; *Alabama Journal* (Montgomery), 12 April 1850; *Southern Museum* (Macon, GA), 20 April 1850. According to these press reports, only four southern senators were absent.

31. *Cong. Globe,* 31 Cong., 1 Sess., quote 656. See also 640-43, 656-65, 704-705. For the clash between Benton and Foote see 762-63.

32. *Cong. Globe,* 31 Cong., 1 Sess., 779-80. Senators from the free states were Cass, Bright, Dickinson, Cooper, Phelps, and Webster. Those from the slave states were Downs, King, Mason, Bell, Mangum, and Berrien.

33. Outlaw to Mrs. Outlaw, 6 May 1850, in Outlaw Papers, SHC.

34. *Cong. Globe,* 31 Cong., 1 Sess., 944-48; Outlaw to Mrs. Outlaw, 9, 12, 15, 19, May 1850, in Outlaw Papers, SHC; Edmund W. Hubard to Robert T. Hubard, 26 May 1850, Hubard Family Papers, UVL; Brown to Crittenden, 18 May 1850, in Crittenden Papers, LC.

## Chapter 4

1. Cole, *Whig Party in the South,* 157-62.

2. For the states' reactions to secession see Ralph A. Wooster, *The Secession Conventions of the South* (Princeton, 1962). See DeBow, *Seventh Census,* xxxiii, for ratio of slaves to total population in 1850.

3. Calhoun to Hammond, 7 December 1849, in Jameson, *Correspondence of Calhoun,* 775-76.

4. Message of Governor Seabrook, 27 November 1849, Legislative System, SCAH, 7-9.

5. *The Spartan* (Spartanburg), 20 December 1849, 14 March 1850; Hammond's Diary, 17 December 1849, in Hammond Papers, SCL.

6. John A. Calhoun to John C. Calhoun, 14 December 1849, in Boucher and Brooks, "Correspondence Addressed to Calhoun," 523-33; Charleston *Courier,* 31 October 1849; Charleston *Mercury,* 14, 15 November 1849; William B. Johnson to Calhoun, 8 November 1849, in Jameson, *Correspondence of Calhoun,* 1208-10; *The Spartan,* 22 November 1849; Calhoun to Hammond, 7 December 1849, in Jameson, *Correspondence of Calhoun,* 775-76; Simms to Nathaniel Bever-

ley Tucker, 30 January 1850, in Mary C. Simms Oliphant, Alfred T. Odell, and T. C. Duncan Eaves (eds.), *The Letters of William Gilmore Simms,* 5 vols. (Columbia, 1952-56), 3:9.

7. *Federal Union* (Milledgeville), 6, 20 November 1849.

8. *National Intelligencer* (Washington, D.C.), 11 March 1850; *Southern Museum* (Macon) 26 January 1850; Shryock, *Georgia and the Union,* 254-55. *The Southern Recorder* (Milledgeville) practically ignored the convention until 19 March 1850.

9. Berrien to Charles J. Jenkins, 7 January 1850, in Berrien Papers, SHC; Johnson to Foote, 19 January 1850; Johnson to Calhoun, 19 January 1850 and 5 November 1849, all in Johnson Papers, DUL.

10. Shryock, *Georgia and the Union,* 223-32; Copy of the ten resolutions, Berrien Papers, SHC; Georgia *House Journal,* 1849-50, pp. 350, 422, 656-58; Georgia *Senate Journal,* 494-95, 648; Proclamation of Governor Towns, 4 March 1850, Executive Minute Book (Georgia), GAH, 108.

11. Hall to Calhoun, 15 January 1850, in Calhoun Papers, SCL; Chapman to Calhoun, 19 October 1849, in Jameson, *Correspondence of Calhoun,* 1207-1208; Message of Governor Chapman, 13 November 1849, Alabama *House Journal,* 12-45.

12. Eufaula (Alabama) *Democrat,* 1 January 1850; Greensboro (Alabama) *Beacon,* 29 December 1849.

13. Denman, *Secession Movement in Alabama,* 23-28. See Appendix A for the list of delegates from each state.

14. Montgomery *Advertiser and State Gazette,* 13 February 1850; Nuermberger, *Clays of Alabama,* 109-10; Dorman, *Party Politics in Alabama,* 38-39; Files of the Montgomery *Alabama Journal,* February-May 1850.

15. Vicksburg *Whig,* 15 December 1849; Executive Journal, 1845-1850 (Mississippi), MAH, 13-30; Message of Governor Quitman, 10 January 1850, ibid., 279-82.

16. J. F. H. Claiborne (ed.), *Life and Correspondence of John A. Quitman,* 2 vols. (New York, 1860), 2:34-35; Executive Journal, 292-94.

17. *The Southron* (Jackson) 15 February, 15, 22 March 1850; Vicksburg *Whig,* 13 March 1850.

18. Calhoun to Yulee, 19 October 1849, in David L. Yulee Papers, UFL.

19. Dorothy Dodd, "The Secession Movement in Florida, 1850-1861," *Florida Historical Society Quarterly* 12 (July 1933): 3-7.

20. Yulee, Morton, and Cabell to Brown, 6 February 1850, in Yulee Papers, UFL; Doherty, "Florida Whigs," 130; Governor Brown to Florida Congressmen, 22 February 1850, in Yulee Papers, UFL;

Morton to Brown, 10 March 1850 and Brown to Morton, 30 March 1850, Pensacola *Gazette,* 13 April 1850.

21. Sydney J. Wienberg, "Slavery and Secession in Florida, 1845-1861" (MA thesis, University of Florida, 1940), 64.

22. Charles Henry Ambler, *Sectionalism in Virginia from 1776 to 1861* (Chicago, 1910), 244-49; Richmond *Whig,* 5 February, 15 January 1850; Richmond *Enquirer,* 16 October 1849; Campbell to John Mercer Patton, 26 January 1850, in David Campbell Papers, DUL.

23. Tucker to Hammond, 4, 27 December 1849, Hammond Papers, LC; William P. Trent, *William Gilmore Simms* (Boston, 1892), 177-83; Tucker to Hammond, 27 January 1850, Typescript in Nathaniel Beverley Tucker Papers, DUL; M. R. H. Garnett, *The Union, Past and Future: How It Works, and How to Save It* (Washington, 1850). Published in *DeBow's Review* 18 (1855): 145-54, 289-97 and 19 (1855): 38-47 under the title "The South and the Union."

24. Richmond *Enquirer,* 15, 25, 29 January, 1 February 1850; Charles Barrow to Powell, 10 February 1850, in Paulus Powell Papers, DUL.

25. Sitterson, *Secession Movement in North Carolina,* 57; Wilmington *Journal,* 25 January 1850; Raleigh *Register,* 23 January 1850.

26. *Cong. Globe,* 31 Cong., 1 Sess., Appendix, 344; Stanly to John H. Bryan, 11 January 1850, in John H. Bryan Papers, NCAH; Stanly to James W. Bryan, 6 April 1850, in Bryan Family Papers, SHC; Hale to William Alexander Graham, 8 February 1850, in J. G. DeRoulhac Hamilton and M. R. Williams (eds.), *The Papers of William Alexander Graham,* 5 vols. (Raleigh, 1957-73), 3:313-14.

27. Raleigh *Register,* 26 June 1850.

28. See accounts in Wilmington *Journal* and Raleigh *Register,* February-March 1850. Haywood to Francis P. Blair, 7 May 1850, Typescript, in Martin Van Buren Papers, NCAH.

29. Wilmington *Journal,* 15 March 1850; Sitterson, *Secession Movement in North Carolina,* 60.

30. Lewis, "Secession Movement in Arkansas," 116-17; *Arkansas State Gazette and Democrat,* 22 February 1850.

31. *Arkansas Banner,* 19 February 1850.

32. Walter L. Brown, "Albert Pike, 1809-1891," (Ph.D. dissertation, University of Texas, 1955), 258-66.

33. Harold T. Smith, "Arkansas Politics, 1850-1861" (MA thesis, Memphis State University, 1964), 7-9.

34. *Arkansas Banner,* 2 April 1850; *Arkansas State Gazette and Democrat,* 5, 19 April 1850.

35. Conway added the B. to his name to distinguish himself from

a cousin of the same name who lived in the same town. John Hallum, *Biographical and Pictorial History of Arkansas* (Albany, 1887), 45-46.

36. Conway to Miss Williams, 30 April and 4 May 1850, in Polk Papers, NCAH. Four years later Miss Williams married William H. Polk, a Tennessee delegate to the Nashville Convention. See description accompanying the Polk Papers.

37. New Orleans *Courier,* 23 January 1850; New Orleans *Picayune,* 29 January 1850; New Orleans *Daily Crescent,* 2 February 1850; Greer, "Louisiana Politics," 574; New Orleans *Bee,* 30 January 1850.

38. New Orleans *Courier,* 2 February 1850; New Orleans *Picayune,* 1 February 1850.

39. Louis M. Sears, *John Slidell* (Durham, 1925), 83-84.

40. New Orleans *Bee,* 23 February 1850.

41. Campbell, "Texas and the Nashville Convention," 13-14, 4-8; *Brownlow's Knoxville Whig,* 20 April 1850; *Texas Gazette* (Austin), 11 November 1849.

42. Nashville *Union,* 27 March 1850; Pensacola *Gazette,* 9 March 1850.

43. *Texas Gazette,* 16 February, 2, 16 March 1850.

44. Baltimore *Sun,* 2 January, 8 March 1850.

45. St. Louis *Reveille,* 6 March, 19 February, 20 March 1850; Merkel, "Slavery Issue and Decline of Benton," 396-98; Raleigh *Register,* 13 April 1850. Benton was defeated for reelection.

46. Mobile *Daily Register,* 18 January 1850.

47. Combs, leading Whig and confidential friend of Clay, was a holder of Texas bonds.

48. Clay to Combs, 22 December 1849, and 22 January 1850, in Colton, *Correspondence of Clay,* 593, 599; Clay to James Clay, 6 March 1850, ibid., 601-602; New Orleans *Bee,* 9 March 1850.

49. Campbell, *Attitude of Tennesseans Toward the Union,* 52; William F. Cooper to Joseph Varnum, 7 April 1850, in Cooper Family Papers, TSL.

50. Republican *Banner,* 15 October 1849, 19 February 1850; Nashville *Union,* 16 February 1850.

51. St. George L. Sioussat, "Tennessee, the Compromise of 1850, and the Nashville Convention," *Mississippi Valley Historical Review* 2 (December 1915): 321-22.

52. Nashville *Union,* 22, 29 December 1849, 23 January 1850.

53. Sioussat, "Tennessee and National Political Parties," 252. See also Governor Trousdale's message for his position on the slavery question, in Robert H. White (ed.), *Messages of the Governors of*

*Tennessee,* 8 vols. (Nashville, 1952-72), 4:302-303; Nashville *Union,* 8, 16 February 1850.

54. Johnson to James Buchanan, 20 January 1850, in Buchanan Papers, HSP; Cooper to Joseph Varnum, 7 April 1850.

# *Chapter 5*

1. Herbert D. Foster, "Webster's Seventh of March Speech and the Secession Movement, 1850," *American Historical Review* 27 (1921-22): 245-70.

2. Mobile *Daily Register,* 4 March, 2 April 1850; Ames, "Calhoun and the Secession Movement," 122-23.

3. New Orleans *Picayune,* 9, 15 March 1850; New Orleans *Bee,* 16 March 1850; Baltimore *Sun,* 8 March 1850; Jackson *Southron,* 22 March 1850; Charleston *Mercury,* 14 March 1850.

4. *Daily Constitutionalist,* 19 April 1850, as quoted in Helen Greene, "Politics in Georgia, 1830-1854" (Ph.D. dissertation, University of Chicago, 1945), 225; New Orleans *Courier,* 19 March 1850.

5. Manly to Webster, 22 April 1850, in Governor Charles Manly's Letterbook, 1849-50, p. 348, NCAH; James Graham to W. A. Graham, 21 April 1850, in Hamilton and Williams, *W. A. Graham Papers,* 3:320-21; Cooper to Joseph Varnum, 7 April 1850, in Cooper Family Papers, TSL.

6. William O. Goode to R. M. T. Hunter, 20 April 1850, in Charles H. Ambler (ed.), *The Correspondence of R. M. T. Hunter, 1826-1876,* American Historical Association *Annual Report, 1916,* pt. 2 (Washington, 1918): 110-12; Mobile *Register,* cited by the *Nashville Union,* 21 May 1850.

7. New Orleans *Bee,* 5 April 1850; Richmond *Enquirer,* 19 March 1850; Ames, "Calhoun and the Secession Movement," 123-24.

8. New York *Herald,* 21 March, 10, 12 April 1850. *The National Intelligencer* was active in promoting the idea that the convention was disunionist.

9. Davis to Franklin H. Elmore, 13 April 1850, in Dunbar Rowland (ed.), *Jefferson Davis Constitutionalist, His Letters, Papers and Speeches,* 10 vols. (Jackson, MS. 1923), 1:323.

10. Albert B. Moore, *History of Alabama and Her People,* 3 vols.

(Chicago, 1927), 2:240-41; Montgomery *Alabama Journal,* 19, 24 April, 13, 22 May 1850.

11. Mobile *Daily Advertiser,* 25 March 1850; Copy of a letter Hilliard wrote to a friend in Tuskegee, 20 March 1850, in *Republican Banner* (Nashville), 23 April 1850.

12. Beirne to Berrien, 6 April 1850, in Berrien Papers, SHC. Nuermberger, *The Clays of Alabama,* 109-10; Montgomery *Advertiser and State Gazette,* 4, 23 May 1850. Local conventions chose J. S. Hunter and William M. Byrd to fill vacancies.

13. Shryock, *Georgia and the Union,* 256; Augusta *Daily Chronicle,* 22, 27, 30 March 1850; *Southern Museum* (Macon), 16 March 1850.

14. See files of *Federal Union* and *Southern Museum,* Democratic papers, and *Southern Recorder* and *Augusta Chronicle,* Whig papers, January-June 1850.

15. Official returns in Georgia Executive Minute Book, 119; *Federal Union,* 9 April 1850; William H. Hull to Howell Cobb, 3 April 1850, in Howell Cobb Papers, UGL.

16. *Southern Recorder,* 28 May 1850; *Federal Union,* 7 May 1850; Henry G. Lamar to John T. Smith, 21 May 1850, in Telamon Cuyler Papers, UGL; *Southern Museum,* 25 May 1850.

17. Harris to Berrien, 25 April 1850; Jenkins to Berrien, 15 May 1850; Strong to Berrien, 19 May 1850; Howard to Berrien, 5 May 1850, all in Berrien Papers, SHC.

18. Warner to Cobb, 17 March 1850, in Phillips, *Correspondence,* 2:186-87. Warner's brother served as a delegate to the Nashville Convention.

19. *Florida Sentinel* (Tallahassee), 5, 19, 26 March, 23 April, 7 May 1850; *The Floridian and Journal* (Tallahassee), 23 March, 4 May 1850.

20. As quoted by *National Intelligencer,* 2 April 1850; Haywood to Francis Blair, 7 May 1850, Typescript in Van Buren Papers, NCAH; Wilmington *Journal,* 10 May 1850.

21. Holden to David S. Reid, 1 June 1850, in David S. Reid Papers, NCAH; Raleigh *Register,* 25 May 1850.

22. Mayo Cabell to Joseph C. Cabell, 13 March 1850, in Joseph C. Cabell Papers, UVL; Tucker to Hammond, 13, 26 March, 18 April 1850, Typescript in Tucker Papers, DUL; Crallé to R. M. T. Hunter, 23 March 1850, in Ambler, *Correspondence of R. M. T. Hunter,* 106-108; Richmond *Whig,* 9 April 1850.

23. Goode to Hunter, 20 April 1850, in Ambler, *Correspondence of R. M. T. Hunter,* 111; Richmond *Whig,* 29 March, 8 May 1850; Richmond *Enquirer,* 19 March-10 May 1850. Richmond meeting in 30 April issue.

24. Shanks, *Secession Movement in Virginia,* 32-33; Ambler, *Sectionalism in Virginia,* 247.

25. Richmond *Enquirer,* 10-31 May 1850; *Cong. Globe,* 31 Cong., 1 Sess., Appendix, 599-600.

26. Cooper to Joseph Varnum, 7 April 1850.

27. Nashville *Union,* 13 March, 15 April, 3 May 1850.

28. McNairy to Crittenden, 19 March 1850, in Crittenden Papers, LC.

29. Nashville *Union,* 13 April, 2 May 1850.

30. *Republican Banner,* 7 May 1850; Robert B. Satterfield, "Andrew Jackson Donelson, A Moderate Nationalist Jacksonian" (Ph.D. dissertation, Johns Hopkins University, 1961), 423.

31. See *Union* and *Banner,* May 1850; Giles and Bedford meetings in *Union,* 9, 10 May 1850.

32. Johnson to Buchanan, 14 April 1850, in Buchanan Papers, HSP; Johnson to Donelson, 10 May 1850, in Andrew Jackson Donelson Papers, LC.

33. Nashville *Union,* 1 June 1850.

34. *Brownlow's Knoxville Whig,* 30 March, 20 April 1850.

35. Nashville *Union,* 13 May 1850, list of delegates; *Republican Banner,* 13 May 1850, claimed "perhaps a half dozen persons" were present.

36. Nashville *Union,* 21 May 1850; *Brownlow's Whig,* 20 April 1850.

37. Nashville *Union* and *Republican Banner,* May 1850.

38. Files of the *Arkansas Banner* and *Arkansas Gazette and Democrat,* February-May 1850; Brown, "Albert Pike," 267-76.

39. *Arkansas Banner,* 21, 28 May, 18 June 1850; *Arkansas Gazette and Democrat,* 31 May 1850.

40. Hearon, "Mississippi and the Compromise of 1850," 118; Jackson *Southron,* 19 April, 3 May 1850; Vicksburg *Sentinel,* 3 April 1850.

41. Clipping from the *Mississippian* (n.d.), John A. Quitman Scrapbook in John A. Quitman Papers, MAH; Vicksburg *Sentinel,* 25 May 1850; Sharkey to the editor of the *Southron,* 21 June 1850; Richard A. McLemore (ed.), *A History of Mississippi,* 2 vols. (Hattiesburg, MS, 1973), 1:303.

42. Hamer, *Secession Movement in South Carolina,* 58.

43. De Saussure to Unknown, 6 March 1850, individual file, SCL; Joel Ward to Lewis Ward, 7 May 1850, in Lewis Ward Papers, DUL.

44. Boucher, "Secession and Cooperation Movements in South Carolina," 86-87; Charleston *Mercury,* 31 May 1850; *Spartan,* 16, 23 May 1850.

45. Tucker to Hammond, 7 May 1850, Typescript in Tucker Papers, DUL; Benjamin F. Perry, MS Journal, 10, 6 June 1850; Williams to Lieber, 12 February 1850, in Francis Lieber Papers, SCL.

46. Hammond to Calhoun, 5 March 1850, in Jameson, *Correspondence of Calhoun,* 1210-12; Hammond's Diary, 17 March 1850, SCL; Hammond to Simms, 26 March 1850, in Hammond Papers, LC.

47. Hamer, *Secession Movement in South Carolina,* 10.

48. Simms to Hammond, 17 December 1849, in Oliphant, Odell, and Eaves, *Letters of Simms,* 2:574-77. Jamison was chosen as a delegate, but Simms was not.

49. Boucher, "Secession and Cooperation Movements in South Carolina," 96; Yancey to Chairman of Committee, Abbeville, 20 April 1850, in Benjamin C. Yancey Papers, SHC. B.C., a brother of W. L. Yancey, was not chosen.

50. Yeadon to Poinsett, 1 March 1850; Poinsett to Yeadon, 6 March 1850; Yeadon to Poinsett, 9 March 1850; Poinsett to Yeadon, 18 March 1850, all in Joel R. Poinsett Papers, HSP.

51. Holman Hamilton, *Prologue to Conflict,* 66, 126-32. J. Hamilton did request John Bell, a member of the Senate Committee of Thirteen, to work for the provision of an additional slave state from Texas in the committee's report. Hamilton to Bell, 1 May 1850, in John Bell Papers, LC.

52. Hayne to Hammond, 3 May 1850, in Hammond Papers, LC. Elmore died on 29 May, four days before the convention met.

53. Hamer, *Secession Movement in South Carolina,* 47-48.

54. Simms to Tucker, 30 May 1850, in Oliphant, Odell, and Eaves, *Letters of Simms,* 3:43-44.

# Chapter 6

1. Goode to R. M. T. Hunter, 29 March 1850, Ambler, *Correspondence of R. M. T. Hunter,* 109; William Gilmore Simms, "The Southern Convention," *Southern Quarterly Review* 18 (September 1850): 215; Cooper to D. R. Arnell, 10 June 1850, in Cooper Family Papers, TSL; Gordon to Mrs. Gordon, 6 June 1850, in Gordon Family Papers, UVL.

2. Biographical sources include Allen Johnson and Dumas Malone, *Dictionary of American Biography,* 22 vols. (New York,

1928-1958); *Biographical Directory of the American Congress,* 1774-1961 (Washington, 1961); individual biographies; state and county histories; newspapers; private collections; and manuscript returns of the seventh census of the United States, 1850, schedule no. 1: free inhabitants, and schedule no. 2: slaveholdings. See Appendix B for biographical tables for each state delegation.

3. Report of Samuel Otterson, South Carolina delegate, *The Spartan* (Spartanburg), 17 October 1850. No information on selection of any Louisiana delegates was available.

4. Manuscript census returns give age, place of birth, occupation, and amount of real estate. Other sources, not previously cited, include: Emily B. Reynolds and Joan R. Faunt (comps.) , *Biographical Directory of the Senate of the State of South Carolina, 1776-1964* (Columbia, 1964); John R. May and Joan R. Faunt, *South Carolina Secedes* (Columbia, 1960). Mrs. Faunt personally supplied additional information. Benjamin F. Perry, *Reminiscences of Public Men* (Greenville, 1899); Joshua H. Hudson, *Sketches and Reminiscences* (Columbia, 1903); John B. O'Neal, *The Annals of Newberry* (Charleston, 1859); J. B. O. Landrum, *History of Spartanburg County* (Atlanta, 1900); Elizabeth Merritt, *James Henry Hammond, 1807-1864* (Baltimore, 1923); Robert C. Tucker, "James Henry Hammond, South Carolinian" (Ph. D. dissertation, University of North Carolina, 1958); Laura A. White, *Robert Barnwell Rhett: Father of Secession* (1931; rpt. Gloucester, MA, 1965); J. H. Easterby (ed.), *The South Carolina Rice Plantation as Revealed in the Papers of Robert F. W. Allston* (Chicago, 1935); Archie Vernon Huff, Jr., *Langdon Cheves of South Carolina* (Columbia, 1977).

5. Cooper to D. R. Arnell, 10 June 1850, in Cooper Family Papers, TSL. J. H. Ingraham (ed.), *The Sunny South, or the Southerner at Home: Embracing Five Years Experience of a Northern Governess in the Land of the Sugar and the Cotton* (Philadelphia, 1860), 132-33. The governess who attended the convention wrote under the assumed name, "Kate Conynham."

6. Based upon the categories used by Kenneth Stampp, i.e., large planters 50 slaves or more, small planters 20 to 50 slaves, farmers less than 20 or no slaves. See Kenneth M. Stampp, *The Peculiar Institution: Slavery in the Antebellum South* (New York, 1956), 30. Census enumerators followed no consistent pattern in labeling "planters" and "farmers." Slaves were enumerated by the county of residence of the owner. It is entirely possible that any delegate might have owned additional slaves in other counties or even in another state.

7. Chauncey S. Boucher, *The Nullification Controversy in South Carolina* (Chicago, 1916), 53-56, 104, 276-79; Yates Snowden (ed.),

*History of South Carolina,* 5 vols. (Chicago, 1920), 2:586-87 contains the names of all those who signed; Francis W. Pickens, "Private Notebook, 1835-1869," 11 May 1835, SCL.

8. White, *Rhett,* 105-106; Rhett to Calhoun, 19 July 1849, in Boucher and Brooks, "Correspondence Addressed to Calhoun," 517-18.

9. *Dictionary of American Biography,* 9:604-605.

10. Hammond to Edmund Ruffin, 8 February 1850, in Ruffin Papers, SHC; Hammond to Calhoun, 5 March 1850, in Jameson, *Correspondence of Calhoun,* 1210-12; Hammond's Diary, 17 March, 26 May 1850, in Hammond Papers, SCL; Hammond to William B. Hodgson, 2 April 1850, in Hammond Papers, DUL.

11. Benjamin F. Perry, MS Journal, 19 May and 9 July 1850, SHC.

12. Dallas T. Herndon, "The Nashville Convention of 1850," Alabama Historical Society *Transactions* 5 (1905): 229-30 contains a list of delegates from each state for each session.

13. Charles Robert Lee, Jr., *The Confederate Constitutions* (Chapel Hill, 1963), 22-26, 147.

14. *Dictionary of American Biography,* Suppl. 1:689-90.

15. Dunbar Rowland (ed.), *Encyclopedia of Mississippi History,* 2 vols. (Madison, WI, 1907), and *The Official and Statistical Register of the State of Mississippi* (Nashville, 1908); Goodspeed's *Biographical and Historical Memoirs of Mississippi,* 2 vols. (Chicago, 1891); William B. Hamilton, "Holly Springs, Mississippi, to the Year 1878," (MA thesis, University of Mississippi, 1931). Biographical files in the Department of Archives and History, Jackson, were useful. The only biography of a Mississippi delegate is Robert W. Dubay, *John Jones Pettus, Mississippi Fire-eater: His Life and Times, 1813-1867* (Jackson, 1975). Dubay claims Pettus did not attend the Nashville Convention, but he is listed as a delegate in the official journal.

16. *Southron* (Jackson), 7 June 1850; Message of retiring Governor Matthews, 7 January 1850, *Journal of the House of Representatives,* 13-30; Ingraham, *The Sunny South,* 137.

17. Address of the States Rights Committee to the People of Mississippi, 10 December 1850, in J. F. H. Claiborne Papers, SHC; *Mississippi Free Trader* (Natchez) 30 September 1850; Rowland, *Encyclopedia,* 2:695-96. Smith's name appeared on the bonds Gen. Narciso Lopez, the Venezuelan adventurer who tried to raise a force of American volunteers to free Cuba, put in circulation.

18. T. J. Word to W. P. Donnell, 22 April 1850, as cited by Hearon, "Mississippi and the Compromise," 123; *Speech of Honorable S. S. Boyd Delivered at the Great Union Festival Held at Jackson, Mississippi,* published in pamphlet form (Natchez, 1851), 9.

19. Vicksburg *Daily Sentinel,* 23 April 1850; Sharkey to the editors of the *National Intelligencer,* 4 April 1850, reprinted in the *Black River Watchman* (Sumterville, S. C.), 11 May 1850; Sharkey to the editor of the *Southron,* 24 May 1850.

20. As cited by Hearon, "Mississippi and the Compromise," 120; *Southron,* 28 June 1850, second letter; *Mississippi Free Trader,* 22 June 1850; Samuel Otterson in *Spartan,* 17 October 1850.

21. *Southron,* 21 June 1850; Vicksburg *Daily Sentinel,* 5 October 1850; Henry S. Foote, *The War of the Rebellion* (New York, 1866), 146.

22. See Chapter 9 of this study. None of the June delegates from Mississippi attended the second session.

23. Editorial comments, *Southern Quarterly Review* 17 (April 1850): 255.

24. Ralph A. Wooster, "The Secession Conventions of the Lower South: A Study of their Membership" (Ph. D. dissertation, University of Texas, 1954).

25. Neil is credited with having raised the Thirtieth Infantry Regiment, particularly noted for "dash, brilliancy and courage."

26. Shryock, *Georgia and the Union,* 264-65.

27. Simpson Fouche and Obediah Warner were not listed on the 1850 census returns, but Fouche was listed on the 1860 census.

28. No published biographies for any of the delegates exist. The general card file for biographical information and a few county tax digests on microfilm at the Department of Archives, Atlanta, were useful. A scrapbook of Lizzie Mitchell's history of Pike County arranged by Elsie Story, 1932, supplied information for Gibson.

29. *Southern Museum* (Macon), 27 July, 10, 24 August 1850; Benning to Cobb, 1 July 1849, in Phillips, *Correspondence,* 168-72; Benning to Cobb, 29 March 1850, in "Howell Cobb Papers," *Georgia Historical Quarterly* 5 (September 1921): 37-40.

30. *Southern Museum,* 23, 2, 30 March 1850; *Federal Union,* 28 May 1850; John H. Lumpkin to Cobb, 21 July 1850, in Phillips, *Correspondence,* 207.

31. Dodd, "Secession Movement in Florida," 8.

32. C. Seton Fleming, "Observations on Original Members," *Florida Historical Quarterly* 3 (January 1924): 12, 14.

33. *The Florida Sentinel* (Tallahassee), 5 March, 7, 14 May 1850.

34. Herbert J. Doherty, Jr., *Richard Keith Call* (Gainesville, 1961), 126.

35. *Dictionary of American Biography,* 4:526-27; Nevins, *Ordeal of the Union,* 1:316-17.

36. William Garrett, *Reminiscences of Public Men in Alabama* (Atlanta, 1862); Thomas M. Owen, *History of Alabama and Diction-*

*ary of Alabama Biography,* 4 vols. (Chicago, 1921); Willis Brewer, *Alabama: Her History, Resources, War Record and Public Men, 1549-1872* (Montgomery, 1872); James E. Saunders, *Early Settlers of Alabama with Notes and Genealogies* (New Orleans, 1899); William C. Harris, *Leroy Pope Walker: Confederate Secretary of War* (Tuscaloosa, 1962); Glenn N. Sisk, "John Anthony Winston, Alabama's Veto Governor" (MA thesis, University of Alabama, 1934); George W. Duncan, "John Archibald Campbell," Alabama Historical Society *Transactions* 5 (1904): 107-51; Justine Staib Mann, "The Political and Constitutional Thought of John Archibald Campbell," (Ph.D. dissertation, University of Alabama, 1966); James R. Maxwell, Jr., "John Archibald Campbell, States Rights and the Federal Union, 1829-1861" (Senior thesis, Princeton University, 1958). The only published biography of an Alabama delegate is Henry G. Conner, *John Archibald Campbell* (Boston, 1920).

37. *Alabama Journal* (Montgomery) 19 April 1850; Joseph Hodgson, *The Cradle of the Confederacy* (Mobile, 1876), 278; J. E. D. Yonge, "The Conservative Party in Alabama, 1848-60," Alabama Historical Society *Transactions* 4 (1899-1903): 503.

38. *Florida Sentinel* (Tallahassee), 19 March 1850.

39. John A. Campbell, "Slavery in the United States," *Southern Quarterly Review* 12 (July 1847): 91-134; Maxwell, "Campbell," 34; Mann, "Political and Constitutional Thought of Campbell," 96. According to the census, he owned 17 slaves in 1850. Duncan, "Campbell," 121.

40. Dorman, *Party Politics in Alabama,* 45; Albert B. Moore, *History of Alabama and Her People,* 3 vols. (Chicago, 1927), 2:241. The Yancey collection at the Department of Archives and History, Montgomery, contains nothing useful for this period. Various authors, including his biographer, John W. DuBose, have more adequately covered his role after the convention.

41. Montgomery *Advertiser and State Gazette,* 22 May 1850. This article states that Yancey also addressed the meeting in favor of resolutions approving the Nashville Convention.

42. Harris, *Leroy Pope Walker,* 10-18; Sisk, "John A. Winston," 13-15.

43. William H. Brantly, Jr., "Alabama Secedes," *Alabama Review* 7 (July 1954): 169, 180.

44. Ingraham, *The Sunny South,* 134.

45. E. G. Swem, *Virginia Historical Index,* 2 vols. (Roanoke, 1934) was helpful in locating material. There are biographies of two delegates: Armistead Gordon, *William Fitzhugh Gordon* (New York, 1909), and Robert J. Brugger, *Beverley Tucker: Heart Over Head in the Old South* (Baltimore, 1978). Vernon L. Parrington, *Main Cur-*

*rents in American Thought,* 3 vols. (New York, 1927), 2:30-35 includes a good account of Tucker.

46. Richmond *Enquirer,* 11 May 1850; Richmond *Whig,* 29 March 1850; Goode to R. M. T. Hunter, 11 May 1850, in Ambler, *Correspondence of Hunter,* 112-13.

47. Tucker to Hammond, 18 April 1850, in Tucker Papers, DUL.

48. Richmond *Enquirer,* 11 March, 9 April, 14 May 1850.

49. Tucker to Hammond, 7 May 1850, in Tucker Papers, DUL; Newton to the editor of the Richmond *Times,* 20 April 1850, reprinted in Richmond *Enquirer,* 30 April 1850; Gordon to Hunter, 2 July 1850, in Ambler, *Correspondence of R. M. T. Hunter,* 113-14; Goode to Hunter, 20 April and 11 May 1850, in ibid, 110-13; Richmond *Enquirer,* 17 May 1850.

50. Tucker to Hammond, 27 January, 8 February 1850, in Tucker Papers, DUL; Tucker to his nephew, 25 March 1850, *William and Mary Quarterly,* ser. 1, vol. 18 (July 1909): 44-46; Tucker to Hammond, 7 May 1850, in Tucker Papers, DUL.

51. Josiah H. Shinn, *Pioneers and Makers of Arkansas* (Little Rock, 1908), 80.

52. Unidentified delegates are followed by an asterisk in Tennessee's list in Appendix A.

53. The late Dr. Daniel M. Robison very graciously contributed his compiled information on all delegates who had served in the Tennessee legislature. Biographical sketches and other data at the Tennessee State Archives, Nashville, were helpful. Other useful sources, not previously cited, include: John P. Campbell (ed.), *The Nashville, State of Tennessee and General Commercial Directory* (Nashville, 1853); Herschel Gower and Jack Allen (eds.), *Pen and Sword: The Life and Journals of Randal W. McGavock* (Nashville, 1959); William S. Speer, *Sketches of Prominent Tennesseans* (Nashville, 1888); Goodspeed's *History of Tennessee* (Nashville, 1886-87); W. Jerome D. Spence and David L. Spence, *A History of Hickman County, Tennessee* (Nashville, 1900); James McCallum, *Settlement and Early History of Giles County, Tennessee* (Pulaski, 1876); W. W. Clayton, *History of Davidson County, Tennessee* (Philadelphia, 1880); Ursula B. Beach, *Along the Warioto: A History of Montgomery County, Tennessee* (Nashville, 1964); William B. Turner, *History of Maury County, Tennessee* (Nashville, 1955); Jill K. Garrett (comp.), *Maury County, Tennessee, Newspapers (Abstracts), 1846-1850* (Columbia, 1965). Mrs. Garrett and Mrs. Jack P. Lightfoot, both of Columbia, personally supplied information. *Speeches, Congressional and Political and Other Writings of Ex-Governor Aaron V. Brown of Tennessee* arranged by the editor of the Nashville *Union and American* (Nashville, 1854); Patricia P. Clark, "A. O. P. Nicholson of

Tennessee: Editor, Statesman and Jurist" (MA thesis, University of Tennessee, 1965); and genealogical data attached to the McGavock Papers, SHC.

54. Hammond to William Gilmore Simms, 16 June 1850, in Hammond Papers, LC.

55. Cooper to D. R. Arnell, 10 June 1850, Cooper Papers, TSL; Johnson to James Buchanan, 6 June 1850, in Buchanan Papers, HSP.

56. Quoted by Satterfield, "A. J. Donelson," 423; Nashville *Union,* 15 April, 23 June 1850.

57. Sioussat, "Tennessee, Compromise, and Convention," 339; Hammond to Simms, 16 June 1850, in Hammond Papers, LC.

58. Philip M. Hamer, *Tennessee: A History 1673-1932,* 4 vols. (New York, 1933), 2:1021-22. Civil War Centennial Commission, *Tennesseans in the Civil War,* 2 vols., (Nashville, 1964), vol. 2 passim.

59. Ingraham, *The Sunny South,* 130.

# Chapter 7

1. There were 2,028 slaves, 511 free Blacks, and 7,626 whites. United States Bureau of Census, *Seventh Census of the United States* (Washington, 1853), 575, 397, 399.

2. Gordon to Mrs. Gordon, 6 June 1850, in Gordon Family Papers, UVL; F. Garvin Davenport, *Cultural Life in Nashville on the Eve of the Civil War* (Chapel Hill, 1941), 1-2; Jesse C. Burt, *Nashville: Its Life and Times* (Nashville, 1959), 47-50.

3. Clayton, *History of Davidson County,* 207; First American National Bank, *Firsts in Nashville: A Pictorial History* (Nashville, 1966), 19-20; Charles E. Roberts, *Nashville and Her Trade* (Nashville, 1870), 40-41.

4. Davenport, *Cultural Life in Nashville,* 32-33, 84; Joe C. Guild, *Old Times in Tennessee with Historical, Personal and Political Scraps and Sketches* (Nashville, 1878), 487; Henry McRaven, *Nashville: "Athens of the South"* (Chapel Hill, 1949), 87.

5. Nashville *Union,* 13 June 1850; William Gilmore Simms, "The Southern Convention," *Southern Quarterly Review* 19 (September 1850): 215. Simms claimed that when the delegates first assembled "their reception was a cold one"; Ingraham, *The Sunny South,* 130-31.

6. Nashville Union, 4 June 1850; Felix Robertson, son of James,

and the first white male child born in Nashville, was a delegate. Biographical sketch, TSL; Staff of McKendree Methodist Church (eds.), *The March of McKendree, 1787-1962* (Nashville, 1962), a 35 page monograph; John Wooldridge (ed.), *History of Nashville, Tennessee* (Nashville, 1890), 455-56; Cullen T. Carter (ed.), *History of Methodist Churches and Institutions in Middle Tennessee* (Nashville, 1956), 15-17; Ingraham, *The Sunny South,* 140.

7. Cooper later stated that his position as secretary was conferred as part of the secret history of the convention, in order that his "pen" might be used, if necessary, in the convention's defense. Cooper to D. R. Arnell, 10 June 1850, in Cooper Family Papers, TSL.

8. *Resolutions, Address, and Journal of Proceedings of the Southern Convention, Held at Nashville, Tennessee, June 3rd to 12th, inclusive in the Year 1850* (Nashville, 1850), 23-24. Official journal of the first session published by order of the convention and located at Harvard University Library. The journal includes the resolutions introduced, but it does not contain speeches. Hereafter cited as *Official Journal.* The Nashville *Union* (Democrat) and the Whig papers, the *Republican Banner* and the *True Whig,* the best accounts of the convention among the city's press, were useful as supplements.

9. Nashville *Union,* 5 June 1850; Nashville *Gazette* and Nashville *True Whig,* 4 June 1850; *Official Journal,* 26-28.

10. Ingraham, *The Sunny South,* 131; Johnson to James Buchanan, 6 June 1850, in Buchanan Papers, HSP.

11. Nashville *Union* and *Republican Banner,* 3 June 1850. Davidson County delegates who signed the petition for the meeting included T. D. Moseley, Washington Barrow, Jacob McGavock, J. N. Esselman, and Felix Robertson. See Nashville *Gazette,* 29 May 1850.

12. Nashville *Union,* 1 June 1850. They were C. J. Dickerson, George Gantt, R. A. L. Wilkes, R. G. Payne, and William H. Polk.

13. Charleston *Mercury,* 8 June 1850; Huntsville *Democrat,* 6 June 1850.

14. Ingraham, *The Sunny South,* 129-30, 132, 135-36.

15. *Official Journal,* 34-37.

16. *Republican Banner,* 5, 7 June 1850.

17. Ingraham, *The Sunny South,* 136, 140; Charleston *Mercury,* 11 June 1850.

18. A delegate's figure of speech, in Ingraham, *The Sunny South,* 131.

19. First American National Bank, *Firsts in Nashville,* 20; Gordon to Mrs. Gordon, 6 June 1850, in Gordon Family Papers, UVL.

20. *Official Journal,* 45-50.

21. Charleston *Mercury,* 11 June 1850; Minority Report, *Official Journal,* 21-22.

22. *Official Journal,* 53-56. Tucker's plan included seventeen points.

23. Ingraham, *The Sunny South,* 71-73, 136-37; Davenport, *Cultural Life in Nashville,* 118-19; Republican Banner, 8, 20 June 1850; McRaven, *Nashville: "Athens of the South,"* 87. One Georgia delegate related that he and others visited the Hermitage. *Federal Union,* 18 June 1850.

24. *Official Journal,* 57-60. For Campbell's resolutions see 29-32. Huntsville *Democrat,* 13 June 1850; Cooper to D. R. Arnell, 10 June 1850, in Cooper Papers, TSL.

25. Henderson to Rusk, 22 June 1850, in Thomas J. Rusk Papers, UTxL.

26. *Speech of Samuel S. Boyd Delivered at the Great Union Festival Held at Jackson, Mississippi* (Natchez, 1851), 9-10, 13. A copy of this pamphlet, 19 pages in length, is in LC.

27. *Official Journal,* 3-8, complete resolutions and 9-21, address. See also *Resolutions and Address of the Southern Convention, June 8, 1850* (Nashville, 1850), an official publication without the proceedings. A copy of this publication is in TSL.

28. Boyd's description in *Boyd's Speech,* 12.

29. Charleston *Mercury,* 17 June 1850; *Official Journal,* 60-63.

30. *Official Journal,* 64; Nashville *Union,* 12 June 1850; *Republican Banner,* 13 June 1850; Cooper to D. R. Arnell, 10 June 1850; Ingraham, *The Sunny South,* 137-38.

31. Nashville *Union,* 12 June 1850; *Republican Banner,* 13 June 1850; Ingraham, *The Sunny South,* 133; Cooper to D. R. Arnell, 10 June 1850; Simms, "The Southern Convention," 227. Simms was reporting what he had heard, as he was not present.

32. Hammond to Simms, 16 June 1850, in Hammond Papers, LC; Hammond's Diary, 10 August 1850, in Hammond Papers, SCL; *Republican Banner,* 13, 14 June 1850.

33. Cooper to D. R. Arnell, 10 June 1850; Simms, "The Southern Convention," 217; "Southern Convention: Remarks of the Hon. Beverley Tucker of Virginia," a 16-page pamphlet at VHS; Ingraham, *The Sunny South,* 134.

34. *Republican Banner,* 15 June 1850. Simms, "Southern Convention," 224-27 includes extracts from Sharkey's speech and Hammond's reply. Hammond's Diary, 10 August 1850, in Hammond Papers, SCL; Cooper to D. R. Arnell, 10 June 1850.

35. Nashville *True Whig,* 15 June 1850; Nashville *Union,* 13, 14 June 1850.

36. Hammond to Simms, 16 June 1850, in Hammond Papers, LC.

See also Hammond's Diary, 10 August 1850, in Hammond Papers, SCL.

37. Easterby, *The South Carolina Rice Plantation,* 445-46; Charleston *Mercury,* 7 September 1850.

38. *The Spartan* (Spartanburg, S. C.), 17 October 1850.

39. *The Southron* (Jackson) 5 July 1850; White, *Rhett,* 108-109; Hammond to Simms, 27 June 1850, in Hammond Papers, LC.

40. Gordon to Hunter, 2 July 1850, in Ambler, *Correspondence of R. M. T. Hunter,* 113-14; Tucker to Hammond, 17 July 1850, in Tucker Papers, DUL.

41. Henderson to Thomas J. Rusk, 22 July 1850 in Rusk Papers, UTxL.

42. *Boyd's Speech,* 10-11; *The Southron,* 25 October 1850.

43. Nashville *Union,* 1 July 1850; *Republican Banner,* 26 June 1850.

44. Cooper to D. R. Arnell, 10 June 1850, in Cooper Papers, TSL.

45. Press accounts during the summer and autumn. See especially *Federal Union* (Milledgeville), 10 September; *Southern Recorder* (Milledgeville), 20, 27 August; Charleston *Mercury,* 22 October; *Alabama Journal* (Montgomery), 24 July; *Mississippi Free Trader* (Natchez), 31 August, 7 September; Vicksburg *Daily Sentinel,* 27 July 1850.

46. Charleston *Mercury,* 21 June 1850. Special correspondent's reports 17, 18 June 1850; Nashville *Union,* 19 June 1850; Boucher, "Secession and Cooperation Movements," 98; Simms, "The Southern Convention," 215-231; Benjamin F. Perry, MS Journal, 23 June 1850, SHC.

47. *Federal Union,* 4, 25 June 1850; cited by the Raleigh *Register,* 13 July 1850.

48. Cited by the *Southern Press* (Washington), 25, 26 June 1850.

49. Lumpkin to Howell Cobb, 21 July 1850, in Phillips, *Correspondence,* 206-208.

50. *Mississippi Free Trader* (Natchez), 22 June 1850; Vicksburg *Daily Sentinel,* 20, 25 June 1850; *The Southron,* 5 July 1850.

51. Denman, *Secession Movement in Alabama,* 33-35; DuBose, *Life and Times of Yancey,* 1:248.

52. Huntsville *Democrat,* 13, 20 June 1850; *Alabama Journal,* 21, 24 June 1850; Eufaula *Democrat,* 11 June 1850; cited by *Republican Banner,* 19 June 1850.

53. *Floridian and Journal,* 29 June 1850; *Florida Sentinel* (Tallahassee), 25 June 1850; Pensacola *Gazette,* 15 June 1850; Wienberg, "Slavery and Secession in Florida," 68.

54. Nashville *Union,* 14 June 1850. At this time Editor Eastman also endorsed the Compromise. See editorials beginning in May. *Republican Banner,* 19 June 1850. See other issues of this paper and the Nashville *True Whig* for this period; Memphis *Enquirer* cited by the Nashville *Union,* 19 June 1850.

55. Shanks, *Secession Movement in Virginia,* 35-36; Richmond *Enquirer,* 21 June 1850; Lynchburg *Virginian,* 20 June 1850.

56. *Arkansas State Gazette and Democrat,* 28 June 1850.

57. Raleigh *Register,* 26 June 1850.

58. J. D. B. DeBow, "The Cause of the South" *DeBow's Review* 9 (July 1850): 22, and "The Nashville Convention Again" (August 1850): 250; New Orleans *Bee,* 21 June 1850; New Orleans *Courier,* 20 June, 27 May 1850; Baton Rouge *Gazette,* 15, 22 June 1850.

59. *Southern Press,* 20 June 1850; Nashville *Daily Gazette,* 12 June 1850; cited by Raleigh *Register,* 22 June 1850.

60. Nashville *Daily Gazette,* 12 June 1850; cited by *Southern Press,* 25 June 1850.

61. Cited by *Southern Shield* (Helena, Arkansas), 29 June 1850; New York *Herald,* 7, 23 June 1850.

62. Washington *Union,* 18, 19, 20, 21, 22 June 1850.

63. Gordon and Paige, *Works of Daniel Webster,* 5: 429; King to Buchanan, 11 June 1850, in Buchanan Papers, HSP. King was a member of the Senate Committee of Thirteen.

# *Chapter 8*

1. Henry Clay to Thomas Clay, 31 May 1850, in Henry Clay Papers, LC; *Cong. Globe,* 31 Cong., 1 Sess., Appendix, 612-16.

2. *Cong. Globe,* 31 Cong., 1 Sess., Appendix, 571, for committee addition. Ibid., 31 Cong., 1 Sess., 1134, 1146, for Berrien and Yulee amendments. The latter extended the Constitution to a territory. See ibid., Appendix 902, 911, for Soulé's amendment which permitted admission of a state from the western territory regardless of its slave or free status.

3. *Cong. Globe,* 31 Cong., 1 Sess., 1216.

4. Nevins, *Ordeal of the Union,* 1: 327-30; Hamilton, *Zachary Taylor,* 2:374-80. Outlaw to Mrs. Outlaw, 24 June 1850, in David Outlaw Papers, SHC.

5. There are controversial versions of these interviews. Some

accounts claim Stephens accompanied Toombs on his 3 July visit. See Ulrich B. Phillips, *The Life of Robert Toombs* (New York, 1913), 83. Hamilton belives the final interview occurred on 3 July and that Stephens was not present. Hamilton, *Zachary Taylor,* 2: 380-81.

6. *National Intelligencer,* 4 July 1850; Taylor was also planning to reorganize his Cabinet with a decided northern preponderance. Nevins, *Ordeal of the Union,* 1: 332-34.

7. Robert J. Rayback, *Millard Fillmore: Biography of a President* (Buffalo, 1959), 186-87, 224-37; Claude M. Fuess, *Daniel Webster,* 2 vols. (Hamden, Conn., 1963), 2: 235; Gordon and Paige, *Works of Daniel Webster,* 5: 412-38.

8. Henderson to Quitman, 22 July 1850, in Claiborne, *Life of Quitman,* 2: 41-42; Campbell, "Texas and the Nashville Convention," 12.

9. *Cong. Globe,* 31 Cong., 1 Sess., Appendix, 1390, 1405-15; David Outlaw to Mrs. Outlaw, 22 July 1850, in Outlaw Papers, SHC.

10. *Cong. Globe,* 31 Cong., 1 Sess., 1481-82, 1489-91; ibid., Appendix, 1456, 1463, 1470-85; Hamilton, *Prologue to Conflict,* 107-17, quote, 112.

11. Douglas to Charles H. Lanphier and George Walker, 3 August 1850, in Robert W. Johannsen (ed.), *The Letters of Stephen A. Douglas* (Urbana, 1961), 191; Andrew Ewing to Edwin Ewing, 2 August 1850, in Andrew Ewing Papers, DUL.

12. Rayback, *Fillmore,* 250-51; George F. Milton, *The Eve of Conflict: Stephen A. Douglas and the Needless War* (New York, 1963), 72-78; George D. Harmon, "Douglas and the Compromise of 1850," *Journal of the Illinois State Historical Society* 21 (January 1929): 453-99. See Hamilton, *Prologue to Conflict,* 191-92, for Senate roll-calls on all Compromise measures.

13. *Cong. Globe,* 31 Cong., 1 Sess., Appendix, 1533, 1535.

14. Copy of this agreement in Hopkins L. Turney to Robert Barnwell Rhett, 1 May 1852, in the Robert Barnwell Rhett Papers, SHC. Southern senators who signed were Turney, Butler, Atchison, Yulee, Soulé, Davis, Clemens, Mason, Morton, and Barnwell.

15. *Cong. Globe,* 31 Cong., 1 Sess., Appendix, 1535, 1537-38. Barnwell had been appointed to fill Calhoun's vacancy when Franklin Elmore, the first appointee, died.

16. *Cong Globe,* 31 Cong., 1 Sess., 1573.

17. *Cong. Globe,* 31 Cong., 1 Sess., 1574. In this protest Hunter's name appears instead of Clemens in the group who signed the 2 August agreement. Although Foote voted against the California bill, he opposed this protest. Hearon, "Mississippi and the Compromise of 1850," 143.

18. W. A. Graham to James Graham, 25 August 1850, in Hamilton and Williams, *Papers of William Alexander Graham,* 3: 369.

19. *Cong. Globe,* 31 Cong., 1 Sess., 1589, 1660, 1829-30, 1683-86; David Outlaw to Mrs. Outlaw, 5 September 1850, in Outlaw Papers, SHC.

20. *Cong. Globe,* 31 Cong., 1 Sess., 1762-64, 1769-76, 1806-07, 1810-12, 1837. See Hamilton, *Prologue to Conflict,* 195-200, for House rollcalls on the Compromise measures; Millard Fillmore to Robert L. Caruthers, 20 August 1850, in Robert L. Caruthers Papers, SHC.

21. Harris to John M. Berrien, 2 August 1850, in Berrien Papers, SHC; Benjamin F. Perry, 14 September 1850, MS Journal, SHC.

22. Simms to Beverley Tucker, 11 September 1850, in Oliphant, Odell, and Eaves, *Letters of Simms,* 3: 65. Barnwell to Hammond, 25 July, 9 September 1850; Hammond to Samuel J. Ray, 12, 27 August 1850 and to Simpson Fouche and others, 26 September 1850, all in Hammond Papers, LC.

23. White, *Rhett,* 111. Nashville Convention delegates from Georgia who spoke at this meeting were Walter T. Colquitt, James N. Ramsey, and Obediah Gibson. *Southern Museum,* 24 August 1850; Chapman to Stephens, 31 August 1850, in Alexander H. Stephens Papers, LC.

24. *Federal Union,* 24 September 1850; Green, "Politics in Georgia," 242; Shryock, *Georgia and the Union,* 296-97.

25. Hamer, *Secession Movement in South Carolina,* 65-67; Lieber to Henry W. Hilliard, 11 August 1850, in Lieber Papers, SCL.

26. Seabrook to John A. Leland, 18, 21 September 1850; Seabrook to the governors of Alabama, Virginia, and Mississippi, 20 September 1850; Towns to Seabrook, 25 September 1850, all in Seabrook Papers, LC.

27. Hearon, "Mississippi and the Compromise of 1850," 148-55; Huston to Quitman, 19 September 1850; Barnwell to Quitman, 19 September 1850, all in J. F. H. Claiborne Papers, MAH.

28. Copy of proclamation in Claiborne, *Life of Quitman,* 2:43; Quitman to McRae, 28 September 1850, in ibid., 44-46; Quitman to Seabrook, 29 September 1850, in Seabrook Papers, LC; Quitman to his daughter Louise, 1 October 1850, in Quitman-Lovell-Duncan Papers, SHC.

29. Seabrook to Towns, 8 October 1850, in Seabrook Papers, LC. See also Richard Yeadon to Benjamin F. Perry, 17 October 1850, in Benjamin F. Perry Papers, AAH; Seabrook to Quitman, 23 October 1850, in Claiborne, *Life of Quitman,* 2: 37-38.

30. Pickens to Perry, 30 October 1850, in Perry Papers, AAH.

31. Denman, *Secession Movement in Alabama,* 36-42. Allan Nevins divides the lower South in practically the same manner in *Ordeal of the Union,* 1: 357-58.

32. Campbell to H. W. Collier, 5 October 1850, clipping from an

unidentified Mobile newspaper in A. W. Venable Scrapbook, 1849-50, pp. 78-81, DUL; *Alabama Journal,* 1, 4, 16 November 1850; Tocca Cozart, "Henry W. Hilliard," Alabama Historical Society *Transactions* 4 (1904): 277-99.

33. Dorman, *Party Politics in Alabama,* 48; T. B. Bethea to the Montgomery Union Meeting, 28 October 1850, in *Alabama Journal,* 6 November 1850; King to Bolling Hall, 19 November 1850, in Bolling Hall Papers, AAH.

34. Denman, *Secession Movement in Alabama,* 46-50; DuBose, *W. L. Yancey,* 1: 251-52.

35. The Democrats won control of the legislature. John Meador, "Florida and the Compromise of 1850," *Florida Historical Quarterly* 29 (January 1960): 16-33.

36. Governor's message, *Texas State Gazette* (Austin), 17 August 1850; Duval to R. M. T. Hunter, 13 August 1850, in Ambler, *Correspondence of R. M. T. Hunter,* 115.

37. Nevins, *Ordeal of the Union,* 1: 349-50; *Texas State Gazette,* 21 September, 16, 23, 39 November 1850; Love to Crittenden, 24 September 1850, in Crittenden Papers, LC.

38. Melvin J. White, "Louisiana and the Secession Movement in the Early Fifties," *Proceedings* of the Mississippi Valley Historical Association 8 (1916): 278-86; Greer, "Louisiana Politics," 577-78.

39. Files of the Richmond *Enquirer* and the Richmond *Whig,* September-December 1850.

40. Tucker to Hammond, 15 October, 21 September 1850, in Tucker Papers, DUL; Mason, *Life and Diplomatic Correspondence of Mason,* 84-85.

41. Shanks, *Secession Movement in Virginia,* 39-41; "Proceedings and Address of the Central Southern Rights Association of Virginia to the Citizens of Virginia," adopted 10 January 1851 (Richmond, 1851), copy at VHS; Ambler, *Sectionalism in Virginia,* 249-50.

42. Lewis, "From Nationalism to Disunion," 143-67; *Arkansas State Gazette and Democrat,* 28 June, 9 August, 4 October, 8 November, 13 December 1850. The Democratic State Convention drafted Johnson, who defeated his Whig opponent by traditional Democratic strength and his promise to abide by the Compromise.

43. Wilmington *Journal,* 13 September 1850.

44. Sitterson, *Secession Movement in North Carolina,* 72-79, citing *North Carolina Standard,* 13 November 1850; Governor Manly's Message to the General Assembly, November 1850, in Governor Manly's Letterbook, 1849-50, NCAH; Willie P. Mangum to Charity A. Mangum, 30 November 1850, in Henry Shanks, (ed.), *The Papers of Willie Person Mangum,* 5 vols. (Raleigh, 1950-56), 5: 192-93.

45. Nashville *Union,* 18 September 1850; *Republican Banner,* 16

September 1850; Nashville *Daily American,* 13 September 1850. Eastman was the former editor of the *Union* and a secretary at the Nashville Convention.

46. Washington *Union,* 2 October 1850, citing Winchester (Tennessee) *Independent;* Johnson to Buchanan, 10 November 1850, in Buchanan Papers, HSP.

47. *Republican Banner,* 1, 3, 10 October 1850. Tennessee congressmen thought it was "inexpedient" to accept the banquet.

# *Chapter 9*

1. Charleston *Mercury,* 16 September 1850; Barnwell to Hammond, 9, 26 September 1850, in Hammond Papers, LC.

2. Hammond to Simms, 30 September 1850; Hammond to Seabrook, 18 October 1850; Seabrook to Hammond, 23 October 1850, Gregg to Hammond, 4 November 1850; M. L. Bonham to Hammond, 3 November 1850; and Hammond to Simms, 11 November 1850, all in Hammond Papers, LC. See also Hammond's Diary, 29 November 1850.

3. W. F. Cooper to D. R. Arnell, 23 November 1850. See Appendix D for a list of delegates by states.

4. *Journal of the Proceedings of the Southern Convention, at Its Adjourned Session, Held at Nashville, Tenn., Nov. 11, 1850, and Subsequent Days* (Nashville, 1850). Official journal of the second session, located at New York Public Library, does not include Young's name, but the *Republican Banner* (Nashville), 19 November 1850 does include his name. The official journal, hereafter cited as *Official Journal,* Second Session, gives the residence for all delegates except those from Tennessee and one Georgia delegate. No other personal information was available for either Bradley or Wilson. Allston to Dr. James Bradley, 1 November 1850, in Bradley Family Papers, SCL.

5. John D. Freeman, in *Cong. Globe,* 32 Cong., 1 Sess., Appendix, 338; Hearon, "Mississippi and the Compromise of 1850," 175.

6. Georgia Executive Minute Book, 26 October 1850, p. 151, GAH; Troup to Unknown, 10 October 1850, in Edward J. Harden, *The Life of George M. Troup* (Savannah, 1859), 529; Executive Minute Book, 26 October 1850, p. 151 for Snell; 5 November 1850, p. 154, for Hunter and Jones; Sneed to Towns, 13 June 1850, in Telamon

Cuyler Papers, UGL. This is a letter of acceptance to the second session, but no record of his appointment is in the Executive Minute Book.

7. John H. Lumpkin to Howell Cobb, 25 August 1850, in Howell Cobb Papers, UGL; Green, "Politics in Georiga," 244.

8. Owen, *Alabama History and Biography,* 3: 285, 342; 4: 1771. The manner of selection was not determined.

9. Williams, "Florida in the Union," 512, 517-18; Rosa Calphin, "Address of John C. McGehee Before the Southern Rights Association of Madison County," *Florida Historical Quarterly* 5 (October 1926): 67-87.

10. *Arkansas State Gazette,* 4 October 1850; Special Correspondent, Charleston *Mercury,* 20 November 1850.

11. Gregg to Hoke, 21 August, 25 September 1850, in William A. Hoke Papers, SHC; Sitterson, *Secession Movement in North Carolina,* 64-65.

12. Charleston *Mercury,* 16 September 1850; *Federal Union,* 5 November 1850.

13. First American National Bank, *Firsts in Nashville,* 20; *Republican Banner,* 20 November 1850.

14. Charleston *Mercury,* 15, 20 November 1850; Gordon to Mrs. Gordon, 10 November 1850, in Gordon Family Papers, UVL.

15. Conversation with Mrs. Eva Jean Wrather, who is writing a history of the church; Wooldridge, *History of Nashville,* 494-95; Nashville *Union,* 12 November 1850. Representative Andrew Ewing expressed his opposition to the Missouri line in a speech in Nashville on Saturday before the convention met on Monday. Charleston *Mercury,* 23 November 1850.

16. The *Republican Banner* is fairly good, but the *Union* is poor because of Watterson's opposition. The editorials in the Nashville *Gazette* are significant for their severe criticism. In addition to the *Official Journal,* another good primary source is a letter of W. F. Cooper to D. R. Arnell, 23 November 1850.

17. *Republican Banner,* 12 November 1850.

18. The contrast between McDonald and Sharkey is significant. One Georgia politician thought McDonald's name had "done more for the cause of ultras" than everything else. Luther J. Glenn to Howell Cobb, 21 September 1850, in Phillips, *Correspondence,* 213.

19. *Official Journal,* Second Session, 3-5; Nashville *American,* 12, 13 November 1850; Charleston *Mercury,* 15 November 1850.

20. *Official Journal,* Second Session, 6-13; Nashville *American,* 14 November 1850; *Republican Banner,* 14 November 1850.

21. *Official Journal,* Second Session, 13-17, 20-23; Nashville *American,* 15, 17 November 1850. The special correspondent of the Charleston *Mercury,* on 20 November, reported that the Georgia

resolutions "did not come up to the mark fully." See also Cooper to D. R. Arnell, 23 November 1850, in Cooper Family Papers, TSL.

22. Although the Tennessee delegates appointed Brown and Nicholson to prepare these resolutions, they are primarily the work of Brown. Editor of *Union and American* (ed.), *Speeches, Congressional and Political and Other Writings of Ex-Governor Aaron V. Brown of Tennessee* (Nashville, 1854), 319-22.

23. Nashville *Union,* 16 November 1850; *Official Journal,* Second Session, 17-20; Charleston *Mercury,* 20 November 1850. The *Mercury* reporter described Claiborne as "an old man, but one of few who are decided in this state." Claiborne does appear more ultra than most Tennesseans.

24. Cheves to Mrs. Charles T. Haskell, 7 October 1850, in Langdon Cheves Papers, SCHS; *Speech of Langdon Cheves to the Southern Convention at Nashville, Tennessee, November 14, 1850,* published by the Southern Rights Association, 1850 (30 pp.), LC. Both the Nashville *American* and the *Republican Banner* published this speech on 16 November 1850; Charleston *Mercury,* 20 November 1850.

25. Nashville *American,* 16 November 1850; W. F. Cooper to D. R. Arnell, 23 November 1850, in Cooper Papers, TSL; Nashville *Gazette,* 16 November 1850.

26. The press later published their undelivered speeches. Although Brown's speech was especially critical of the Compromise, it was a rhetorical appeal to abide by the laws with the motto "resistance for the future." *Brown's Speeches,* 307-18. See *Official Journal,* Second Session, 31-34 for preamble and resolutions.

27. Nashville *American,* 17, 19, 20, 21 November; Charleston *Mercury,* 19 November 1850; Cooper to D. R. Arnell, 23 November 1850. The preamble and resolutions adopted 18 November 1850 are also included in *Resolutions and Address Adopted by the Southern Convention, Held at Nashville, Tennessee* (Columbia, S. C., 1850), 24-27.

28. In Greek mythology Radamanthus or Rhadamanthus was the son of Zeus and a judge in the lower world.

29. Nashville *Gazette,* 19 November 1850.

30. Hammond to W. H. Gist, 2 December 1850, in Hammond Papers, LC.

31. Charleston *Mercury,* 21 November 1850; Governor Quitman's Message to the Legislature, 18 November 1850, in Quitman's Official Correspondence, 38, MAH; Quitman to Rhett, 30 November 1850, in Seabrook Papers, LC; Vicksburg *Whig,* 7 December 1850.

32. John Edmond Gonzales, "The Public Career of Henry Stuart Foote, 1804-1880," (Ph. D. dissertation, University of North Carolina, 1957), 86-89; Vicksburg *Whig,* 7 December 1850.

33. Shryock, *Georgia and the Union,* 301-19; Myrta Lockett Avary (ed.), *Recollections of Alexander H. Stephens* (New York, 1910), 27; John H. Lumpkin to Howell Cobb, 5 October 1850, in Phillips, *Correspondence,* 214-15, notes the "swing to the right."

34. Savannah *Morning News,* 27 November 1850. See the *Southern Museum,* 7 December 1850, for the official returns of the election. No Nashville Convention delegates were elected to the Georgia convention.

35. Savannah *Morning News,* 11, 13, 14, 16, 17 December 1850; Shryock, *Georgia and the Union,* 325-36. Toombs, Stephens, Cobb, Jenkins, and W. C. Dawson were the most prominent members.

36. Shryock, *Georgia and the Union,* 354.

37. Ambler, *Sectionalism in Virginia,* 249-50; Sitterson, *Secession in North Carolina,* 81-94; Brown, "Albert Pike," 287-89; Campbell, *Attitude of Tennesseans Toward the Union,* 61-63.

38. Meador, "Florida and the Compromise of 1850," 21-24; Doherty, "Florida Whigs," 162-68.

39. Denman, *Secession Movement in Alabama,* 56-64.

40. Gonzales, "Henry Foote," 98-101; McLemore, *History of Mississippi,* 304-305; Reuben Davis, *Recollections of Mississippi and Mississippians* (Boston, 1889), 317; Oscar Lieber to Francis Lieber, 5 September 1851, in Francis Lieber Papers, SCL.

41. Davis resigned his Senate seat on 23 September 1851 before the election in November, but Foote held his Senate seat during the campaign and did not resign until 8 January 1852, after his election as governor. McLemore, *History of Mississippi,* 307.

42. Gonzales, "Henry Foote," 119-23, returns by counties. Hudson Strode, *Jefferson Davis,* 3 vols. (New York, 1955-64), 1: 234-36. Reuben Davis says Davis contracted pneumonia after a three weeks' canvass and was confined to bed until after the election. Davis, *Recollections,* 320.

43. Rowland, *Davis Correspondence,* 2: 335.

44. Gonzales, "Henry S. Foote," 123-24; Hearon, "Mississippi and the Compromise of 1850," 216-19; Rowland, *History of Mississippi,* 1:739-41.

45. Boucher, "Secession and Cooperation Movement in South Carolina," 105-12; N. W. Stephenson, "Southern Nationalism in South Carolina in 1851," *American Historical Review* 36 (1931): 316-20; James O'Hanlon to Perry, 15 November 1850, in Perry Papers, AAH; Perry MS Journal, 17, 20 November 1850, SHC; Lillian Kibler, *Benjamin F. Perry: South Carolina Unionist* (Durham, 1946), 248.

46. Hammond's Diary, 30 November 1850; Hammond to Gist, 2 December 1850, in Hammond Papers, LC.

47. As quoted in Hamer, *Secession Movement in South Carolina,* 76-77.

48. James Louis Petigru to Jane Petigru North, 19 December 1850, in James Petigru Carson (ed.), *Life, Letters and Speeches of James Louis Petigru: the Union Man of South Carolina* (Washington, 1920), 285-86; Seabrook to Quitman, 17 December 1850, in Claiborne, *Life of Quitman,* 2: 39-40; Perry MS Journal, 29 December 1850, SHC; R. F. W. Allston to Adele Petrigu Allston, 30 November, 14, 17 December 1850, in the R. F. W. Allston Papers, SCL.

49. Harry Hammond to James H. Hammond, 9 December 1850, in Hammond, Bryan, and Cumming Families Papers, SCL; Resolutions on Federal Relations, 7, 11, 14 December 1850, and extracts from the act providing for the southern congress and state convention in the files of the Legislative System, SCAH; White, *Rhett,* 114-15; Lewis M. Ayers to Hammond, 18 December 1850, in Hammond Papers, LC.

50. George Harris to Isaac Harris, 15 December 1850, in Wright-Harris Papers, DUL.

51. Harold S. Schultz, *Nationalism and Sectionalism in South Carolina, 1852-1860* (Durham, 1950), 28; Hamer, *Secession Movement in South Carolina,* 84-87.

52. Charleston *Mercury,* 29 April 1851.

53. Charleston *Mercury,* 17 May 1851; Orr's speech in unknown newspaper, SCL files; (Nathaniel Beverley Tucker), "South Carolina: Her Present Attitude and Future Action," a review of the *Proceedings of the meeting of Delegates from the Southern Rights Associations of South Carolina; held at Charleston, May 1851,* in the *Southern Quarterly Review* 20 (October 1851): 273-98.

54. Stephenson, "Southern Nationalism in South Carolina," 329-30; Schultz, *Nationalism and Sectionalism in South Carolina,* 29-30; Christopher Williams Dudley, 2 June 1851, SCL files.

55. Charleston *Mercury,* 30 July 1851; Stephenson, "Southern Nationalism in South Carolina," 329-32.

56. Barnwell to Orr, 25 August 1851, in Orr-Patterson Papers, SHC. See also Waddy Thompson to Orr, 29 July 1851, in ibid.

57. Hamer, *Secession Movement in South Carolina,* 121-25. Three weeks before the election Rhett became ill and took a trip to Europe to recuperate. See White, *Rhett,* 123, as quoted in Charles E. Cauthen, *South Carolina Goes to War, 1860-1865* (Chapel Hill, 1950), 5.

58. Hamer, *Secession Movement in South Carolina,* 126-43, quote, 142; White, *Rhett,* 130-33.

# *Bibliographical Essay*

The combined footnotes form a complete bibliography of the sources used in this book. Primary references include manuscript collections, edited works, official records, newspapers, and contemporary books and pamphlets. Secondary accounts comprise general works, biographical and state studies, monographs, theses and dissertations, and periodical articles.

The starting point for any serious study of the crisis of 1850 is Holman Hamilton's excellent bibliographical essay in *Prologue to Conflict: the Crisis and Compromise of 1850* (Lexington, 1964). Repeating all of my sources or duplicating those of Professor Hamilton would be pointless; what I propose to do in this essay, therefore, is to indicate the way some historians have viewed the Nashville Convention and to discuss briefly some of the most significant and rewarding materials dealing with the entire southern unification movement.

James Ford Rhodes in his *History of the United States from the Compromise of 1850*, 9 vols. (New York, 1893-1922), points out that if Congress had passed the Wilmot Proviso or abolished slavery in the District of Columbia, "the Southern Convention would have been a very different affair from the one that actually assembled at Nashville" (p. 135). Yet neither Rhodes nor other historians of his time were much impressed with the convention. Melvin J. White in *The Secession Movement in the United States, 1847-1852* (New Orleans, 1910), however, views the Nashville Convention as one of the factors that finally brought about the passage of the Compromise measures. Three years later, Cleo Hearon published her doctoral dissertation, "Mississippi and the Compromise of 1850," in the Mississippi Historical Society *Publications* 14 (1913): 7-229. Although her work has a distinct value in regard to Mississippi's call for the convention and state developments, she concludes that "the convention had little or no influence on the progress of the Compromise measures through Congress" (p. 128). St. George L. Sioussat's article "Tennessee, the Compromise of 1850, and the Nashville Convention" (*Mississippi Valley Historical Review* 2 [December 1915]: 313-47) is especially valuable for several reasons—his examination of Tennessee's attitude, politics, and participation, his accounts of both sessions, and his comments on the Nashville press. Sioussat observes that "it is hardly possible . . . to avoid the impression that the Nashville Convention was really more important than it had been thought to be" (p. 347).

Three important studies, primarily concerned with South Carolina, were published in 1918. Philip May Hamer's work, *The Secession Movement in South Carolina, 1847-1852* (Allentown, PA, 1918) made a definite contribution in regard to Calhoun's role, the call for the convention, and developments within the state. Hamer believes that in early 1850 little difference existed between the positions of Calhoun and those who desired immediate secession. Herman V. Ames' article "John C. Calhoun and the Secession Movement of 1850," published in the University of Pennyslvania *Lectures* 5 (Philadelphia, 1918): 103-30, asserts that Calhoun was largely responsible for the assembling of the convention and that he hoped to guide its proceedings. Ames was convinced that a careful study of the southern convention movement would lead to the conclusion "that it was of much greater importance and a more serious menace to the Union" than historians had generally recognized (p. 129) A monograph by Chauncey S. Boucher entitled "The Secession and Cooperation Movement in South Carolina, 1848-1852," published in the Washington University Studies 5, Humanistic Series, pt. 2, no. 2 (St. Louis, 1918), 65-138, suggests that the convention call and exhortations to send as delegates men who would no longer yield "may have had something to do with the prompting of the compromise" (p. 95).

One of the most frequently cited articles dealing with the crisis is Herbert D. Foster, "Webster's Seventh of March Speech and the Secession Movement of 1850," *American Historial Review* 27 (1921-22): 245-70. Foster builds a strong case for Webster's influence in checking the radical objectives of the meeting and seems to echo the judgment so succinctly expressed by contemporary legislator Robert Winthrop of Massachusetts: "Webster's speech has knocked the Nashville Convention into a cocked hat."

Avery Craven, Allan Nevins, Holman Hamilton, and David Potter have made the most significant contributions to the historiography of the 1850 crisis. Craven's two books are *The Coming of the Civil War* (New York, 1942) and *The Growth of Southern Nationalism* (Baton Rouge, 1953), a volume in the *History of the South* series. He believes that the convention, which opened in the "unfriendly atmosphere" of Nashville, was "doomed to failure," as most southerners attached little importance to the meeting. But the outcome of the meeting did have important effects on events in Washington, for it strengthened those who worked for the Compromise. The first volume in Nevins' *Ordeal of the Union,* 2 vols. (New York, 1947) covers the period 1847-1852. Nevins claims only two groups of men showed any enthusiasm for the assemblage—the old nullifiers and "the fiery young men who worshiped Calhoun." Moreover, he views the Nashville ultimatum as "too late and too weak. . . . The Convention passed into history like the far-off rumble of a storm that might have been disastrous, but had dissolved without loosing a single thunderbolt" (p. 317). The radicals, however, learned much from the Nashville "fiasco." Hamilton has contributed the best biography of

President *Zachary Taylor* 2 vols. (Indianapolis, 1941-51) and the most complete study of the Compromise in his *Prologue to Conflict: The Crisis and Compromise of 1850* (Lexington, 1964). In his biography of Taylor, Hamilton gives the most detailed account of the president's position and concludes that if Taylor's death had not reversed the national picture, the November session "might have been entirely different and indeed threatening" (p. 373). It is doubtless true, he asserts, that many delegates and their friends ardently wished to threaten secession. In his *Prologue to Conflict,* Hamilton indicates that Clay's leadership was of "dubious value" and the northern Democrats were the most consistent pro-compromise group, but he devotes little space to the convention. David Potter died in 1971 before completing *The Impending Crisis, 1848-1861,* which Don E. Fehrenbacher completed and published five years later (New York, 1976). Potter states that the Nashville Convention "proved an obstacle to secession rather than an instrument for it" (p. 485).

Six authors have chosen the Nashville Convention as a specific topic for an article or thesis. In 1905 Dallas Herndon published a thirty-five page article entitled, "The Nashville Convention of 1850" in the Alabama Historical Society *Transactions* 5 (1905): 203-37. He believes that prospects of success were encouraging up to the early spring of 1850 with apprehension created in parts of the North. Herndon cites several reasons for failure, but "the final stroke" that killed the hope of uniting the South was the passage of the Compromise. Seven years later, Farrar Newberry, apparently unaware of Herndon's previous work, wrote an article, "The Nashville Convention and Southern Sentiment of 1850" for the *South Atlantic Quarterly* 11 (1912): 259-73. Although this article has some merit as a general account, it is rather superficial and is even less satisfactory than Herndon's work.

The Nashville Convention has been the subject for four MA theses. The first by Andrew Pickens Johnson was completed at Vanderbilt in 1927. Johnson's work, based on very limited sources, is rather poor. He concludes that the probable effects of the convention were doubtless far-reaching, but in what manner he does not specify. Four years later at George Peabody College, Margaret Randolph Cate wrote an MA thesis entitled "Basis and Significance of the Southern Convention of 1850." Ms. Cate interprets the call for the convention as "avowedly a popular and not a political movement" that caused great agitation in the North. She concludes that the gathering was largely responsible for the adjustment of the problems which motivated the convention, that men destined to be southern leaders a decade later attended the meeting, that the convention forecast the alignment of states in 1861, and that it marked the beginning of a breakdown in parties. Thus the convention was by no means a failure. In 1947 Abram John Foster submitted his thesis, "The Nashville Convention of 1850" at Duke University. Foster concludes that probably the principal reason for the first session of the convention was to influence Congress to act more favorably toward the South, that agitation for the meeting caused some apprehension in the North, that in many respects the Nashville Convention was similar to the Hartford Convention of 1814, and that the failure of the assemblage to gain southern public approval may have been a turning point in the movement toward disunion and thus caused a postponement of secession for a decade. Although the Nashville Convention indicated a prevailing disaffection of the southern mind, it demonstrated clearly that the southern people were unwilling to dissolve the Union. The latest study is an MA thesis entitled "Southern Sentiment and the Nashville Convention of 1850" written in 1965 by Thomas S. McFerrin IV at Florida State University. McFerrin takes issue with the traditional viewpoint that the delegates met with the idea of secession foremost in their minds and were unrepresentative of southern sentiment in general. Because the prospect of secession had been eminent, however, the proposed convention had promoted an adjustment.

Numerous manuscript collections were explored in repositories of most of the southern states and the Library of Congress. The work in the collections of the Southern Historical Collection, at the University of North Carolina at Chapel Hill, Duke University, and the South Caroliniana Library at the University of South Carolina proved most rewarding, but valuable materials are scattered far and wide. Chapel Hill's most significant offerings include the John M. Berrien Papers, David Outlaw Papers, and the Benjamin F. Perry Manuscript Journal. The Robert Barnwell Rhett Papers were a disappointment; in fact very few Rhett letters for this period are extant. The David Campbell Papers, Herschel V. Johnson Papers, Nathaniel Beverley Tucker Papers (Typescript) are important collections at Duke. Dr. W. Edwin Hemphill was most generous in giving me access to the large collection of photo copies of Calhoun's correspondence at the South Caroliniana Library. The R. F. W. Allston Papers and James Henry Hammond's Diary are also significant at South Caroliniana. Other Hammond Papers are located at Duke, but the most important collection is at the Library of Congress, which also includes the valuable John J. Crittenden papers and the Whitemarsh B. Seabrook Papers. The Cooper Family Papers at the Tennessee State Library and Archives contain some valuable letters of W. F. Cooper, Convention secretary. Of important aid were the collections of John Francis H. Claiborne at the Mississippi State Department of Archives and History and at Chapel Hill, the David L. Yulee Papers at the University of Florida, the Bolling Hall and Benjamin F. Perry Papers at the Alabama State Department of Archives and History, the Telamon Cuyler and Howell Cobb Papers at the University of Georgia, and the Joel R. Poinsett and James Buchanan Papers at the Historical Society of Pennsylvania. The Gordon Family Papers at the University of Virginia contain two letters that Nashville Convention delegate William F. Gordon wrote while attending the convention.

A number of edited works and correspondence also provided valuable information. The most significant include J. Franklin Jameson (ed.), *Correspondence of John C. Calhoun,* American Historical Association *Annual Report, 1899,* pt. 2 (Washington, 1900); Chauncey S. Boucher and Robert P. Brooks (eds.), "Correspondence Addressed to John C. Calhoun, 1837-1849," American Historical Association *Annual Report, 1929* (Washington, 1930), 125-533; and Ulrich B. Phillips (ed.), *The Correspondence of Robert Toombs, Alexander H. Stephens, and Howell Cobb,* American Historical Association *Annual Report, 1911,* pt. 2 (Washington, 1913). Charles H. Ambler (ed.), *Correspondence of R. M. T. Hunter, 1826-1876,* American Historical Association *Annual Report, 1916,* pt. 2 (Washington, 1918), contains important letters to and from Virginia leaders. Of a similar nature is Mary C. Simms Oliphant, Alfred T. Odell, and T. C. Duncan Eaves (eds.), *The Letters of William Gilmore Simms,* 5 vols. (Columbia, S.C., 1952-56), which contain Simms' letters to Hammond, Tucker, and others. J. F. H. Claiborne (ed.), *Life and Correspondence of John A. Quitman,* 2 vols. (New York, 1860) contains some significant letters of Mississippi's radical governor.

The most important official records are the *Congressional Globe;* United States Bureau of the Census, Manuscript returns, Schedules 1 and 2 for the various states; *Resolutions, Address, and Journal of Proceedings of the Southern Convention, Held at Nashville, Tennessee, June 3rd to 12th, Inclusive in the Year 1850* (Nashville, 1850); and *Journal of Proceedings of the Southern Convention at Its Adjourned Session, Held at Nashville, Tennessee, November 11, 1850, and Subsequent Days* (Nashville, 1850).

Newspapers, although very partisan in nature, were good sources for both factual information and southern sentiment. For these reasons I tried to explore as many as possible and to keep a fairly even balance between Whig and Democratic papers. Two of the most important papers were the Whig *Republican Banner* (Nashville) and the Nashville *Union,* a Democratic paper. Of somewhat less importance was the Nashville *Daily American* (Democrat.) Two papers, the Huntsville (Alabama) *Democrat* and the Charleston *Mercury* sent special reporters to the convention. The *Mercury,* edited by the Rhett family, was also significant as the chief organ of the fire-eaters. Other noteworthy Democratic papers include the Richmond *Enquirer,* a most influential paper; the Mobile *Daily Register,* another well edited paper; the *Federal Union* (Milledgeville, Georgia); and the Wilmington (North Carolina) *Journal.* On the whole, Whig papers opposed or gave little support to the convention, but a notable exception was the Montgomery *Alabama Journal,* a widely circulated Whig paper that supported the convention throughout the period. Since material for Arkansas was difficult to locate, the two papers at the capital, Little Rock, have particular significance—the *Arkansas Banner* (Democrat) and the *Arkansas State Gazette* (Whig 1849), which combined with the *Arkansas Democrat* as another Democratic paper, *The Arkansas State Gazette and Democrat.* Other leading Whig papers include the Augusta *Daily Chronicle,* the Raleigh *Register and North Carolina Gazette,* and the Richmond *Whig.* Perhaps the most violent in its opposition was *Brownlow's Knoxville Whig.* Although the New Orleans *Picayune* was one of the leading southern antebellum newspapers, it proved disappointing, as well as other Louisiana papers examined. Undoubtedly, this was true because of the lack of interest in the state. In Florida, the state's most influential Democratic paper was the Tallahassee *Floridian and Journal,* and the chief organ of the Whigs was the Florida *Sentinel* (Tallahassee). The South Carolina press voiced virtually no opposition to the convention. The Charleston *Courier* was the most conservative South Carolina paper, and the *Spartan* (Spartanburg) was a significant up-country paper. The Vicksburg *Sentinel* and the *Mississippi Free Trader,* published in Natchez at the residence of General John A. Quitman who became governor in January 1850, were two of the staunchest Democratic papers in favor of the convention in Mississippi. The Whig *Southron* (Jackson) and the Vicksburg *Whig* supported the resolutions of the October Convention, but they opposed the action of the legislature in making the admission of California a sectional issue and electing a new slate of delegates to the Nashville Convention. Thus the legislative action became something of a partisan press issue, with the Whigs giving less support to the Nashville Convention. *Niles' Weekly Register,* published in Baltimore from 1811 to 1849, a kind of news periodical, was also helpful.

Contemporary works were of limited value except for J. H. Ingraham (ed.) *The Sunny South, or the Southerner at Home: Embracing Five Years Experience of a Northern Governess in the Land of the Sugar and Cotton* (Philadelphia, 1860). The governess, who attended the convention, gave her impressions of the proceedings and certain personnel, which are at least interesting.

Indispensable to this study were a number of state studies relative to the secession movement. Perhaps the most outstanding of these is Richard H. Shryock, *Georgia and the Union in 1850*

(Durham, 1926), a reliable and dispassionate work, chiefly valuable for factual information rather than interpretation. Of a similar nature are Clarence P. Denman, *The Secession Movement in Alabama* (Montgomery, 1933); Henry T. Shanks, *The Secession Movement in Virginia, 1847-1861* (Richmond, 1935); J. Carlyle Sitterson, *The Secession Movement in North Carolina* (Chapel Hill, 1939); and the Hamer work previously mentioned. Less valuable but worthy of mention are Mary E. R. Campbell, *The Attitude of Tennessee Toward the Union, 1847-1861* (New York, 1961); Charles H. Ambler, *Sectionalism in Virginia from 1776 to 1861* (Chicago, 1910); and Lewy Dorman, *Party Politics in Alabama from 1850 to 1860* (Wetumpka, AL, 1935). Since no study for Mississippi dating back to 1850 exists, Dunbar Rowland, *History of Mississippi: The Heart of the South,* 2 vols. (Chicago, 1925) was helpful.

Also essential were biographical studies of outstanding leaders of the period. The most definitive biography of Calhoun is the multivolume study by Charles L. Wiltse (3 vols., Indianapolis, 1944-51), who notes that the overt threat posed by the convention acted for awhile "as a damper upon northern agitation" (p. 458). The best secondary account of the launching of the southern movement is in volume 3 of this study. Other significant biographies include John W. Dubose, *The Life and Times of William Lowndes Yancey,* 2 vols. (Birmingham, 1892), primarily important for source materials; Percy S. Flippin, *Herschel V. Johnson of Georgia: State Rights Unionist* (Richmond, 1931); James Byrne Ranck, *Albert Gallatin Brown: Radical Southern Nationalist* (New York, 1937); Ulrich B. Phillips, *The Life of Robert Toombs* (New York, 1913); Lillian Kibler, *Benjamin F. Perry: South Carolina Unionist* (Durham, 1946); Rudolph Von Abele, *Alexander H. Stephens, A Biography* (New York, 1946); and Laura A. White, *Robert Barnwell Rhett* (New York, 1931), which is the most helpful and the most scholarly of the group. Jon L. Wakelyn, *The Politics of A Literary Man: William Gilmore Simms* (Westport, Conn., 1973); Archie Vernon Huff, Jr., *Langdon Cheves of South Carolina* (Columbia, 1977); and Robert J. Brugger, *Beverley Tucker: Heart Over Head in the Old South* (Baltimore, 1978), an informed intellectual biography that is the best source on Tucker's thought and writings, are important recent contributions.

A number of theses and dissertations have been written on various topics that are relevant to the Nashville Convention and the southern unification movement. Walter L. Brown's extensive dissertation on Albert Pike, (University of Texas, 1954) and Elsie Mae Lewis, "From Nationalism to Disunion: A Study of the Secession Movement in Arkansas, 1850-1861," (Ph.D. dissertation, University of Chicago, 1946) were indeed important resources for Arkansas. In the absence of published, scholarly biographies, I found the following theses and dissertations helpful: Patricia P. Clark, "A. O. P. Nicholson of Tennessee: Editor, Statesman and Jurist," (MA Thesis, University of Tennessee, 1965); John Edmund Gonzales, "Public Career of Henry Stuart Foote, 1804-1880," (Ph.D. Dissertation, University of North Carolina, 1957); and Justine S. Mann, "The Political and Constitutional Thought of John Archibald Campbell," (Ph.D. Dissertation, University of Alabama, 1966). Since there is no published monograph on the secession movement in Florida, these unpublished works were useful: Herbert J. Doherty, Jr., "The Florida Whigs," (MA Thesis, University of Florida, 1949); Sydney J. Wienberg, "Slavery and Secession in Florida, 1845-1861," (MA Thesis, University of Florida, 1940); and Edwin L. Williams, Jr., "Florida in the Union, 1845-1861," (Ph.D. Dissertation, University of North Carolina, 1951).

Finally a few periodical articles should be mentioned because of their distinct contribution. Dorothy Dodd, "The Secession Movement in Florida, 1850-1861," *Florida Historical Quarterly* 12 (July 1933): 3-24, and John Meador, "Florida and the Compromise of 1850," *Florida Historical Quarterly* 29 (1960-61): 16-33, are two excellent articles that provided additional information on the young state of Florida. Randolph Campbell, "Texas and the Nashville Convention," *Southwestern Historical Quarterly* 76 (July 1972): 1-14, is a most welcome supplement to Anna Irene Sandbo's earlier article, "Beginning of the Secession Movement in Texas," *Southwestern Historical Quarterly* 18 (July 1914): 41-73. James K. Greer, "Louisiana Politics, 1845-61," *Louisiana Historical Quarterly* 12 (1929): 403-18, was invaluable in helping me understand the situation in that state. Two significant articles on Missouri, an important border state, were very helpful: Benjamin Merkel, "The Slavery Issue and the Political Decline of Thomas Hart Benton, 1846-1856," *Missouri Historical Review* 38 (1944): 388-407, and Raymond D. Thomas, "A Study in Missouri Politics, 1840-1870," *Missouri Historical Review* 21 (1927): 166-84. The best secondary account of the slavery provisions of the territorial acts passed by Congress in 1850 is Robert R. Russel, "What Was the Compromise of 1850?" *Journal of Southern History* 22 (1956): 292-309. N. W. Stephenson, "Southern Nationalism in South Carolina in 1851," *American Historical Review* 36 (1931): 314-55 is the best article on the cooperationists and single state secessionists' struggle in South Carolina, a subject that needs further investigation.

# *Index*